1971 University of Alabama football team. Row 1 (L to R): Bill Davis, Glenn Woodruff, Greg Gantt, Terry Davis, Billy Sexton, Benny Rippetoe, Johnny Sharpless. Row 2: Butch Hobson, David McMakin, Slade Rhodes, Wayne Adkinson, Johnny Musso, Ronnie Richardson, Paul Spivey, Jeff Blitz, Bobby McKinney. Row 3: Bubba Sawyer, Steve Williams, Robby Rowan, Joe Labue, Steve Wade, Rod Steakley, Ellis Beck, Chuck Strickland, Richard Bryant. Row 4: Lanny Norris, Tom Surlas, Steve Bisceglia, Joe Cochran, Jerry Cash, Robin Cary, Steve Higginbotham, Wayne Hall, Freddie Marshall. Row 5: Andy Cross, Pat Raines, Jim Krapf, Jimmy Grammer, Jeff Rouzie, Terry Rowell, Morris Hunt, Marvin Barron. Row 6: Buddy Brown, Jack White, Steve Root, Rick Rogers, Don Cokely, Jimmy Rosser, John Hannah, Mike Raines. Row 7: Allen Cox, Jeff Beard, Steve Sprayberry, Mike Denson, Wilbur Jackson, Tommy Lusk, Wayne Wheeler, John Croyle, David Bailey. Row 8: Jim Simmons, Jimmy Horton, Robin Parkhouse, Don Groves, Dexter Wood, David Watkins, Skip Kibelius, Jim Patterson, John Mitchell (Jack White Collection).

CAREER IN CRISIS

PAUL "BEAR" BRYANT AND THE 1971 SEASON OF CHANGE

JOHN DAVID BRILEY

Mercer University Press | Macon, Georgia

© 2006 Mercer University Press
1400 Coleman Avenue
Macon, Georgia 31207
All rights reserved
MUP 719

First Edition.
Book design by Burt & Burt Studio

Library of Congress Cataloging-in-Publication Data

Briley, John David, 1955-
Career in crisis: Paul "Bear" Bryant and the 1971 season at Alabama
p. cm.
Includes bibliographical references and index.
1. Alabama Crimson Tide (Football team)—History.
2. University of Alabama—Football—History.
3. Bryant, Paul W.
4. Football—Social aspects—Alabama.
I. Title.
GV958.A4B75 2006   796.332'630975184—dc22

2006013601

DEDICATED TO MY MOTHER AND FATHER,
WHO ARE RESPONSIBLE FOR ANY GOOD DEEDS
I HAVE DONE IN THIS LIFE.

FOREWORD

WHEN COACH PAUL "BEAR" BRYANT OFFERED ME A JOB ON HIS football staff at the University of Alabama in January 1960, it was one of the greatest moments in my life. Gene "Bebes" Stallings, one of Bryant's assistant coaches, had talked with him about me, and Coach Bryant wanted me to join them in Tuscaloosa. It did not take me long to say yes to this wonderful opportunity. At the time, I was the president of the Alabama High School Coaches Association. As a former Crimson Tide athlete and a high school football coach, I was stepping into one of the premier football programs in the country. I can remember thinking, "Bryant and Bama—it can't get any better than that, no matter what position I coach." When I started the job, I was not assigned a position to coach, but Coach Bryant had a plan. I was the recruiting coordinator because of my many connections to the high school coaches in the state. I spent the next twenty-three years working for the best, and I would not change a thing.

When I first came back to the Capstone to help Coach Bryant, we enjoyed a great deal of success. We won national championships in 1961, 1964, 1965, and felt like we were cheated out of another one in 1966. The next two seasons were pretty good, but we did not win the SEC or the national championships. The years of 1969 and 1970 were difficult ones for Paul Bryant and his staff, with Coach Bryant almost leaving us after the 1969 season to take the head coaching job with the Miami

Dolphins. Luckily for us he did not leave, but he read us the "riot act." He let the staff know in no uncertain terms that we were going to have to do our jobs better or we were going to be in the unemployment line.

Alabama had gotten so good that we thought that we could recruit anybody in the country. In doing this, we got away from our natural recruiting bases in and around the state of Alabama. The country was changing, and we were getting a fair amount of kids outside the South who did not know what it meant to be a football player for the University of Alabama. Many of these youngsters were not willing to put forth the effort it took to play football here. In addition to this, we had actively begun recruiting black athletes. This was initially difficult for us given the political situation in the state. We had earlier signed Wendell Hudson to a basketball scholarship. He did a great job on the court and now is one of our associate athletics directors. The first two black football players we signed were Wilbur Jackson and John Mitchell, both fine gentlemen and excellent players. In 1970 the Crimson Tide was a little better, but we had a couple of key injuries and a more difficult schedule that resulted in another six-win season.

Coach Bryant was determined to get back to the winning ways of the 1960s, and we were all with him. The year 1971 was a very special time for us. The seniors on this team were committed to winning and going out as a big success. There were only about a third of them left from their freshman class, and this was their time. The regular season began in Los Angeles and ended in Birmingham.

Bryant also knew that the success of any program is based on the people who work for that particular program, and he believed that the Alabama football program needed the help and support of every person involved. The famous coach understood the importance of every job, from secretaries and coaches, groundskeepers and ticket takers, maids and doctors, to dining hall and ticket office staff. Coach Bryant was tough and strict, yet also intelligent and compassionate. In many of his final decisions he went to his right-hand man, Jim Goosetree, a Tennessee native and former student athletic trainer under General Robert Neyland at the University of Tennessee. Goosetree taught the student trainers many lessons, both on and off the field.

From the ranks of Goosetree's trainers, many went on to prestigious professional careers, including a number of medical doctors, attorneys, and judges. One of those trainers from Tennessee, David Briley, went onto to earn his Ph.D. He now teaches political science at East Tennessee

State University in Johnson City, Tennessee. When David approached me a few years ago with his ideas for a book about the 1971 season, I was excited and wanted to help him any way I could. I have spent many hours over the past five years discussing this important team and how it impacted the future of Alabama football. It really took me back to a time when the players re-dedicated themselves to winning football games. What this team accomplished laid the groundwork for the most successful decade in college football history.

Finally, I have also become reacquainted with a number of players who came to the Bryant Museum to be interviewed for this book. In addition, the athletics department had a thirty-year reunion of this team in 2001. More than forty-five former players and coaches attended. I had a great time recalling these experiences, and I hope that you will enjoy reading about this fascinating account of the 1971 season. I sure did.

Clem Gryska
September 2005

PREFACE

WHILE CLIMBING UP THE TOWER ON THE PRACTICE FIELD TO
give a pack of *Chesterfields* to Paul "Bear" Bryant, I was scared to death
and hoping I did not do something wrong. The head coach of the
Alabama Crimson Tide had just told Ed Parsons, our head student
trainer, to get some cigarettes. We always had a spare carton around for
such emergencies. Parsons relayed the message to me, the nearest student
trainer around, and I completed the task. As I handed them to Coach
Bryant, he simply smiled and said, "Thank you, son." Almost anyone who
ever was around him, be it a fan, player, or coach, wanted to please him.
I was no different, for one of my childhood dreams was to go to the
University of Alabama and work for the "Bear."

I realized this dream as I reported to Tuscaloosa for fall practice at
the beginning of August 1973. I lasted one season at the university, but it
was a memorable one. That year the Crimson Tide won the UPI National
Championship, and only a 1-point loss to Notre Dame in the Sugar Bowl
separated them from a consensus national title. Little did I know that
some thirty years later I would be writing a book about the famous football coach—not about his 1973 squad, but about the 1971 team. While
this work has elements of both a cultural history and a celebrated sports
team history, it is neither per se. It is a hybrid of both. I am writing this
book as a scholar to illustrate the importance of this team, adding to the
literature and understanding of Alabama football. Yet I also approach
writing this book as a Crimson Tide fan, having followed the team

through the years and attended five games during their historic 1971 season.

In order to understand the 1971 team's story, one must go back a few years. Paul Bryant led the University of Alabama to three undisputed national championships during the 1960s; however, at the end of that decade, the program was mired in mediocrity. Back-to-back 6-5 seasons suggested that Bryant had let the game pass him by. The football program was under attack from one of its own student organizations. The Afro-American Student Association sued Bryant and its athletics department for not recruiting black athletes.

The year 1971 changed everything in Alabama football. Bryant's 1971 team included two black players—Wilbur Jackson and John Mitchell—whose courage and skills brought acclaim to themselves, their teammates, and their coach. The Bear abruptly switched to an entirely new run-based attack that was far removed from the pro-style offense mastered in the 1960s by legendary quarterbacks Joe Namath and Kenny Stabler. The success of 1971, in solving both the problems of integration in the Southeastern Conference (SEC) and the challenge of designing a new winning strategy, set the table for another decade of success. In doing so, Alabama football and Paul Bryant himself achieved near-legendary status as one of the great football programs of the late twentieth century.

In researching this book, I conducted in-depth interviews with sixty players, twelve coaches, and numerous others affiliated with the Alabama football program. I utilize these, with additional research materials, to determine the perceived causes of the waning years of the Crimson Tide football team in the late 1960s and to discuss the factors that led to the revival in the 1970s within the context of the demanding social and cultural changes resulting from the politics of upheaval and the Civil Rights Movement. This book is more than a history of a successful team; it examines in detail, with probing interviews and extant manuscript sources, the internal process of cultural change at Alabama that helped the team's and coach's resurgence. A comprehensive behind-the-scenes analysis of the 1971 season demonstrates how this team and this year of football changed the course of the Crimson Tide for the rest of Bryant's career. By adopting a new offensive strategy, Bryant solidified his reputation as winningest coach of the twentieth century. The year 1971 was a turning point for Bryant, the football program, and the university

John David Briley
September 2005

ACKNOWLEDGMENTS

THIS BOOK COULD NOT HAVE BEEN POSSIBLE WITHOUT a number of important people who have assisted me during the last five years. Taylor Watson, curator for the Paul W. Bryant Museum, provided me with a clip file on the forgotten lawsuit against Paul Bryant and emphatically stated that somebody needed to write a book about the integration of the Alabama football team. While this book is not so ambitious, it provides an additional historical niche to approach this subject.

Clem ("Coach") Gryska, current staff member of the Bryant Museum and former long-time assistant coach under the "Bear," has assisted me from the beginning of this project. I could never have completed this endeavor without his assistance in locating former players, coaches, and other contacts associated with the University of Alabama football team. There is not a single living person associated with the Alabama football program since the 1940s who Gryska does not know, and no one, with the exception of Paul W. Bryant, has projected so much goodwill about the Alabama football program in the last half-century. There are not enough words in the English language to convey my thanks to him. In addition, other members of the Bryant Museum have also been a great help to me over the years: Ken Gaddy, Gary Shores, and staffers Esther Cade, Charlene Givens, Brad Green, and Thelma Marchant. Whatever I requested, they were always there to help me. Brad Green in particular had an assortment of good ideas that proved valuable in a number of different ways. The staff members of the W. S. Hoole Special Collections Library were extremely beneficial in looking into the presidential papers of Frank Rose and David Mathews. Special thanks are in order for Tom Land, the institutional records analyst for the Hoole Library, who found records nobody seemed to know about. He was also generous with his time to discuss the general state of Alabama football, from its inception to the present time.

Betty Wagner, a colleague in the Political Science department at East Tennessee State University (ETSU), suggested that I talk to Dr. Robert J. ("Jack") Higgs about this project. Having grown up in middle Tennessee, Higgs had first-hand knowledge of Bear Bryant as a former college football player for Vanderbilt and the Naval Academy. At Vanderbilt, Higgs played against Bryant's team at Kentucky and said that he had never seen so many good players on one team. During his senior year at Navy, his squad defeated Ole Miss in the Sugar Bowl and ranked top five in the final polls. Higgs, a noted scholar and former English professor, has written numerous books and articles about sports. Jack has been extremely helpful in all aspects of this project, and his insight is greatly appreciated. I also want to thank ETSU for a small research grant to study the lawsuit against Bryant.

I conducted all but four interviews in person and take full responsibility for their content. Over three years I interviewed nearly eighty people in and around the Alabama football program. I interviewed sixty players and twelve coaches for this book, and several provided invaluable assistance to me: former players Jimmy Rosser, Jack White, Steve Williams, Wilbur Jackson, Jeff Beard, Lanny Norris, Robin Parkhouse, and Marvin Barron. Rosser, White, Jackson, and Beard gave me permission to use their photographs. Dr. Finus Gaston Jr., a student manager in 1971 and the current associate athletics director at the University of Alabama, also provided me with a couple of great pictures. Allen Cox was extremely helpful in introducing me to a number of the players; in June 2001 he invited me to a reunion of the freshmen teams of 1968 and 1969, who later comprised the 1971 squad. Coaches Jack Rutledge and Jimmy Sharpe, who were also players on the first Alabama squads under Bryant, provided a great deal of insight into understanding Paul Bryant. Larry "Dude" Hennessey, who played for Bryant at Kentucky and coached with him at the Capstone, was also helpful in this endeavor. Ann Barron, an administrative assistant for media relations in the athletics department, was a great source for finding people, places, and things. Her cheerful personality and broad smile always encouraged me to move forward. Harry Lee, former Alabama football player and long-time officer of the "A" Club, was also very supportive in locating former players.

Cathy Whaley, fresh from completing a master's degree in English at Clemson University, worked on the subsequent drafts and revisions of the manuscript. Her expertise in the English language and sports in general were of tremendous help, and she provided additional insights over lunches at the Cottage, a local restaurant near the ETSU campus. I also had help from Jessica Bice and Crystal Stewart, two undergraduate students at ETSU, who transcribed approximately 30 percent of the interviews. I also received a great deal of assistance in the editing of this manuscript from others. One of my childhood friends, Dr. Carroll Van West, a noted historian and now director of historic preservation at Middle Tennessee State University (and who accompanied me to the 1971 Vanderbilt-Alabama game), read the manuscript, and his remarks were greatly appreciated. Dr. Neal Richard "Rick" Boyd read the first several chapters, and his comments were useful in completing the manuscript. Dr. Ken Mijeski, the chair of the political science department at ETSU, was very supportive anytime I needed to be away from school for additional research. I must also thank Phyllis Jennings Corso for her editing assistance early in the process.

I became acquainted with Allen Barra a year ago after I returned a call I received from him. We talked about an hour that day. Since then, we have had a number of telephone calls and emails concerning the state of Alabama football and Paul W. Bryant. Allen has been very helpful in listening to some of my rants about the current state of the world and, in particular, about the Crimson Tide. His recent book *The Last Coach* is the definitive biography of the Bear. I predict that this work will become the standard for Bryant scholars.

Finally, I must thank the people closest to me. My mother, Martha V. Briley, died in the spring before this project began. Her family was responsible for introducing me to Alabama football at a very early age. I was given an Alabama football bobblehead for Christmas when I was seven years old. In the early 1960s, during trips to my grandparents' house in Selma, seeing Bear Bryant in the newspapers and billboards advertising Coke and Golden Flakes Potato Chips ("Great Pair Says The Bear") was a source of a great inspiration to this young fan of the famous coach. My mother was a great admirer of Coach Bryant and would have greatly enjoyed this book. I think about her every day. My father, H. Clayton Briley, took me to my first Alabama football game in Tuscaloosa, the 1970 A-Day game in which the Team of the Sixties was honored. One or both of my parents, along with long-time friend Darold Dunlap, were with me when I attended five games during the 1971 season. My dad also has attended a number of games in the last five years and provided me with whatever help I needed. He was my biggest fan and told everybody in Murfreesboro about this book. He died in July 2005 and will be greatly missed. My wife Susan Widener, while not an Alabama supporter per se, thought a lot of Paul Bryant, primarily because of the scholarship program he established to provide for the children of every player who played for the great coach. She has been very helpful and understanding in my numerous trips to the "Heart of Dixie" and took care of our numerous dogs in my absence. In addition, my special Dalmatian females, Lippy and Oreo, were always there at my feet or sitting on the couch with me, giving me emotional support during this research. Unfortunately, both of them died before I finished. They are also greatly missed.

My last bit of thanks lies with all the players and coaches of the 1971 team. This book stands as a tribute to this historic team, recognizing their accomplishments during this memorable season.

John David Briley
September 2005

WHITHER BRYANT?

PAUL WILLIAM BRYANT WAS BORN ON SEPTEMBER 11, 1913, in Moro Bottom, Arkansas, to a large family that included eleven siblings. Bryant described this area of the rural Deep South as a "little piece of bottom land on the Moro Creek, about 7 miles south of Fordyce."[1] Bryant earned the nickname "Bear" by having wrestled with a bear at a carnival in Fordyce in his early teens. Hank Crisp recruited the All-State end to play for the University of Alabama. While at the Capstone, as the university is called, Bryant became known as the "other end" because the end on the other side of the football was the great Don Hutson (voted in 2000 to the National Football League's all-time team). During his three varsity years, Bryant's teams went 23-3-2. Following Bryant's junior year, Alabama defeated Stanford in the Rose Bowl and won the national championship.

Bryant's coaching career began with assistant positions, first at his alma mater from 1936 to 1939 under Frank Thomas and then under Red Sanders at Vanderbilt from 1940 to 1941. However, World War II intervened; Bryant volunteered for duty in the Navy and served in North Africa and in European theaters until his discharge in August 1945. During this period he coached a military football team at North Carolina Naval Pre-Flight. His first head-coaching job at the University of Maryland would be only a month after his release from service.

In his only season with the Terrapins, Bryant went 6-2-1. Following a dispute with the university president Curly Byrd over who would have final say in personnel matters with the football team, Bryant resigned. When news of Bryant's resignation spread across campus, some students reacted by refusing to go to classes. Only after a meeting with the former head coach did the students decide to return to class.

Maryland's loss was the University of Kentucky's gain. Bryant was immediately signed to coach the Wildcats. In his eight seasons, the Bear would post a record of 60-23-5 (.710 winning percentage), play in four bowl games, and in 1950 lead the team to the only Southeastern Conference (SEC) title ever won by the Wildcats. In 2003, the Sagarin (recognized by the NCAA as an "official" champion) rating system awarded Kentucky the national championship for the 1950 season. In the entire 114-year history of football at Kentucky, among those who coached for four seasons or longer, none were as successful as Bryant. Kentucky has finished in the Associated Press top twenty eight times, five times during the Bryant era. His biggest problem in the Bluegrass State was the competition with the basketball program. Well-publicized spats between Bryant, university president Herman Donovan, and its legendary basketball coach Adolph Rupp were numerous. Bryant then entered a series of discussions with the University of Arkansas regarding their coaching vacancy. These discussions were not successful and Bryant turned his attention to a similar position at Texas A&M University in College Station, Texas.

Bryant's first pre-season training camp at Junction, Texas, was memorable for the Aggie players. The coach took 111 players to camp but only thirty-five remained for the full ten days. That year Bryant endured his only losing season as a head coach, ending with a 1-9 record. During the next season he turned things around for the Aggies, who for the next three years were 24-5-2. During this span they won one Southwestern Conference (SWC) championship in 1956 and two top-ten finishes (1956 and 1957). A&M star John David Crow won the Heisman Trophy in 1957.

After the 1957 season, Bryant returned to Alabama as the head coach and athletics director because "Mama called" after he had turned them down in 1947 and 1954. In *The Legend of Bear Bryant* Mickey Herskowitz tells the story behind the famous above-mentioned quote. Following the last regular season game in which the Aggies lost to archrival Texas by a score of 9-7, Bryant came into the locker room and explained to his players and the media that "I'd like to think that I haven't considered it yet. I'd like to think I have been preparing for Texas. There is only one reason that I would consider [the Alabama job]. When you were out playing as a kid, say you heard your mother call you to do some chores, or come in for supper, you might not answer her. But if you thought she needed you, you'd be there in a hurry."[2] Jim Dent's recent book *The Junction Boys: How Ten Days in Hell with Bear Bryant forged a Championship Season* is a wonderful account of this experience, even though much of it is fictional and not historically accurate.

BRYANT RETURNS TO ALABAMA

The 1958 season was a memorable campaign in which the Crimson Tide achieved their first winning record in five years; having won only three games the previous three years, Bama would go 5-4-1. This would be the only time in Bryant's twenty-five years at his alma mater that the team would not compete in a bowl game. In *Turnaround*, author Tom Stoddard tells a poignant story of Bryant's return to Alabama. Sophomore guard Don Parsons sums up Bryant's first meeting with the players: "He looked like a man on a mission and before he reached the front of the room, you could sense that everyone was beginning to feel new hope."[3] Jack Rutledge, one of the offensive linemen on Bryant's first squad and later long-time assistant coach, tells of this new hope. He recalls that during the first meeting in the summer Coach Bryant instructed "that if they did what he told them to do that they could be national champions."[4] The national championship was realized in 1961 when the team allowed its opponents only 25 points while recording six shutouts en-route to an undefeated 11-0 season.

In 1962, a 1-point loss to Georgia Tech in Atlanta stood between the Tide and another national championship. In 1963, the Tide finished 9-2 and an eighth place finish in the AP final poll. 1964 and 1965 would also be national championship seasons. In 1966, the 11-0 team finished third in the polls. Notre Dame and Michigan State, who had played to a tie during the season, finished ahead of them. Bryant would later say that the 1966 team was his best team in the 1960s, even though the national sportswriters did not award them the top prize. How does the national champion of the past two seasons start out pre-season number one, go undefeated during the season, and fall to third?

The next two years (1967 and 1968) would not be great ones for the Crimson Tide, at least not by the standards of the previous years, during which the Tide won eight games each year. They went to major bowls but lost to Texas A&M in 1967 and to Missouri in 1968, which certainly ruined the off-seasons. The 1969 and 1970 campaigns, however, were low points as Alabama's records slipped to 6-5 and 6-5-1. On the field, the biggest problems were on the defensive side of the football. The defenses in each of these seasons were atrocious and allowed 534 points.

Teams from the years 1959 to 1966 combined on 513 points. Doubts about Bryant surfaced, who was then fifty-seven years old. Had Bryant lost his touch and the game passed him by? Certainly some of the Tide's fans as well as opposing players and coaches thought so. When in 1969 Alabama lost to the University of Tennessee Volunteers in Birmingham, Vol linebacker Steve Kiner claimed that the Tide players "had lost their pride in the red jersey."[5] Was the Coach at fault for the loss of university pride or were there other contributing factors?

HISTORICAL CONTEXT AND THE 1969 CAMPAIGN

The year 1969 was the first of Richard M. Nixon's presidency. It would be the year that the United States became the first country to successfully land men on the moon. Amidst numerous demonstrations against America's involvement in the Vietnam conflict, Nixon would begin to bring back the troops to their home soil. General unrest was pervasive in America. Assaults against traditional authority left no institutions excluded. For instance, the football team at the University of Alabama was just one of many targets. In June 1969, the university's Afro-American Student Association filed a lawsuit against Coach Bryant and university officials, demanding that they recruit black athletes as intensely as they recruit whites and that they grant a significant number of football scholarships proportionate to the number of black and white high school athletes in the state.

The year 1969 was also the 100th anniversary of college football. *Sporting News* magazine polled 100 prominent figures associated with the game and across the country helped commemorate this celebration with the election of the greatest coach of college football's first one hundred years. The magazine unveiled the results in its pre-season issue, which provided coverage of the upcoming season. The issue designated Knute Rockne of Notre Dame as the greatest coach; Bryant ranked sixth and was the only active coach listed in the top ten.[6] In the football press guide issued by the University of Alabama sports information department, Director Charley Thornton predicted that, while strong defensive teams and a strong passing attack had been the trademarks of Bryant teams of the past few years, the 1969 team would be one that relied more on the running game and ball control. The Bear even admitted that "you have to adjust your plans to fit your personnel…and you have to have good balance in your offensive game to win consistently."[7]

The 1969 version of the Crimson Tide reflected another type of adjustment with the team's offense passing much more than in the past. The defense was much weaker than had been the case during the Bryant era. The team was up and down all year. They won their first three games against Virginia Tech, Southern Mississippi, and Ole Miss. At that point in the season, the Tide ranked thirteenth in the nation. It would be the last time they would be ranked in 1969. They stumbled badly and lost against Vanderbilt in Nashville then were blown out by Tennessee in Birmingham before they rebounded against Clemson and Mississippi State. Bama lost a close contest to Louisiana State University in Birmingham and won in a laugher against Miami for homecoming. The final encounter against Auburn was a huge disappointment by a score of 49-26. However, one game remained: the Liberty Bowl in Memphis, Tennessee against the Colorado Buffaloes.

Two days before the bowl game, assistant coach Pat Dye met with Coach Bryant and asked if he could miss the contest. This was a highly unusual request, but one that had some merit. The signing day for new recruits was on the same Saturday as the game and Dye thought it would be more advantageous to sign the upcoming players than to participate in the game. Dye recollected:

I told Coach Bryant that it did not matter one way or the other if Alabama or Colorado won this bowl game. What did matter was that we needed some better players. Coach had been on the staff pretty hard about recruiting better people. I told him that neither one of us were gonna have a job if we did not get some better players. I let him know that I had twelve players that wanted me to be with them as they signed to play for us. He was receptive to this and allowed me to miss the game. I was able to sign them all.[8]

At Memphis, the Tide's offense played better and kept their turnovers to a minimum, but the defense could not contain the high-powered offense of the Buffaloes. A 47-33 loss was the result. Although they actually led 33-31 midway through the third quarter, Alabama could not hold on to the lead. Long-time assistant coach and recruiting coordinator Clem Gryska remembers the game well because of how the team lost in the final quarter and what this suggested about the future of Alabama football. "This was the second time in as many years that we had lost a bowl game in which we were physically manhandled. Danny Ford was our top offensive lineman during that season and he did everything we asked of him physically, but their defensive lineman just threw him down several times because of superior physical skills. That told something very significantly about the type of player we would have to recruit."[9] The era of the lean, quick boys for which Bryant was so noted in the 1960s was over. The coach would now have to recruit bigger, stronger players to compete successfully. The 85-12-3 record of the decade was the best in college football history. Bryant's peers voted him the "Coach of the Decade." However, five of the twelve losses had come in a single season. Another problem hovered over the Crimson Tide that very few people, even those close to the program, knew anything about.

HAD BRYANT HAD ENOUGH?

The problem was that the head coach was looking elsewhere. Paul Bryant had been successful everywhere he had been in college football, and he was looking for a new challenge. More than twenty times he talked or met with the professional Miami Dolphins during and after the 1969 season. All of the assistant coaches who were interviewed except John David Crow admitted that they did not know anything about it at the time. Crow knew about the change, but Bryant had sworn him to secrecy. In fact, John David was just leaving his Tuscaloosa home to catch an 8:00 A.M. flight to Miami to oversee the team's operations until Coach Bryant's arrival the next day when he got an urgent phone call telling him to cancel the trip.[10] However, others like Jack Rutledge had noticed puzzling changes in Bryant's regimen. Rutledge commented about these: "I noticed that Coach Bryant had taken off for about a month earlier in the spring of that year and he had a lot of outside interests and Dr. Mathews had to get him out of the contract that he had made with the Miami Dolphins. The whole attitude thing has changed, as were the game, defenses, and strategies were also changing. This is what was going on in Coach Bryant's mind and he's been successful at the college level. He's thinking that he can do it at the pro level."[11]

Bryant even consulted with former player and New York Jet quarterback Joe Namath about the Dolphins personnel and asked him to evaluate them. Joe Robbie, the Dolphins president, made Bryant an offer he could not refuse. In his autobiography the Alabama coach recounts this episode, describing how he ultimately rejected the offer after an earlier agreement:

> [Robbie and I] drew up the contract in a hotel room in Birmingham. I got my lawyer, Winston McCall, to rewrite Robbie's original. We put in everything I could think of, making the total value so good I'd have had to make about $1.7 million over a five-year period to equal it. A stock option, a place to live, cars—the works. The most important item was $10,000 for Mary Harmon to go back and forth to Tuscaloosa during the season.... That night I told Joe Robbie I'd take the job, but that I had to get the approval of my people first. And when it came to nut-cutting, I couldn't do it.... When it was all over, I really felt guilty. I had tried to convince myself that it was the challenge that interested me. Nobody had ever done it both ways, won in college and the pros, and I knew I could do it. But I think now it was more the money, because I kept thinking about four bedrooms, seven baths, Jockey Club, and Cadillacs and Lincolns, so many things. Things I didn't need or already had. It was ridiculous. And I knew it. Never again.[12]

COULD A REJUVENATED BRYANT
BRING BACK THE TIDE?

The front-page headline of the January 8, 1970 issue of the *Tuscaloosa News* read "Bryant to Stay at Bama." There was no mention of the Dolphin job in the article, except that there had been a review by the athletic director and Dr. Mathews over the state of the football program. Soon afterward Coach Bryant met with his staff and told them how poor recruiting had been and how all the fair-weather fans were trying to take his job. Keith Dunnavant recounts this meeting with his assistants. "Now, I'm not worried about myself. I can get a job. I'm not sure about the rest of y'all. If I was you, I'd get out there and get us some players."[13] The message was clear that Alabama was going to get back to doing what had made them successful in the past, going back to the basics, something they had not been doing very well lately.

Alabama would recruit larger and heavier players than it had before. It was much concerned with the core of its recruiting base, namely the state and the high-school coaches. Of the thirty-one 1970 signees, nine were 6-foot-3 or taller and seven 220 pounds or more. Wilbur Jackson, a wide receiver from Ozark, Alabama, was a diamond in the rough. The first black player his size and speed filled a void missing from the team. Recruiting coordinator Gryska explained the change in philosophy from a smaller quick player to a larger, quick player and how it benefitted the teams future:

> To start with, we got greedy by going nationwide with the recruiting classes of '67 and '68. The first problem with these groups was that they had trouble adjusting to the culture and climate of the region. We had some real average years with those kids, and our offensive system didn't match the talent of the kids we had. Prior to signing John Mitchell and Wilbur Jackson, we decided to go back to our roots in recruiting and stay mostly within the Southern region. If an in-state kid has problems with the program and decides to quit us, it becomes his burden. It is not like he can go home and bad-mouth Coach Bryant, because everybody in this state knows different. As a consequence of this, the analysis is that you don't insult your father in his own house and you respect the rule. This is how malcontents are controlled and our national reputation is not hurt and that was part of the problem during the late sixties.[14]

Long-time assistant at Alabama and former player under Bryant at Kentucky, Larry "Dude" Hennessey, echoed this sentiment when he stated that "all these All-Americans were out-of-state and there were eight to ten of these that we were recruiting in the late sixties and spending a lot of time on them which could have been better spent in our own backyard. We did not get any of these types of players and should have stayed at home."[15]

In February 1970, Coach Bryant announced the scheduling of an eleventh regular season game pursuant to the change in policy from the National Collegiate Athletic Association (NCAA). Rivaling Alabama in this game were the University of Southern California (USC) Trojans. They were by coached by Bryant's long-time friend John McKay. Ironically, McKay (along with Darrell Royal and Charlie McClendon of LSU) had been considered for the Alabama opening in the event that Bryant went to the Dolphins. A two-game contract was signed, the first game in Birmingham in 1970 and the second in Los Angeles in 1971.

USC had the top football program in the West and had great success in the 1960s, winning two national championships in the years 1962 and 1967. They had also been ranked third in the nation in the final polls of 1969. In other seasons USC might have been considered a great opening-day opponent, but not given the kinds of problems that the Crimson Tide had recently been having. They were less confident about facing such a formidable team.

The football squad went through a spirited spring training, which concluded with the annual A-Day game. At the last meeting of the spring practice the Bear delivered a message to his troops. Jimmy Rosser, an offensive lineman, remembered it well:

> Coach Bryant got up at this meeting like any other, and he said many of the same things that he told at the end of the last spring practice like what he expected of us when we came back in the fall. What was different about this one that he was getting more animated as he continued to speak. His voice seemed to pick up the longer he stood before us. Finally, he told us that he was going to get the best athletes available to play for us and that included black players. He then proceeded to tell us that if any of you didn't like that then you could get the hell out of here; because that was the way it was going to be. None of the players left the meeting.[16]

Paul Bryant began preparation for the 1970 season with more vigor than he had displayed during the previous three seasons. With a schedule that included seven of the previous year's top-twenty teams, the Crimson Tide had extra incentive to be ready. They had lost half their starters to graduation but would have the strongest nucleus of sophomores in quite some time. The offense would be very similar to what they had run in the past, with a pro-style offense led by senior quarterback Scott Hunter. Johnny Musso would lead a vastly improved running game complemented by the likes of Joe Labue and Ohio State transfer Dave Brunguard. The defense, however, would look somewhat different. Alabama would discard its basic five-man front and install a 4-3 alignment (four down linemen and three linebackers).

The Crimson Tide was unranked in any of the pre-season top-twenty polls for the first time since 1959. They had only been ranked in the middle of the SEC pre-season forecast. Much of their luster had faded after the Tide's 1969 disastrous campaign of 6-5 and an eighth-place finish in the conference. Many thought the game had passed Bryant by. Some even thought that perhaps he should move out of the way and allow the university to hire a younger and more energetic coach. Alabama's Bear would have none of that kind of thinking. In his comments prior to the 1970 season, Bryant accepted the blame for the decline while sounding more determined and optimistic about the future: "Four years ago we had the finest football team that I had ever seen. In three short years we worked our way down to where the ordinary people are. I believe in three years we can be back on top, and I'm hoping that it doesn't take three. This has to be the first sound basic building year.... This is the first adequate sophomore group we have had in the last four or five years. It's a good sophomore group."[17]

THE USC GAME

The press buildup to this game was enormous. Southern Cal ranked third or fourth in all the pre-season polls, but many analysts thought that the team could be national champions because of the players' enormous talent. The game had been added a few months earlier when the NCAA allowed another game played in collegiate football. This would be the first time that an integrated team outside the SEC had come to Birmingham to play against the all-white Tide (Wilbur Jackson was a freshman at this time and "frosh" were not allowed to play on the varsity until 1972). Alabama state law had previously prohibited such contests, but the civil rights revolution of the 1960s changed that. Legion Field in Birmingham proclaimed itself the "football capital of the south." The game between intersectional powers was a sellout within a couple of days after tickets were made available in the spring. These two schools had combined to win five of the ten national championships in college football in the decade of the 1960s. Jim Murray, sports editor of the *Los Angeles Times*, had been a virulent critic of the social policy of the South in general and Alabama in particular. Murray single-handedly influenced Rose Bowl officials in 1961 not to include Alabama as one of its participants because of the state's segregationist policies. In his editorial assessment, Murray left no stones unturned:

> The front-of-the-bus champions of the universe, the Alabama varsity, is kicking a habit. It's busting up the cotillion, that old gang of mine. The bedsheet-and-burning conference is coming out in daylight of the 20th century.... It's given up on Bobby Lee, Jeff Davis. The news of Appomattox has finally seeped through. They've figured 100 years is long enough to give up the Confederacy. The Southeastern Conference is handing over its sword.... The "whites only" sign have disappeared all over town and the football field was one of the last to go. The USC Trojans' front four won't have to stage a sit-in at Legion Field Saturday night. They've been invited there.... The Birmingham of Bull Run and Bull Connor is as long gone as the plantations of the Mississippi. It lies rotting on the riverbottom along with the Monitor or the Merrimac. It is through fighting with the American ideal. It is coming to terms with history. It is asking for terms from a society it sought to ignore.... Coach Paul Bryant is a rumpled old party who looks as if he takes a shower with clothes on every morning, then dries himself rolling around the ground. He is a multi-millionaire who, if you saw coming, you would cross the street for fear that he would panhandle you. Old Bear looks relieved. His state has finally decided to join football. Paul Bryant was fixing to retire a year ago as soon as he found someone as good to coach 'Bama. But after peering under a few managers, and quizzing an occasional group of three wise men on camelback, he decided not to count on any miracles and stay, on the job himself.... But the point of the game will not be the score, the Bear, the Trojans: the point of the game will be Reason, Democracy, and Hope. The real winner will be the South. It'll be their first since the second day of Gettysburg, or maybe, The Wilderness.[18]

Needless to say, the game did not live up to its advanced billing of two great football programs. The Trojans destroyed the Crimson Tide 42-21 before a sellout crowd of 72,175. The score did not indicate the disparity between the two teams. It could have been much worse. USC piled up 559 yards of total offense and were led by 235-pound fullback Sam Cunningham, who gained 135 yards and scored two touchdowns. Birmingham native Clarence Davis added 76 yards to the Trojan effort. Both Cunningham and Davis were black. Cunningham and other black players from Southern California were apprehensive about playing in the Deep South, but it did not show on the field. Cunningham would later say that a number of black players had pistols and knives in case they needed them, but "I was not one of them."[19] There were no visible racial incidents on the field or in the stands. The real problem for Tide fans was an Alabama team lacking in competitive players versus the larger and faster Trojans. Alabama could only muster 32 yards on the ground and were forced into many "third and long" situations that forced Hunter to pass. One Bama fan was seen muttering as he left the stadium, "Y'all sure brought a great football team down here. Wowee. I'm sure glad McKay and The Bear are friends. If they weren't, it could have been 70-0."[20] The second game could not arrive quickly enough to help get rid of the bad taste in the mouths of Tide players from this massacre. Help, however, would be on the way in the form of Virginia Tech.

COULD THE SEASON GET WORSE?

Alabama bounced back the next week by demolishing Virginia Tech and former Bryant protégé Jerry Claiborne 51-18 in Legion Field. This was much the same team that the Crimson Tide had struggled with in 1969 when they barely hung on to win 17-13 in Blacksburg, Virginia. This time the Tide rolled up 584 yards of total offense, with 364 yards tallied for the ground game. Seven different players scored touchdowns in this rout of the Hokies. The next two opponents would feature the two top passers in the conference (Florida Gator John Reaves and Ole Miss Reb Archie Manning). The Tide's performance in these contests would show Bama fans a far better defense compared to the previous year.

Johnny Musso led the way with 139 yards on twenty-two carries en route to the Crimson Tide's second victory of the season over the Florida Gators with a score of 46-15. Musso's performance earned him SEC "Back of the Week" honors. The offense was also balanced with 286 yards rushing and 200 yards passing. This overall performance was another strong team effort as six different Tide players scored touchdowns. Although John Reaves piled up impressive numbers (24-44 for 238 yards) for the Gators, the Bama defense allowed only 38 yards rushing and intercepted two passes. There was, however, one glaring drawback to this win: Scott Hunter hurt his passing arm shoulder and would not be available for the following week's clash with the University of Mississippi.

The Ole Miss fans were still smarting from the previous year's 33-32 loss to the Tide, as they thought the better team had lost. They were looking for revenge as Alabama arrived in Jackson. They got their recompense when Archie Manning ran and passed his way to victory over the Crimson Tide 48-23. This game was reminiscent of many of the losses in 1969 as the running game stalled for only 27 yards and forced Hunter's substitute, Neb Hayden, into passing situations not to his liking. Hayden completed only 14-32 passes for 205 yards and threw three interceptions. Could Vanderbilt and Tennessee be the double trouble they were a year ago or would a different fate be in store for the Crimson faithful?

The lowly Commodores would not embarrass Paul Bryant for the second time in two years. However, they would have to do without their star passer, whose shoulder was still on the mend. Although they did not have Scott Hunter, their running game got rolling again after a week's absence compiling 344 yards in the 35-11 win in Tuscaloosa. Hunter would be available for the next week's contest against the powerful defense of the Tennessee Volunteers. He would need a lot of help in order to break the three-game losing streak before the capacity crowd sure to be waiting in Knoxville.

All-American Linebackers Steve Kiner and Jack Reynolds had graduated to the NFL by 1970, but their replacements Ray Nettles and Jamie Rotella joined All-American Jackie Walker as the leaders of Tennessee's defense. The Crimson Tide would have Hunter back, although not 100 percent. He would again share quarterbacking duties with Hayden, but neither was effective in the 24-0 loss. Even though Alabama would have more first downs (25-12), passing yardage (271-60), and total offense (358-213) than the Vols, they were undone by eight interceptions between the two defense-pressed quarterbacks. David Bailey, the talented split end who caught twelve passes in the game, remembers how frustrated Tide receivers were with the quarterbacks. When the offense came back onto the field after the sixth interception, Bailey had some interesting remarks for Scott Hunter. Before Hunter could call the play, Bailey told him to "throw the ball to number 44 [Bobby Majors] in the orange jersey and I will see if I can catch it."[21] Hunter was not amused by the comment. The running game was held under 100 yards for the third time. This would be the first shutout that a Bryant-coached team had received in 115 games since a 0-0 tie with Vanderbilt in 1958. A .500 season at the midpoint did not bode well as the Tide traveled to the Astrodome to meet the tough University of Houston Cougars.

A BREAKTHROUGH OR MORE OF THE SAME?

Houston was a very physical team on both sides of the ball. Their offense was explosive and featured the veer-T option, a first cousin of the wishbone. It would take a super effort on the part of the Crimson Tide to leave with a victory. They had just enough in the 30-21 win. Alabama took the lead 23-21 with 6:35 to play as the Cougars were heading for the go-ahead score. Steve Higginbotham intercepted a Gary Mullins pass at the Bama 20-yard line and returned it 80 yards for a touchdown with 1:51 remaining in the game. A balanced offense and some big plays by the defense were responsible for this exciting fourth victory. Some thirty years later, Johnny Musso recounted how important this win had been. "The week of this game Coach Crow (backfield) came to me and told us that we were going back to being a tough and physical team by being able to run the ball like we had done so in the past. This game would set the stage for what we could become the next season and show how far we had come. I believe that after this game we had turned the corner and would have the opportunity to get much better."[22]

The next two games would also be very important to the University of Alabama. The vastly improved Mississippi State Bulldogs would make the 90-minute trek to Tuscaloosa the next week. The Crimson Tide, however, would have little difficulty in winning the contest 35-6 as they amassed over 500 yards total offense for the second time this season. Alabama gained 289 yards on the ground as Johnny Musso led the way with three touchdowns. The improving defense played their best game of the year and held the Bulldogs to only 293 yards and one touchdown. The Tide had some momentum as they welcomed the Louisiana State Tigers to Legion Field the next week. Former Bryant player at Kentucky, Charlie McClendon, coached LSU and had adopted much the same philosophy as his mentor and former coach. McClendon stressed a strong defense, a ball control offense, and a good kicking game. LSU had finished seventh in the country the previous season and held the same rank going into this contest. LSU won a hard-fought struggle with the Crimson Tide 14-9 as Hunter threw four interceptions. The running game was stymied again and held to only 79 yards. The same pattern had occurred in earlier losses over the past two years. When Alabama could not consistently run the ball, they were forced to rely on the pass. Even though they had Hunter, one of the better quarterbacks around, they were unable to overcome mistakes when their pass protection broke down. As Dude Hennessey later said concerning this phenomenon,

"When you can't stop anybody and can not hold the ball for any length of time, then your defense will wear out."[23] However, the defense held their own. It was the offense that could not move the football. The stronger Tigers won the interior line play.

The tenth opponent of the 1970 campaign was the University of Miami Hurricanes. This small private school played its home games in the Orange Bowl, where the seating capacity was more than 72,000. Miami, however, rarely drew even half that crowd for their home games. Only 25,469 were on hand to see Alabama defeat the Hurricanes 32-8. Bryant commented on the lack of Hurricane fans to longtime Tide announcer Doug Layton: "I am tired of coming down here to play and nobody shows up, when our contract is up with them Miami.... We're through coming to the Orange Bowl unless it is on New Year's Day."[24] After the 1974 season the two teams would play each other only twice, both in the Sugar Bowl with national title aspirations on the line.

The Auburn Tigers would be the Crimson Tide's final opponent in the annual Iron Bowl at Legion Field. Two outstanding players led Auburn: gifted quarterback Pat Sullivan and speedy receiver Terry Beasley. The famous "Sullivan to Beasley" combo would be heard in football circles all over the Southeast and to distant parts of the country. The rivalry between the Tigers and the Tide was rapidly becoming the best in college football. Alabama charged ahead in the game 17-0 by the end of the first quarter but could not hold the talented Tigers as Sullivan completed 22 of 38 passes for 341 yards. Auburn won its second consecutive game over its top rival by 33-28. The Tide finished with more yards total offense (513-457), more first downs (31-22), and more yards rushing (301-140), but they did not have Pat Sullivan to make the crucial plays. The defense could not stop him when they had to. It would the only time in the year that Alabama out-rushed its opponent and did not win the game.

Even though the Tide had another 6-5 season, they were invited to play in the New Year's Eve Astro-Bluebonnet Bowl in Houston against perennial national power, the University of Oklahoma Sooners. The two teams were mirror images. Both had had mediocre seasons with a great deal of talent returning for 1971. The Sooners were 7-4 and ran the wishbone offense. This triple-option offense was highly explosive and time-consuming. Jack Mildren, a talented option quarterback, and three excellent backfield runners, Joe Wylie, Greg Pruitt, and Leon Crosswhite, led the Sooners. By the end of next season, every college football fan would know their names. The 53,822 fans in the Astrodome undoubtedly got their money's worth in seeing this 24-24 tie. Both teams were very resourceful on offense (over 400 yards apiece), but neither could consistently stop the other team. The wishbone was a ball control offense that relied on the run, while Alabama was more much balanced in their approach. The Crimson Tide had a great chance to win the game as they drove inside the 20-yard line with over a minute to play. They ran a couple of dive plays up the middle to get lined up for a would-be winning field goal. However, Richard Ciemny missed badly with the attempt on the game's final play, ending the contest in a deadlock. This game would later be viewed as one that foreshadowed the next decade's two top programs in college football.

WHY THE DECLINE?

In analyzing the 1969–1970 decline from previous excellence, most people tend to lump the years together. Certainly the records were the same, the scores were similar, and the defense experienced some of the same problems. The big difference was that in 1969 the Crimson Tide had not had the players to be successful. Maybe Bryant himself was not as motivated or had not asked enough of his staff. The 1970 team was quite different. It had better personnel. Many were sophomores who matured throughout the season. The schedule was much tougher in 1970—so were Coach Bryant and his staff. It would take a few years for all this to yield results.

The primary reasons for the decline were in coaching and recruiting. The two are related to one another. The head coach sets the tone and philosophy of the team. He makes personnel decisions based on the players available. If the right types of players are not available, tone must question why they are not there. One reason is that they were not recruited. It took the staff a while to realize that to be successful bigger players were needed. Consider Gryska's earlier observation after the Liberty Bowl loss. Another reason involves success and the team's response to it. Mal Moore, long-time Bryant offensive assistant and current athletics director, addressed this issue:

> Well, I think that in my mind we won national championships in '61 and back to back in '64 and '65 and none of us had experienced that type of success. I felt that we went through a period of time and I think

that this included Coach Bryant as well... We assumed that players would come and we had a couple of lean recruiting years... Now you realize that it is harder to recruit because people recruit against us by saying that you will sit there two or three years because of all the players there. You're losing players for that season and recruiters tell them from other schools that [a prospective player] will sit there for a while. One of the things that you realize now (and it may go back that far as well) is that one of the most important factors in this process is the sooner you play is very important to perspective recruits. I do think that this had an effect on our recruiting and we realized that we did not have the type of players that we were supposed to have. We had been beat on several players and it shows up in '68, '69, and '70 in recruiting.[25]

Pat Dye, another Bryant assistant during this period and later head coach at Auburn, seconded this notion in his autobiography *In the Arena*:

You get to thinking that you are invincible. And at Alabama, maybe we thought we were just automatically going to go out there and recruit the top players, who were supposed to come, because we were winning. It's just human nature that you lose that urgency in recruitment and kids can sense it. Somebody's telling them, "We got to have you." And you walk in there and say, "Here's a scholarship. If you want it, fine. If you don't we're gonna line up and beat you anyway." And you can find yourself playing inferior people, which won't win for you.... There's a lot of truth to something Coach Bryant once said...: 'if you take an axe and hit one lick on a big tree every day, for a long time it will be fine, and look fine, but there'll come a day when it will fall.' That's what happened to us, gradually, at Alabama.[26]

Jimmy Sharpe, one of Bryant's former players and offensive line coach, agreed with the others but thought something else had impacted the decline in 1969 and 1970:

We signed a lot of good players in '68 and '69, but they quit us. More players quit during this period than in previous times. All of a sudden, we ran out of lineman. Times were changing. We went through a period of time and I was coaching the offensive line. I can remember in a staff meeting and somebody that had started at linebacker and the other coaches thought he was not good enough to play that position and they gave him to me. In addition to not having enough players on the line, the culture was changing and a lot of the staff had not recognized this.... I could not believe it myself. I'm seeing all this stuff about antiwar and drugs and I'm saying to myself, this can't be happening because this is Alabama football. What is going on? The majority of coaches were disconnected from this. It was a whole another world in which it was impacting the youngsters much more so than us. This was a big problem during this period.[27]

Kirk McNair worked in the sports information department for eleven years beginning in 1969. He left in 1979 to start his own publication, *'Bama: Inside the Crimson Tide*. For the last twenty-seven years he has been the editor of this monthly magazine, which primarily covers football but includes all other University of Alabama sports programs. McNair agreed with some of the above perceptions but disagreed with others, adding that "Coach Bryant and his coaches were not bad coaches, so obviously the material fell off. I think a lot of people point to Scott Hunter, but I think that is unfair because we were moving the football and that Scott did not play defense. We were not stopping anybody. We just got down, we had won a bunch of national championships and Coach would say it all the time that the staff got a little fatheaded. I'm sure the staff did not think so and were working hard and whatever reason we did not get the players."[28]

Jack Rutledge had a somewhat different opinion of the decline in the late 1960s as he related how success on the field changed the way coaches prepared the younger players. He did not look at single seasons, but rather what he called "three-year cycles." Rutledge described this idea with great precision:

> You have to go back to 1958 where Coach Bryant told us that we could be national champions in 1961. We were. The '62 team was pretty good and we should have won [the national championship again] and a lot of carryover to '63, '64. You think of these three years and where you've come from and it takes about two and a half to three years to make it work and there was never any starting over for any of these kids because you kept winning. In '67, '68, and '69 we did not teach the basics; they [the players] had lived with the whole thing and we did not have the fundamentals being taught the same way that we had earlier been taught.... I see this in three-year increments. Now then you go to '68, '69 and it was not as important as it had been before. In 1970 he told us that we're gonna start it back and build it up again. We would do the 6-on-6s and the 3-on-3s and gut-check the players like we had done before and teach in-depth fundamentals to a degree that we had not previously done.[29]

Dude Hennessey observed another factor that contributed to the problem in recruiting. This one had nothing to do with the coaches but everything to do with the external environment in which they were working. Recruits knew that they could be successful players elsewhere and not have to put up with the regimen Bryant required for those who came to the University of Alabama. Hennessey agreed with Dye and Moore's assessment of outside recruiters but added the following:

> The culture changes in the country gave us a different kind of athlete. It was much more difficult to recruit out of our geographical area because of these changes. Most of the athletes in the South were basically the same, but the other ones outside were much different. It was very hard to get them to come to campus. If we could get them to come to campus and he meets Coach Bryant, he'll get him. If he can't close that deal then we did not really want them. We had this one situation which explains what I'm talking about. I am recruiting Mike Curtis [later All-Pro linebacker for the Baltimore Colts] and he has a great deal of respect for Coach Bryant and the Alabama program, but will not visit the university. He says that if he does he knows that Coach Bryant will sell him and he will sign, but he does not want to do that. Go figure! You do not always realize where you are in recruiting until it's too late and it shows up on the field.[30]

One can readily agree with the above evaluations as to why the Alabama football program deteriorated at the end of the 1960s. But these were not the only problems facing the Bryant regime. Another concern was one the entire South, not just Alabama, had to confront. This issue was how to best deal with racial integration and with what some historical observers have called the "second reconstruction."

A SECOND RECONSTRUCTION

ON JULY 2, 1969 THE UNIVERSITY OF ALABAMA CHAPTER OF the Afro-American Student Association filed a lawsuit in federal court against Paul Bryant, the University of Alabama, its board of trustees, chairman of the executive committee John A. Caddell, university president Dr. David F. Mathews, and Robert Finch, secretary of the U. S. Department of Health, Education, and Welfare (HEW). The suit charged that Bryant and representatives of the university and its athletics department had not recruited black athletes with the same diligence used to recruit white athletes. The court was asked to order Bryant and the university to recruit and offer black athletes scholarships in proportion to their population in the state. It also asked HEW to suspend federal funds to the university immediately until the athletics department complied with the Civil Rights Act of 1964. While Bryant had met with the student leaders on a couple of occasions, facing a lawsuit against him was a big surprise.

Paul Bryant explained his position on the most explosive domestic issue of the times—race—in his autobiography, *Bear*. Bryant was a man of his times. He grew up in the Deep South with blacks as friends, but in many areas of his life society separated them. Bryant grew up during the Great Depression and knew of hard times firsthand. People from this period did not challenge authority like the generation of the late 1960s, which was much more comfortable financially. In this sense Bryant was no different. He understood what the civil rights leaders were saying and often times agreed with them, but the political situation in his state constrained what he could do about the problem. He believed that people hated because they were ignorant. Comparing attitudes toward the blacks of the 1960s to the view of Catholics in the 1920s, Bryant noted: "You don't change people's thinking over night…. Shoot, when I was back in Arkansas, some of those ignorant country boys thought it was awful that Al Smith [Democratic candidate in 1928] was running for President. Smith was a Catholic, see, and Catholic was a bad word. They didn't know any better. When folks are ignorant, you don't condemn them, you teach them."[31]

Bryant was a football coach and he would do what he needed to help his team. He did not create the circumstances that were before him, but would have to deal with them nonetheless. Like it or not, the state of Alabama was at the heart of the civil rights movement, and its most prominent citizen was affected. In order to understand where Paul Bryant stood on this issue, some historical background is in order.

NOT A PRETTY PICTURE

The monumental *Brown* and *Brown II* decisions by the US Supreme Court in the mid-1950s authorized school districts to implement desegregation with "all deliberate speed."[32] Afterward, in 1956, two black students, Autherine Lucy and Polly Myers, applied for and were granted admission to the University of Alabama. This occurred a mere two months after Rosa Parks refused to go to the back of the bus in Montgomery, Alabama. Parks's refusal led to a year-long bus boycott by blacks that became the seminal event in the modern civil rights movement. A number of on- and off-campus incidents made it difficult for the university to protect the new students. Seven years passed before the political atmosphere would allow the university to make its next integration attempt. John Patterson won the governorship in 1958 by playing the racial card. His losing opponent was George C. Wallace. Wallace vowed that he would never get "outnigguged" again in a campaign. He won the governorship in 1962 and vowed to back "segregation now, segregation tomorrow, and segregation forever" in his inauguration speech in Montgomery in 1963.[33] He made good on this pledge by standing in the schoolhouse door at the Foster Auditorium at the University of Alabama in June of that year. Even though Wallace was not successful in stopping the university's integration, he made himself a national political figure.

Later in 1963, the country saw up close in Birmingham what happened when blacks pressed for equal rights. They were greeted with fire hoses, dogs, and whatever force police commissioner Eugene "Bull" Connor deemed appropriate in keeping the races separate. Martin Luther King, Jr., was in jail for nine days in Birmingham for his acts of civil disobedience. As if this were not enough, white terrorists bombed the Sixteenth Street Baptist Church during Sunday services. Four young black girls were killed. This was the picture Alabama sent the rest of America, and it was not the image Paul Bryant wished to portray.

At the same time Bear Bryant's all-white football teams were winning in a big way. This certainly gave white Southerners something to cheer about. This image was much different from those projected all over the country concerning the civil rights struggles. The all-white football teams won three national championships during the tumultuous decade of the 1960s. Yet this victory might have been greater had the state been more progressive in approaching the integration problem. During this decade at least two instances involving racial politics had negative consequences for the Bryant-coached teams. The first had to do with the snub of the Rose Bowl Committee during the 1961 season after several bowl officials indicated that they would love to have the Crimson Tide play in their postseason bowl game. The campaign by Jim Murray, Melvin Durslag, and others in the Los Angeles area sports media to exclude Alabama because of their state's political stand on civil rights was successful and hurt Bryant's image in certain parts of the national media. The second instance involved the 1966 team's loss of the national championship after completing eleven games undefeated and finishing third in the nation behind Notre Dame and Michigan State, who had earlier tied during the regular season. One of the voters in the Associated Press poll acknowledged such a bias that cost the Crimson Tide an unprecedented three national championships in a row. Bud Collins from the *Boston Globe* claimed that the football team suffered because of the state's negative image on the predominant domestic political issue of the day. "It has Selma to live down, as well as Lurleen [sic] and George, and Sheriff Bull Connor's [sic] police dogs. Surely there's something worthwhile there. Yes—it has the best football team," stated Collins.[34]

Many have asked, why the state of Alabama? Why not somewhere else? It was not as if this were the only state in which prominent racist tendencies held sway. Although segregation existed, there were differences of degrees. There was formal segregation in the South, enacted and upheld by laws and state courts. In the North, there was informal segregation, in which minorities might choose to do things among themselves but were not prohibited by law from inter-mixing with the whites if they chose to do so. The current dean of Communications at the University of Alabama, E. Culpepper ("Cully") Clark, addressed the issue of Alabama and racism in his brilliant work *The Schoolhouse Door: Segregation's Last Stand at the University of Alabama*: " Nowhere did the images of freedom's struggles or the faces of evil show themselves in sharper relief than in Alabama. Alabama was to the civil rights movement what Virginia was to the Civil War—its significance leading itself to enlargement in the public mind because the most memorable engagements occurred on its soil...."[35]

THE ATHLETICS DEPARTMENT'S FIRST ATTEMPT AT INTEGRATION

On April 6, 1967, the *Tuscaloosa News* printed on the front page of its sports section an article titled "Bryant Checks Negro Hopefuls." This story detailed the first instance of the football team's attempt at integration. Five black athletes reported for spring drills: Doc Roane, Andrew Pernell, Melvin Leverett, Arthur Dunning, and Jerome Tucker. Four of the five were from the state of Alabama; Tucker was the exception. He was a Southerner—a native of Georgia. As it turned out Tucker was academically ineligible and unable to compete for a position. These four non-scholarship athletes, called "walk-ons," were among the fifty who tried to make the squad that spring. Roane was an offensive guard while the other players were running backs. Pernell and Roane dressed for the annual A-Day spring game. These two non-scholarship players would remain on the squad into fall practice. Coach Bryant was questioned about the first two black players in his 1970 deposition associated with the lawsuit:

> Well, I can tell you a lot about Doc Roane. We all thought that maybe he would help us some day; we thought he was a good kid and that particular spring, Doc is the first one we ever had, he came to see me and sure, we love to have him.... I talked to the squad about it and the squad handled it and I think our kids, we respected Doc. I don't know, I don't think that he would ever be a starter, but I think he would have played

some day and he got into academic problems and got drafted...I think Andrew came out the spring after Doc, but anyway, he did; Andrew was out there and Andrew stayed, I think, longer than any of them, but the two that we had out there might have helped us someday were doing good, were Doc and Andrew.

Bryant was also asked whether Andrew Pernell was on some type of community scholarship.

> We didn't know that, of course; he had been out there, I guess a year before that came up. He didn't put this on his first—when he filled out our first eligibility blank and it turned out he was getting some type of loan or help in some way from a church... Well, anyway, when that came about we had—there was five of them, four white boys and Andrew and we have a rule, a Conference rule that prohibits them from playing unless they were counted in our scholarship number, and of course, they were not; and even if we would have wanted to have counted. We couldn't have, because we were out. I didn't like—I was in sympathy, particularly with Andrew and a boy named Orville, Orville worked and paid a terrific price to be out there. Anyway, we called the Commissioner, and then later we had correspondence back and forth, we had to ask them to not come out, and there were five of them, and Pernell was one of them.[36]

Keith Dunnavant, in his biography *Coach*, asserted that sometime in 1968, after a meeting with several prominent university alumni (including George Wallace, who was not governor at the time but was running for president), Bryant gave his staff a green light in recruiting black athletes.[37] Yet Dunnavant does not mention his source for this information, nor has one been uncovered. On the other hand, the veteran head coach had strongly hinted three years earlier in *Look* magazine that black players would soon play in the SEC.[38] There is additional evidence that on March 3, 1967, Bryant sent a memorandum concerning recruitment of black players to then-university president Frank Rose. In this correspondence, titled "Colored Athletes," Bryant admitted to not actively recruiting black athletes. As he put it, they did not qualify academically or athletically, but he nonetheless welcomed them to come out on their own. At the end of this memo he remarked, "Finally, we do not plan to recruit colored athletes from out-of-state at this time, but certainly would be interested in any that qualify within the state."[39] This memo acknowledges the existence of a double standard at the time. Bryant was a racial moderate who understood the politics of his state and insisted on a go-slow incremental approach to integrating his football team. This position was no different from any of the other schools of the Southeastern Conference. Yet it pointed to problems in the broader culture associated with blacks trying to gain equal rights in Alabama. If the timing of the integration had been an issue, in his mind Paul Bryant had already made the decision to integrate his squad, but he did not want to get ahead of Alabama's political climate. He was a football coach, not the state governor.

THE FUNDAMENTALS OF THE LAWSUIT

In the two years leading up to the lawsuit, Bryant and other members of the athletics department had met on a number of occasions with the Afro-American Student Association's representatives. Ed Nall was the president of this group and served as the key liaison with the athletics department in the effort to expand recruitment of black athletes. Nall stated that Bryant convinced him that the department would recruit the best athletes available, black or white.

Nall felt that he had been misled given Bryant's slow progress in recruiting black athletes. Earlier in the spring, the basketball team had signed Wendell Hudson as its first black player. Yet this did not impress Nall or the group who viewed it as mere "tokenism." Nall stated that "our suit is aimed primarily at the football program, because football is the main sport at the University, we hope that the ice can be broken there."[40] This lawsuit was Nall's idea and would be funded by the NAACP Legal Defense Fund.

There were a number of other plaintiffs (complete list appears in the appendix at the end of the book) listed in the suit, including President-elect Percy C. Jones, Jr., Andrew Pernell, and the Tuscaloosa Citizens for Action Committee (TCAC). Attorney U. W. Clemon, of the Birmingham law firm of Adams, Baker, and Clemon, served as counsel for the plaintiffs. J. Rufus Beale was the Board of Trustees' General Counsel. He essentially subcontracted the work to the Birmingham firm of Thomas, Taliaferro, Forman, Burr, and Murray. Andrew Thomas was the chief litigator while Beale remained available for consulting purposes and to keep the major participants at the university apprised of the proceedings. Federal US district judge Frank H. McFadden presided over the case.

Paul Bryant and the other football coaches were out of town and unavailable for comment the day the lawsuit was filed. A football spokesman from the sports information office told the *Tuscaloosa News* that Alabama had offered scholarships to three black players the previous fall, but the three had chosen other schools. The athletes were James Owens, who went to Auburn, Frank Dowsing, who signed with Mississippi State, and Greg Davis, who chose Chattanooga. The spokesman also added that coaches had recruited players from fifty all-black high schools during spring and fall 1968. In a memorandum to his coaching staff dated the same day that the suit was filed, Bryant stated that there would be no change in recruiting policy in reply to this suit: "our recruiting policy shall continue just as it has been in the past—with the lone purpose of recruiting WINNING STUDENT-ATHLETES, regardless of color. While we welcome individuals and groups to call our attention to prospective student-athletes and to aid us in the recruiting, we shall also continue to reserve the right to make the selection of stu-dent-athletes we want to recruit for the University of Alabama."[41] The head coach left no question as to who would make decisions on athletic scholarships.

U. W. Clemon, on the other hand, had a different opinion. Clemon's perspective was influenced by having grown up black in the Deep South and experiences in his daily life. Clemon grew up in Birmingham and graduated from Miles College in 1965. He had been active in the civil rights activities in Birmingham during the early 1960s. Clemon under-stood the political culture in his state and described how the suit evolved:

These small cadres of black students were concerned that there were no black players on the football team and more importantly that Bear Bryant was continuing the tradition of an all-white football team which had been a winning team nationally and gave credence to the separate-but-equal nature of it.... Over the period of two to three years they had met with various officials of the university and the athletics department including Bear Bryant. In their opinion of these meetings, he had misled them. They were convinced that he was not going to have blacks on the team. Shortly after I took the case, we filed the lawsuit. We did quite a bit of discovery. We talked with a fair number of black coaches who told us that Bryant was not serious in the recruitment of black athletes. We took his deposition. He was a very gracious guy. We thought that we had set him up and we were prepared to show this. He equivocated a lot in his deposition. We were prepared to show that the contacts with the black coaches were superficial and they were convinced that he was not really serious. What really incensed the group and Ed Nall in particular was that the Owens guy had gone down to Auburn and they were apparently serious in recruiting black athletes and Alabama was not.[42]

There was little press coverage of this event. In its July 8, 1969 edition, school newspaper the *Crimson-White* endorsed the actions taken by the Afro-American Student Association toward the athletics department in its supposed non-recruitment of black athletes. The paper did not dispute the athletics department's spokesman on the matter but wondered "how conscientious they were in their recruitment of black athletes. With all the resources available to their department, it is quite unrealistic to think that no blacks can be found to play football for the Crimson Tide." Furthermore the paper wondered about the issue of federal infringement would figure into any calculation about the suit:

> Intermixed in the Afro-American's struggle for more black athletes here is a classic one of the state vs. federal government. Should the court deliver a ruling in favor of the Afros, then the cry of federal encroachment surely will flood Alabama just as it has too many times in the past. The case is a simple one of the athletics department's obvious oversight in keeping the Crimson Tide white. The Afro-American Association has quietly sought to alleviate the situation through conversations with University officials. They evidently have received nothing but platitudes, so the only remaining recourse they had was the courts. As in past situations in this state, we have here what looks like a case of the state forcing a group to seek relief from the federal government because of the former's inaction....[43]

Bad publicity would continue for the university and its athletics department. In a July 15, 1969 article in *Presbyterian Life*, Wilmina Rowland accused both the university and its athletics department of being racist, stating, "A varsity football player who was black could be regarded by some as an embarrassment to the University of Alabama." The student in question was Andrew Pernell, previously mentioned as one who came out for the team in spring 1967. This had to do with the SEC rule regarding players who were not on athletic scholarships but had received other financial aid; such students were added to the school's total number of players. When informed of this article, Williard Gray, chairman of the Faculty Committee on Intercollegiate Athletics, immediately responded with a letter to the publication. He was sympathetic to Pernell's plight, as Bryant would later state in the deposition. Gray pointed out in this September 3 letter to Bryant that this was a conference regulation and had nothing with the university or its athletics department: "A Southeastern Conference (SEC) rule limits the number of scholarship holders on the football team to a total of 125 students, at a rate of forty per year. Your correspondent, Andy, joined the team after this allotted number had been filled.Fortunately for his education, he chose the scholarship. Unfortunately for the football team, which did want him to play, he could not play."[44]

Within three weeks of the lawsuit filing date, the university's Student Government Association (SGA) had a meeting with Paul Bryant and Sam Bailey to discuss the problems and implications of the suit. The three members of the SGA present at the meeting were president Warren C. Herlong, Jr., vice president Joe Estep, and secretary-treasurer Henry Agee. They were generally complimentary in a July 29 letter sent to Bryant. The group offered their assistance in any phase of the recruiting process and wished to be kept up to date on any progress that the department was making recruiting black athletes.

On August 28, the SGA received another correspondence from Paul Bryant. The contents of the letter included a list of four black athletes who had been recommended for football scholarships and presented to the committee at the proper time in December. The correspondence also listed six additional players the department planned to watch closely in the next few weeks; these students might be recommended for scholarships based on the evaluations. One of these players was Wilbur Jackson.[45]

On September 28, Judge McFadden gave the university thirty days to respond to the complaint filed by the Afro-American Student Association. Four weeks later, Coach Bailey sent to the HEW's regional office in Atlanta a list of all predominately black high schools the coaching staff visited in the proposed recruitment of black athletes. This included forty-eight schools the staff had visited in the previous year and a half, three-quarters of which were in Alabama. The other two states recruiters called upon were Georgia and Mississippi. While there were no scholarships offered from the list of schools, Bailey pointed out that this did not mean the university was not interested in the athletes from the abovementioned schools:

> Recruiting of a student athlete must begin with grades and physical ability. Many times we are interested in a boy because of his physical ability, but in checking his grades and A.C.T. grade we find he cannot possibly qualify for admittance to our school. If this is not the case, we do not spend anytime except for public relations.... You have on file records of black athletes that we have tried to recruit, unsuccessfully.

Our coaches spend just as much time in recruiting these athletes as is spent on any athlete. We are trying to win in our Athletic Program. If a boy is a prospect physically and qualifies academically, we want him regardless of color.[46]

Bailey's comments on what drew the coaching staff's attention were misplaced. Physical ability was clearly more important in determining whether one received an athletic scholarship, but the athlete had to be academically qualified for university admittance. Still, academics were a secondary concern.

For the next six months, the attorneys engaged in a flurry of legal correspondence. In December, the US attorney filed a motion to drop Secretary Finch from the lawsuit. The university agreed with this action. In February, Judge McFadden called for lists from the plaintiffs for all persons who had been discriminated against. A month later, the judge dropped the plaintiffs to only three: the Afro-American Student Association, Isiah Lockett, and Andrew Pernell. U. W. Clemon responded to the defendants in May by requesting interrogatories concerning times, dates, lists, methods, etc. that the athletics department employed in recruiting prospective athletes. Since both sides were preparing for a July trial date, the athletics department responded to this request within a couple of weeks. Coach Bryant was be deposed in federal court on July 8, 1970. This deposition provided many interesting details that illuminated the issues in the case. Coach Gryska assisted Bryant in this endeavor, as would the attorneys for the university.

THE BRYANT DEPOSITION

In eighty-seven pages of the ninety-two page deposition, U. W. Clemon questioned Bryant. A. J. Cooper, from the Mobile firm of Crawford, Fields, and Cooper, presented the final questions. J. Rufus Beale did not recall Bryant "even being prepped by our attorneys for the deposition."[47] Bryant was a smart man who had been acquainted with the courtroom, specifically in the *Saturday Evening Post* trial of the early 1960s. He had confidence in himself and in the principles that guided his life.

Clemon asked Coach Bryant about a situation from the mid-sixties involving a prospective black player from the Mobile area who wanted to attend the University of Alabama. Bryant recalled the event and described what he might have done had this been his own son:

> ...it was not a player; I was in Mobile and a coach, you are going to ask his name and I don't remember it, but a very fine coach came to me and said he had a terrific athlete that wanted to come to the University.... I told him if he comes up there we are going to treat him just like anybody else, but from one coach to another, if he was my kid, right now I believe it is a little too soon, I would direct him some place else. I said, we want to win, color doesn't mean anything to us, but it is—we are going to have to play in Starkville, Mississippi, and Oxford, Mississippi, and Tuscaloosa, Alabama, and it might be just a year or two from now, but I said, right now if he was my kid, I would try to direct him some place else.[48]

Bryant's genuine concern with the player's safety and well-being is quite obvious, yet he seemed to realize that the time might not have been appropriate for integrating the football team. Given the fact that Bryant lived his whole life in the South or at least on its borders, he was well versed in the racial climate of the times. One can not help but remember some of the problems encountered in integrating the university.

Another issue arose when the famous head coach acknowledged how the recent history of the state would constrain any attempts to recruit black athletes from outside Alabama's immediate geographical region. In addressing questions concerning "all the black high schools out of state," Bryant explained:

> Well, actually, year before last, as I said, we started on border states, Cleveland, Tennessee, and Tupelo, Mississippi, but up until then, we felt we had to start in Alabama and we got to get the good ones, you know, in Alabama, and it was kind of ridiculous for us to think that we could go to California, like we did this year, and try to get a black athlete with the image that we have here in Alabama, but then this year, after losing all those games, we said the hell with it, we are going to go anyway and try to get them any place. To answer your question, we hadn't gone out up until two years ago to really look for them out of State; I think we wasted our money this year.[49]

Bryant's last comment is in line with some assistant coaches' earlier comments in the late 1960s that recruiting out-of-state players would be a waste of resources. It is also quite clear that the high schools in

Alabama lagged behind the entire country, even behind the rest of the South, in integration. As late as 1969–1970, at least fifty black high schools remained open in the state. In the fall of 1970, the state finally fell in line with the rest of the country. In places where integration did exist, it involved only a handful of individuals. There were more all-black high schools in Alabama than in Kentucky and Tennessee combined. The white Alabama High School Athletic Association and the black Alabama Interscholastic Athletic Association merged at the beginning of the 1968–69 school year. In 1969, black football players took part in the annual high school all-star game for the first time. Three players participated in this summer event, which usually took place a week or two before the Crimson Tide fall practice opened. The university had difficulty when trying to recruit black athletes from outside the region. Bryant thought it was necessary to be more careful in the beginning so he could show that it was okay for other black athletes to follow. The state of Alabama was his core recruiting area.

Bryant became quite testy in some of his responses in the deposition. He recalled the meetings with both the Afro-American Student Association and the SGA. Bryant seemed to develop a "bunker mentality,":

> [Edward Nalls] came to see me and another young man and I was very much impressed with him; we visited and they said they wanted to help and so on and so forth, and we visited a time or two and I think we had some names, entertain a boy or two for us, and then later on when some question in my mind arose [as to] what their objectives were, I am afraid they weren't what mine was, ...but then they started talking to me...wanted me to offer an individual a scholarship, and I wasn't going to do it, and finally,—heck, I guess they changed their attitude toward us and then last year, not this year, the President of the Student Government Association, a couple of them from Student Government had come to me because they had complaints; I told them exactly, hell, we want a football team, I don't care what color, we want winning players, so on and so forth, and they understood; so, then, they said well, we would like to kind of help as liaison and I said I haven't got time, I am not going to take time to sit up here and try to talk me into picking somebody; I said, the alumni doesn't pick them; so, since then, this came up and I haven't had any contact with them; and I am sorry about this, because see all it does, although they want to help, all it does is hurt, because again it doesn't help our image with the black athlete in Kentucky or black athlete in Mississippi or somewhere else.[50]

Perhaps this summed up Bryant's frustration with the process. He felt that he was trying to get the best players available, and lawsuits were not productive means toward that end. Coach Bryant probably felt some intrusion by these organizations like the afro-american student organizations and the SGA on the athletics department's decision-making. Everywhere he had coached before returning to Alabama, others had made unwanted advances upon what he considered his turf. When that happened, he eventually left the school. Although this does not suggest that he was contemplating another option, it gives some perspective and context to his reply in the deposition.

On July 20, the plaintiff and defendant's attorneys held a meeting with Judge McFadden. During this discussion Clemon agreed that if a black football player could be recruited within the next year, the plaintiffs would dismiss the case. The next day, Coach Gryska sent to the staff a memorandum titled "Recruitment of Black Athletes" that informed the athletics department that the trial was postponed until May 10, 1971. It went on to add that the department would now keep a complete file on the matter of recruiting black athletes: "As directed by Coach Bryant, I am setting up a complete file on this category. Forms are available in my office to get a resume of contacts. Any visit, questionnaire, phone call, transcript, principal's office visit, ball games, programs, evaluation, campus visit, correspondence etc. must be filed. Come May 10, 1971 we plan to hand this file over to the plaintiffs. Your complete attention must be thorough in this matter."[51]

A "Report to the President" of the list of grievances that the Afro-American Student Association submitted to President Mathews was completed and made available for viewing on August 19, 1970. In response to the demand of the alleged discriminatory practices of the athletics department, the report stated that the following steps had been taken since fall 1968 in the recruitment of black athletes:

1) In 1968, five black athletes were offered football scholarships, but none accepted. Six black athletes were offered basketball scholarships and one accepted.

2) In 1969, ten black athletes were offered football scholarships and two accepted. Six black athletes were offered basketball scholarships and two accepted.

3) In 1970 thirteen black football players and nine black basketball players are already under consideration for scholarships.[52]

In the supplementary documents associated with this summary, some discrepancies were evident. The documents indicated that in 1968 the department had offered only three football scholarships, not five. The indication that two players had accepted football scholarships in 1969 was technically correct, but one of the students, William "Bo" Matthews, could not get into the school because of academic requirements. The rest of the figures appeared to be accurate.

CORRECTING A MYTH?

The September loss in Birmingham to the University of Southern California by a score of 42-21 might have played a factor the integration process, but perhaps not in the same way that previous Bryant biographies indicate. The comment that "Sam Cunningham did more for integration in the South in sixty minutes than Martin Luther King, Jr., did in twenty years"[53] has been vastly overstated. David Mathews thinks the affect of this game was way out of line with reality. "We had already integrated the basketball team and Wilbur Jackson was playing on the freshmen team. Paul was actively seeking other black football players even before this game. The USC game in Birmingham may have been important to outsiders, but on the inside, the impact was marginal at best."[54] However, the plaintiff's attorney saw it differently. U. W. Clemon indicated that during the discovery phase of the trial, the plantiff attorneys had interviewed a number of black high school football coaches in 1969–1970. All of the coaches had indicated that they did not think Bryant was serious in recruiting black athletes; after this, Clemon stated, "Along came the game with USC and from that point on, the black coaches impressed upon us that serious efforts had been made. All we were seeking was a good faith effort and if there were a serious effort there would be blacks on the football team. Hell, these players wanted to play for the University of Alabama."[55]

HOW ABOUT THE PLAYERS?

Another important aspect of integrating the football team involved the players. Generally speaking, younger people in the South were much more comfortable with integration than many of the political leaders, who were one or two generations older. The Alabama football players as a group appeared to have little problem with this change. This did not mean that every player was in favor of integration, but of nearly sixty players interviewed, none would go on record as having opposed integration. Several occurrences in 1971 lend credence to this point. The first was the signing of John Mitchell. Mitchell accepted a scholarship in January 1971 to join Wilbur Jackson as one of the first two black football players on scholarship. John attended junior college in Arizona, but Mobile was his home. Mitchell moved into the dorm a couple of days before the spring semester. His roommate Bobby Stanford was a lineman from Georgia. They soon became good friends. Stanford explained how it happened:

> I remember walking into the dorm and Coach White wanted to talk to me. I didn't think that it was a big deal. He said he wanted me to do him a favor. I said sure. He started telling me about a new player that we got from junior college, and that he needed a roommate. He told me that he was black. It really didn't faze me that much. Even though they didn't integrate my high school until my senior year, I had been around black people my entire life. Most of the people who worked at Bob's [a candy company in Albany, Georgia, where Stanford's father was a vice president] were blacks. We played together at company outings and such.[56]

Stanford's comments might not have spoken for all the white players, but the group expressed a great deal of goodwill toward their new black teammates.

The second example of a generally positive attitude toward integration was a conversation that occurred between Rod Steakley and Wilbur Jackson as they rested in their motel room before a road game. Steakley recalled this discussion some thirty years later:

> Will and I were back in the room. We were lying around watching television. It was an episode of the old historical program entitled *You Were There.* This was a show in which actors reenact some event in history. This particular episode was on the Underground Railroad that operated in the 1850s and during the Civil War. We were lying around and watching this and this was about slavery. It was about slaves escaping from the South to freedom in the North. It was really getting to me, and I did not know what to say. I had to say something, given who I was and who Will was. At some point toward the end of the program, I looked to Will and said: "Will, I don't know what to say, but I want to

tell you how sorry I am that that's a part of our history, and I hope...."
He cut me off. He said, "Rod, you don't have to say anything. I know
you're not like that." That's all that was said and it was all right. I guess
from my perspective, it was all right, but it was some of the most
uncomfortable few minutes I've spent in my life when you think of the
era and timeframe.[57]

Both of these players were at the University of Alabama to win football games, but that did not mean they did not have a conscience. This
fairly enlightened conversation certainly did not appear to be happening
in the state a decade earlier.

The final instance that demonstrated white players' support of integration involved the team's outing to the pre-game movie *Shaft*. This was
the first movie about black characters and black themes that was mar-
keted to a black audience. It quickly became a crossover hit among
whites. The University of Alabama football team was no exception. John
Mitchell remembered seeing the movie and how he started refering to
himself as Shaft. The nickname soon caught on with the other players.
The fact that Bryant decided upon the movie and the players seemed to
like it speaks volumes about this new social experiment.[58]

ANALYSIS OF THE LAWSUIT

Lawsuits often involve differences in perception. The old cliché of
whether the glass is "half full" or "half empty" applies. This analogy questions not reality, but the perception of reality. Thus, perception is reality.
The Afro-American Student Association tried to communicate with
Bryant and help recruit black athletes. They were not successful and perceived that Bryant was trying to keep the team completely white. He
wanted to protect his football team and athletics department. They
played in the SEC and had to make trips to Mississippi. Bryant did not
think that the state of Alabama was ready for this, but when it was he
would integrate the team. On the other hand, Bryant was the one coach
in the South who could have bucked the system and integrated in the
mid-sixties. He saw himself as a football coach, not an agent for social
change.

Bryant certainly was not a racist. U. W. Clemon acknowledged this
with a qualification: "I do not think personally that Bryant was a racist. I
do think that he was catering to the political culture at the time."[59]

Perhaps he was catering to politics. He was not, however, the governor of the state or even the university president. He knew his place in terms of the chain of command. Recruiting coordinator Gryska explained:

> What you must understand about Coach Bryant was that he was not an innovator, but he knew how to read the personalities of his coaches, players, and people in general. He was looking for the right players who would make the transition without causing any added attention to the program. We did not need another schoolhouse door episode. The University of Alabama is a public institution. The University of Alabama president and the state approve the budget. On the issue of integration, Coach Bryant was not opposing them over school or state policy. By going along with the policy, he could protect his program and offer the program to black athletes when the program was at its most desirable and at a time when the state government would find the change most acceptable. If it had not been for the Wallace factor in this state, we would have integrated much earlier.[60]

One cannot underestimate the last comment about the "Wallace factor." During the segregationist phase of his career, Wallace was not only governor in the state, but a national political figure who as a third-party presidential candidate in 1968 received nearly 14 percent of the popular vote. There is no evidence to suggest that Coach Bryant shared Wallace's beliefs on the issue of race, but he would not cross the governor in a public manner. Bryant knew his limits. He was a football coach and had complete control in that theater, but when he went outside his element, he was more circumscribed in his approach. Bryant had earlier spoken of these constraints in an unsuccessful negotiation with the Governor of Arkansas to be the head coach at the university there. He had also been made aware of his place when he attempted to integrate the football squad at Kentucky. Bryant described this encounter in his autobiography: "When I was at Kentucky, I told the president, Dr. Herman Donovan, that we should be the first in the Southeastern Conference to have black players. I told him he could be the Branch Rickey of the league. But I didn't get anywhere."[61] In Bryant's view, his power base extended over the football team and among the other college coaches, but not beyond that. He would use this power to enhance his football team and athletics department, but he was very leery of going outside that environment.

Finally, assessing the larger lesson of this lawsuit will be left for historians to sort out. History is constantly being revised in response to new information and materials not previously known. Judge Clemon surmised, "Well, I think that if nothing else the lawsuit showed Bear Bryant that black folks were not going to forget their constitutional rights to equally participate in all aspects of college life. Because of that on the one hand, his feet were going to be kept to the fire in the courts. The other was self-interest for the University of Alabama to get back on the winning track on the football field. This made it easier for him to do which ran against the grain of white political culture in this state."[62]

Viewed from another perspective, one could surmise that this case was less influential in the larger scheme of things. The documents from the athletics department indicate that they were already moving in the direction of integration. General counsel for the university, J. Rufus Beale, stated, "I think everyone at the university was ready to do this. I don't really think that the lawsuit had much of an impact whatsoever on integrating the team, because we were already trying to do it when the lawsuit came around."[63] From Clemon's viewpoint, he did not see any black athletes on the squad. He had also grown up in the state and knew its history.

From the athletics department and Coach Bryant's point of view, one can only speculate. The evidence suggests that Bryant wanted to integrate the football team as soon as possible, but outside forces would constrain the speed by which he could do so. Once the team did integrate, the Bear downplayed any mention about the subject. He saw this as a side issue for those with a political agenda and he was not going to let it affect his team. Bryant was moving forward as if nothing had ever happened. His job was to win football games. That was what he intended to do. This is what leadership is all about.

CHANGES IN THE AIR

FORMER PRESIDENT THEODORE ROOSEVELT AND PAUL W. BRYANT had similar beliefs about what it takes to be successful in life. When Roosevelt was vice president, he delivered a speech in Chicago, Illinois, on this subject. In the oration, titled "The Strenuous Life," Roosevelt explained that life presents us with two kinds of success. In the first, people are born to succeed and no amount of training or willpower will change that. Very few people fit this bill. The second kind of success, one accessible to all people, requires that a person work hard and pay the price, physically and/or otherwise, to achieve the goal. Roosevelt, who described himself as "a rather sickly and awkward boy," knew firsthand that he "never won anything without hard labor and working long in advance."[64] No one knows whether Bryant ever read this speech, but certainly his philosophy of life fit quite nicely with Roosevelt's second idea of success. Paul Bryant was not born a successful football coach; he made himself into one. He believed that his players would have the best chance of winning if he pushed them to the limit.

Bryant's philosophy of life is born out of his experience with poverty in Moro Bottom, Arkansas, a place that taught him the lessons of hard work and to which he never wanted to return. When his family moved to Fordyce, Paul was able to go to a better school where he performed well in athletic competition. This allowed him to win a scholarship to the University of Alabama. He performed admirably as a player but was never the superstar like a Dixie Howell or Don Hutson. He later coached teams of his own at Maryland, Kentucky, and Texas A&M before returning to Alabama in 1958. Bryant, with cowriter John Underwood, summed up this history in his autobiography: "The point is that we stressed conditioning, believing that a better conditioned athlete can whip a superior athlete who isn't in top shape. If my 75 percent boy plays 15 percent over his ability and your 100 percent boys slogs around and plays 15 percent under his, we will beat you every time."[65]

In a couple of highly publicized instances, Bryant's coaching tactics and the philosophy they reflected were brought into question. One occurred at Texas A&M ("Aggies"), the other at Alabama. Both of these situations hardened Bryant and reinforced his idea of what it takes to be successful.

Bryant's first pre-season training camp at Junction, Texas, was memorable for the players who attended. Of the 111 players he took to camp, only 35 remained for the full ten days. Jim Dent's recent book *The Junction Boys: How Ten Days in Hell with Bear Bryant forged a Championship Season* calls into question Bryant's coaching tactics, suggesting that he was brutalizing his players. [66] That year Bryant endeared his only losing season as a head coach, with a 1-9 record. During his next season he turned things around for the Aggies, leading them to maintain a three-year record of 24-5-2. During this span they won one Southwestern Conference (SWC) championship (1956) and two top-ten finishes (1956, 1957). In 1957 A&M star John David Crow won the Heisman Trophy. In 2002, the sports network ESPN based a movie on Dent's earlier book that sensationalized the account at Junction, Texas. The movie, like the book, was amusing, but often times it blurred the line between fact and fiction.

In the second instance that called into question Bryant's tactics, a hit by one of his Alabama players caused an opposing team member a broken jaw and a concussion. In this 1960 contest Darwin Holt, a transfer from Texas A&M, hit Chick Graning[67] from Georgia Tech with a forearm. The move created a firestorm between both teams, one made worse by the rivalry between the cities of Atlanta and Birmingham, the two coaches, and media from the two states. Atlanta was on its way to become the capital of the New South, as Birmingham was falling way behind in a number of ways. In addition to the city rivalry was that between Bryant and Bobby Dodd, the Georgia Tech head coach. The two coaches differed in matters of philosophy: Dodd wanted his players to have fun practicing, while Bryant drilled his system into his players over and over again until it became second nature. Dodd felt his players needed to be rested in order to play their best game, while Bryant thought the game was a reward for hard practices. The Holt-Graning incident resulted in a story the following year by *Atlanta Journal* sports editor Furman Bisher, who wrote a piece in the *Saturday Evening Post* that accused Bryant of encouraging his players to be brutal. The article "College Football Going Berserk" claimed that Bryant was the worst offender of such controlled violence.[68] Bryant countered with a $500,000 libel suit against Bisher and the *Post*.

A subsequent article in the *Saturday Evening Post* accused Bryant and University of Georgia athletics director Wally Butts (former football coach) of fixing and rigging the 1962 game between the two teams. In this game, which Alabama won 35-0, the Crimson Tide players were 17-point favorites and ranked second in the nation. The story alleged that Bryant and Butts exchanged information about each team that resulted in the lopsided Tide win. The evidence came from Atlanta-area insurance man George Burnett, who picked up the telephone conversation on a party line by mistake. Burnett's notes were the basis of the *Post* article.[69] Bryant sued for $5 million while his earlier suit was still pending. Butts sued for $10 million. Ultimately both Bryant and Butts won monetary judgments against the magazine. Butts went to trial and was awarded over $3 million, which was reduced to $300,000 on appeal, while Bryant's case was settled out of court for $360,000 and a retraction from the publisher.[70] Comments by Frank Rose, the president of the University of Alabama, seem to put into context the pain associated with these lawsuits: "I think that it was one of the meanest things that I have ever seen done to an individual in my lifetime. We all suffered through it and while Coach Bryant won his case and several hundred thousand dollars, I don't think that anyone can ever re-pay him for the suffering that was his." Bryant would lament that he thought the lawsuits took ten years off of his life.[71]

OFF-SEASON PROGRAM RETURNS TO BASICS

The off-season conditioning program was another indicator of Bryant's philosophy. He had been confronted by his seniors in a meeting immediately after school reconvened in January that they were tired of losing and wanted to reclaim the Alabama tradition of winning. The head coach challenged the seniors and told them that some of them would not be around next season. Bryant's words were quite prophetic. After this January meeting, ten scholarship players left the team before the first game in September. However, none of these players were from the surviving thirteen 1968 class members. This occurred against the broader backdrop of the younger-generation counterculture that was sweeping the country. While not as pervasive in the South as the rest of the United States, rebellious attitudes had filtered into the university campus. The counterculture stood against traditional discipline and values. It also challenged anything repetitive, believing that monotony turned people into robots. These strands of individualism flew in the face of what Bryant was trying to teach his players. His seniors seemed to buy into the structure and discipline that was missing from the counterculture. It might be that these players had the traits that would make them "winners" in fall 1971. The winners were those who were willing to pay the price physically or otherwise in order to be successful. Bryant himself was a winner. He had relied on this type of player in the past and he would continue to do so in spite of the counterculture.

The off-season conditioning program[72] started when school was back in session after the Christmas and bowl-game breaks. These sessions met three times a week and each lasted an hour. The classes were considered voluntary, but in reality they were mandatory. These classes involved twenty-five to thirty players at a time and took place in different rooms in the Coleman Coliseum. Once they began, there were no rest periods until the session ended. Large garbage cans were placed in the corners for those who vomited as a result of the physical demands. Once a player was finished with this unfortunate upheaval of food, he had to restart the drill—there were no exceptions. Jimmy Rosser, an offensive lineman from Birmingham, recalls such an ordeal: "Coach Donahue stopped the entire drill and said 'that we would not start back until Mr. Rosser had relieved himself.' He singled me out to make a point."[73] Jim Goosetree, the trainer, was the assistant coach in charge of these sessions. "Goose," the only Whitworth regime holdover Bryant had kept on his staff, was also in charge of the summer conditioning program. J. B. "Ears" Whitworth had been the previous coach who only won four games in three years.

Players usually had to complete three to four stations in order to graduate the "class." These stations consisted of "grass drills," "wrestling," "weights," and other agility exercises. The duration of each station would begin at five to six minutes and increase to fifteen to sixteen minutes by the end of the semester. Each week the duration would increase in two-minute increments. These "classes" continued until the formal beginning of spring practice, eight to ten weeks in duration. Not all the drills were conducted in the same place, and players may have had to run to another floor in the coliseum for the next drill. During grass drills the player moved up or down depending on the coach's whistle. In wrestling drills two players grappled on a mat while each tried to pin the other, with no rules to govern the contestants. During weights sessions, barbells were aligned and the players usually had to perform to exhaustion an array of exercises for various body parts. The agility drills could consist of many things, including push-ups, sit-ups, side-to-side movements, basketball, etc. These exercises challenged the players to do what they thought they could not. Many of the players have stated that this was the most difficult part of their football experience at Alabama. Other more experienced players were used to it and knew what to expect. Jimmy Rosser did not think it was that difficult, particularly after the first time: "I stayed in shape the year round and it only lasted about an hour. The two-a-days and those practices that lasted three to four hours were much tougher."[74] Yet there were others like Terry Davis, a quarterback from Bogalusa, Louisiana, who remembered it differently: "The off-season conditioning was brutal and difficult to take, but other than that we knew it was coming and adjusted to it accordingly. That was some of the toughest things for me. It was constant motion all the time three days a week."[75] Dexter Wood, a flanker from Ozark, Alabama, thought the 1971 off-season program was "much more difficult than it had been in the past three years. It was clear to me that some things were getting ready to change."[76] John Mitchell's first spring was very memorable to him and indicates that he obviously was not among the more experienced players:

> My first off-season program was brutal, getting in shape for the spring practice.... I had never had anything like this before either in high school or junior college.... Physically and mentally, it made me grow up. I knew that if I was going to have any chance to play, I had to be physically tough to get through that. In doing that, it made me mentally tough having to compete three days a week. It was a challenge. Coach Bryant did not come down there every day, but usually once a week and everyday that he came, things would pick up a notch....During these six-week periods, Coach Bryant and the others would find out who wanted to play. If you could endure that, you would be ready for spring practice.

It was very grueling and a lot of guys could not take it. You had a lot of casualties.[77]

In spite of these difficult times, the pre-spring drills included some lighter moments. Bubba Sawyer told one of the more humorous stories:

There was one time that I remember in our last spring that Moose [Johnny Musso] and I were partners in the wrestling part of the drills. We had already discussed it before we hit the mat. We got down and going through the motions with a lot of moaning like we were really straining. We were great actors. The coaches thought that we were really getting after it. It was one of the few times we ever fooled them. After we were through with our time on the mat, the coaches exhorted the players to do it like "Musso and Sawyer just did it."[78]

Finally, by the time spring training started, most players were glad to get out of these gym classes. Spring training did not seem to look that bad for many on the Alabama squad, but they just might have found out different.

MORE CHANGES IN THE AIR?

From time to time during the off-season, Paul Bryant would call a team meeting. Such meetings were not that common after the season ended. A week before spring practice was scheduled to begin, he called one of these meetings. Usually when the players were convened they had some inkling about the subject of the meeting, as members of the football squad engaged in lots of small talk as to the "why" of any particular meeting. This one, however, was impromptu and literally came out of nowhere.

A number of accounts from various players and coaches depict this particular episode, but among the versions some constants remain. Coach Bryant stated that it had come to his attention that some players were doing things that were not in accordance with the team's guidelines, nor were they legal. He then made a comment to the effect that if he were nineteen, he might be doing these things himself. But he was not a teenager, and these things were against the law. Bryant looked down at his watch and said that there were agents going through the dorm. John Croyle, a defensive end from Gadsden, Alabama, recalled that "there were about five guys sitting close to me and they were really squirming."[79] Others such as Jimmy Grammer, a center from Hartselle, Alabama, did not know what to think, adding, "I was naïve and really did not know anything about dope at that time. I had heard things, but I did not have any direct knowledge of it."[80] On the other hand, some players were quite familiar with the drug scene. Terry Rowell, a defensive tackle from Heidelberg, Mississippi recalled this:

> Dope was everywhere at that time. I was as far away from it as I could be. Coach Bryant had a few of the players to his office and had asked us about this problem. He swore us to secrecy on this matter.... Most of the players did not give specific names to the coach.... After the team meeting we went back to the dorm and he called a number of players to meet with him on the second floor of the dorm in the study room. He read them the riot act and you didn't see them any more. He told them that they could stay in school, but he was not paying for it. Coach Bryant did not want to see these guys hanging around the dorm with his football team. After that, it was a different world.[81]

Three players were given the choice of leaving the team and their scholarships or dealing with the legal authorities. Bryant told these players that they could stay in school but they were being kicked off the football team. The newspaper accounts only mentioned that they had violated team rules and were dismissed from the squad. Cecil Quick, Brian Faino, and Steve Paulsen would all have contributed in the fall had they been allowed to stay on the team. Quick, a defensive end and letterman from Collins, Mississippi, was expected to be a starter that fall. Faino, a promising defensive back from Des Moines, Iowa, was a starter on the undefeated freshmen team and probably would have played quite a bit. Steve Paulsen, another freshman from Des Moines, was a lineman and was expected to compete for a starting position.

By spring 1971, drugs were creeping into the culture of the country. Even though the football team was somewhat insulated from the rest of the campus, the players were not immune to what was going on around them. Most of them were from small towns, were socially conservative, and had been raised similarly. Yet this did not include everyone. A few players probably engaged in smoking marijuana but were not caught, and thus remained on the team. However Bryant's actions sent a strong message and were an effective deterrent to others who might have been tempted. Jeff Rouzie, a linebacker from Jacksonville, Florida, and later long-time assistant at the University of Alabama, saw this kind of message as "typical Bryant": "Coach Bryant always faced problems head on. After the coaches did the dorm search, it created a situation that eliminated the kind of stuff that needed to be gotten rid of. It got us focused on what we were here for."[82]

THE TERMITES SPEECH

A week later, just before the first spring practice, Bryant called another meeting. This was the second meeting he had called within a week. The players knew something significant must be underway, but they did now know what it was. Gary White, one of Coach Bryant's administrative assistants, recalled what occurred next:

> Coach Bryant walked up to the board in a meeting room over at the coliseum, and he drew a wall, little bricks, and such. He was talking to the players about termites. Termites eating the foundation, and he'd rub a brick out, and he'd take a little bit more and rub out another brick. He said, "You know that these termites are eating the foundation away, and it'll crumble," and he drew that thing crumbling. He said, "That wall's crumbling." He told them, "Now, I know how to coach football, what it takes to win football games and that has not changed any. You may think that it has, but it has not changed. The same ingredients it took ten or twenty years ago, it takes right now. I am not going to change that philosophy. If you want to play, you're going to play the way I know how to coach to do whatever till you love ends and whatever you want to do."[83]

This was vintage Bryant. He took full responsibility for the team's last few seasons. One of the larger criticisms from this period was that he had let the game pass him by. Bryant was ready to remedy this problem. He had made certain adjustments in response to the cultural changes facing the country, like letting the players grow their hair a little longer and allowing them to bring their dates into the dorm, but he was not going to change in regards to his core beliefs. These beliefs were built on discipline, putting the team ahead of the individual, and mental and physical toughness, among others. On the outside, Bryant's long-haired players blended in with the other students on campus, but inside and on the football field, they were no different than his teams at Maryland,

Kentucky, Texas A&M, or Alabama. They were molded in his philosophy, one that had been successful in the past and would be in the future.

A NEW BRYANT?

At the time there were many who did not recognize the significance of Bryant's actions. In hindsight, it seems quite clear that the famous coach was taking back his team and reasserting control, an element some had felt was lacking. Delbert Reed, copy editor (and in summer 1971 named sports editor) of *The Tuscaloosa News* at the time recalled what Bryant had said in an interview before spring training 1971. The esteemed head coach had told him, "I am through tip-toeing around and I'm through pussy-footing. I'm going to go back to being Paul Bryant; if anybody does not like the way that Paul Bryant does things, you can get the hell out of here."[84] There is no way to misinterpret this. The Bear was in control and intended for things to be different in 1971.

THE BEAR REASSERTS HIMSELF

SPRING PRACTICE MEANT A NUMBER OF THINGS TO PAUL Bryant. During this time he stressed fundamentals to a greater degree than at any other time of the year. Once players mastered these, they could work on the little things, the details Bryant knew made the difference between winning and losing football games. This would also be a time the coaches would further note just how much football meant to the players: freshman and junior college transfers would get a closer look when pitted against the varsity. Finally, spring practice would stress discipline. Coach Bryant thought the most disciplined team would often make the difference in the fourth quarter when the game was on the line. He believed that players who were pushed to their breaking points in practice and then could dig down for a little more would perform their task the best during the game. This was one way to separate the men from the boys in their quest to build another championship team, the type that had been missing the last couple of years.

TIME TO GET DOWN TO BUSINESS

In his fourteenth spring training since returning to the Capstone, Paul Bryant wanted a distinct type of spring practice, one that would be markedly different from previous years. Unlike his first "Junction-like" spring practice in 1958, when he ran off a number of players in order to send a big message, this would not be business as usual. He was determined to get back to winning football games at the University of Alabama, and one way to achieve this was to make the players more focused. The winter conditioning program was part of the process, using challenging methods to make the players more mentally alert and put them in a better frame of mind to approach spring practice. They needed to learn how to become better football players, because in the more recent past, Bryant believed, too many of his players had not been concentrating. For a number of these players football had been low on the list of priorities, but this was going to change. In an interview conducted before the start of spring practice by the *Orlando Sentinel* sports editor Bill Clark, the Bear further explained his position:

> When we sign football players at the University of Alabama, we expect them to have good character. They need to be devoted to their family and religion. After that, we expect them to be good students. Football should be next on their list. The last few seasons around here, we have a number of players who wanted to do a number of things before playing football. Some of them were interested in the ladies, the parties, and the social scene. I understand that, but we brought them here to help us win football games. Playing football was way down the list of their priorities. This spring practice is going to help us [the coaching staff] find out how important playing football is to some of these guys.[85]

EXPECTATIONS

Going into spring training the expectations for the 1971 squad were high. Given the team's prior two seasons with 6-5 and 6-5-1 records, Bryant was quite emphatic when he told the local media that "we need to get off the bottom and get back to playing Alabama type of football." He explained that this would be "a strong defense and a sound kicking game." The head coach expressed his disappointment with the previous two seasons when he stated, "We were back among the ordinary folks, and I don't like it."[86] These seasons were generally recognized as those in which the Crimson Tide had been able to move the ball down the field offensively by passing the football, putting points on the scoreboard but not preventing their opponents from doing the same. Even though they had Johnny Musso, one of the greatest running backs in the country, the offense could not maintain the football for long periods. Consequently, the defense was on the field more than necessary and was often worn out in the fourth quarter, when the game was on the line and there was little margin for error. There was little depth on the defensive side of the football. If some key players were injured, there were too few quality athletes to replace them. This problem was less evident during the last half of the 1970 season, as some of the more experienced players were meeting expectations while some of the younger and more talented players were gaining experience and confidence. If the defense could slow and hold the opposition as Bryant-coached teams had before in 1969 and 1970, then good things would follow. Ninety-three players were on the numbered roster for spring 1971, not to mention the thirty to forty walk-ons not listed. The precise number of walk-ons varied depending on different practice schedules and rosters. Of the official spring roster, forty-seven players were sophomores, twenty-five were juniors, and twenty-one were seniors.

LENGTH OF SPRING PRACTICE

One hundred-plus players began spring practice on Wednesday, March 31. A four-day weekly practice schedule would be required until they completed twenty practices, which was the NCAA's limit on official practices in the spring. The players would also have a week off during the university's spring break. The annual A-Day spring game was scheduled for May 1, 1971. That left four additional practices after the Saturday exhibition to complete the spring regimen. Players who competed in the spring sports of track and baseball had to complete their spring practice with the football team before they could play the other sports. However, there were a few exceptions for the 1971 session. Tight end Glenn Woodruff was excused to catch for the baseball squad. Speedsters Steve Williams (defensive back) and Jerry Cash (wide receiver) were also allowed to miss spring practice to compete with the track team. Williams was a 9.6-second sprinter in the 100-yard dash, while Cash competed in the hurdles, high jump, and decathlon. John Hannah, an up-and-coming star offensive lineman, did double duty in the spring as he participated in the football drills and threw the shot put and discus for the track squad.

SPECIAL GUESTS TO HELP?

In the week leading up to the beginning of spring practice, a number of stories had circulated in the press about ex-Alabama players returning to Tuscaloosa to help the coaching staff in their preparations. The ex-players included Ray Perkins (Baltimore Colts), Paul Crane (New York Jets), Joe Namath (New York Jets) and Tommy Brooker (Dallas Texans and Kansas City Chiefs). All of them had played professionally and all were in their off-seasons except for Brooker, who retired after the 1966 campaign. Namath was the most prominent, and many observers would be attending practice just to get a glimpse of the famous professional quarterback. This was twenty-six months after "Joe Willie" had shocked the world by leading the New York Jets of the American Football League (AFL) to a 16-7 Super Bowl victory over the highly favored Baltimore Colts of the National Football League (NFL). This outcome had figured prominently in the NFL's decision to merge the professional leagues into one. Most of the sports journalists considered Namath, competing in the largest market in the country, the best quarterback playing at the time. His popularity off the field was even bigger than his expertise on the field. Jets assistant coach Buddy Ryan's comments about the colorful quarterback were right on the mark when he said, "Joe's a man's man and a ladies' man. And that's some kind of combination."[87] The whole country knew that Namath was successful in endeavors both on and off the field.

A week before spring practice, Namath was in Tuscaloosa to celebrate the opening of his fourth "Bachelors III" supper club. There were over 200 guests in attendance to help celebrate the launching of his newest restaurant. The Bryants were there to help kick off the festivities. The feisty head coach called Namath "the best player that I ever coached." Namath would act as an unofficial coach who would do whatever Braynt's staff wanted him to do. He had broken a wrist during the latter part of 1970, which had sidelined him for the rest of the year, so he would be testing the injured wrist. He told the public, "I'll be out for all the practices I can. I won't be on the field coaching, actually coaching—I'm not a coach—but Coach Bryant asked me if I wouldn't observe our quarterbacking and talk with Mal Moore about my impressions."[88] When Bryant called, few of his ex-players could resist helping him out in any way possible.

HOW PRACTICES WERE ORGANIZED

On the bottom-floor dressing room of the Coleman Coliseum, a posted schedule of the day's practice hung on the bulletin board, awaiting incoming players as they came in dressed for practice. In addition, a depth chart placed in public view showed where each player ranked on the chart for that day's practice. The players wore different colored jerseys to indicate their status on the depth chart. The first team offense wore red jerseys ("Reds"), while the first team defense donned white jerseys ("Headhunters"). Other colors included orange, purple, blue, and green, depending on where players were situated on any given day. The practice schedule and the depth chart were always the first things players saw when they came into the locker room. The head coach made up the practice schedules and depth charts and did not delegate these, even though the assistant coaches did have some input. Bryant always had the final say in these instances.

Coach Bryant always believed that the best-prepared players performed at the highest level on the football field, and it was up to him and his assistants to see that his players were the best prepared. He watched practice from a 30-foot tower so that he could see all the various drills going on at the same time. Certain objectives were to be accomplished in these practices, which were divided into a number of periods that dealt with particular functional areas of concern. There were usually six to seven periods per practice, each at a given time. They might be as short as fifteen minutes or they might have no time limit ("no-timers"). The periods could focus on areas such as blocking drills, tackling drills, goal-line situations, and specialty periods. The head manager would blow a whistle to designate the end of one period and the beginning of the next one. Occasionally, if Bryant was not pleased with a player's progress in the previous period and wanted to make comments, he would blow the whistle after the manager did. At the end of practice, that period would be repeated until the head coach was satisfied. Players were required to run, not walk, to the next designated area. Those who were not hustling enough would be notified or—God forbid—reported to Paul Bryant himself.

Senior All-American tailback Johnny Musso would lead the offensive team of the Crimson Tide for 1971, which had six returning starters. The 5-foot-11, 196-pound star was also an Academic All-American and consensus All-SEC pick in 1970. Paul Bryant said flat out that he is the "best running back that he has ever coached."[89] This would place Musso in pretty select company considering that John David Crow, one of Bryant's former running backs and now assistant coach, won the Heisman Trophy in 1957. Musso was nicknamed the "Italian Stallion," which covered both his ethnic roots and his running ability. Musso ran for 1,137 yards for an average of 5 yards per carry and caught thirty passes for 160 yards scoring nine touchdowns. He also threw two touchdown passes out of three passing attempts. Even though these statistics were quite impressive, his blocking ability may have been even better than his running game. The Birmingham native had known that he wanted to play for the University of Alabama even before he went to Banks High School, where he was All-State his senior year. When he was eleven years old, an older cousin asked Musso if he wanted to go with him to the Iron Bowl (the annual Alabama-Auburn contest held in Birmingham). Musso was more than ready and accompanied the older relative to Legion Field for the 1961 version of this famous event. The only problem was that when they got there, Musso found out that they did not have tickets: "My cousin got caught scaling the fence by security and was thrown out, but I had already gone over and was in the stadium. My heroes like Pat Trammell and Lee Roy Jordan were playing and I knew right then and there that I wanted to play for the University of Alabama."[90] This was in spite of Musso having an older sister who went to Auburn.

The other running back slot in the backfield was an open question and was not without some promising talent. In Alabama's offense, this could be either a halfback or a fullback. The leader for the other spot besides Musso was Paul Spivey, up from the undefeated 5-0 freshmen squad. Spivey, a 5-foot-eleven, 190-pound speedster and a true halfback from Montgomery, led his Robert E. Lee Generals to a state championship his senior season. He was a huge Tide fan growing up and would later say when remembering this period, "it was a no-brainer for me. I had always wanted to come to the University of Alabama and play for Coach Bryant. All they had to do was offer me a scholarship."[91] The other contenders for this position included Joe Labue, red-shirts Ellis

Beck and Steve Dean, and junior college transfer Steve Biscelgia. Labue was probably a little ahead of the others and would have lettered in 1970 since he played a great deal the first half of the 1970 season, but a freak knee injury in sweat clothes on the day before the Tennessee game put the running back on the sidelines for four games until the season finale with Auburn. Labue was one of those players who had enough quickness and speed to be a halfback or enough blocking skills to be a fullback. He grew up in Birmingham and was a big Alabama fan. Labue moved to Memphis during his high school years and played at Central High. Labue recalled, "It was a dream come true when I signed those scholarship papers to play at Alabama. Going there meant that you would get the opportunity to play for a national championship."[92] Ellis Beck was another candidate for the other running back position. Nearly identical in height and weighing 5 pounds more than Labue, Beck was more a true fullback. Having been red-shirted in 1970, this Ozark native was ready to make the most of this opportunity, one he almost did not get. He nearly went to Florida State, but their head coach told him that he would never play for Alabama and he would be just wasting his time going there. That changed his mind and he signed with Bama at the first opportunity.[93]

Two of the other running back contenders, Steve Dean and Jesse Causey, were from Florida. Dean, another red-shirt from the previous year, hailed from Orlando. He was a high school teammate of Robin Parkhouse and Wayne Wheeler, two other players on the Crimson Tide who were expected to contribute during the 1971 season. During his senior season of 1967 Causey was considered by many of the recruiting services to be the top runner in the country and he probably would have competed for the other running back position, but he quit the team in February and went back to Florida. Causey had great ability but had been injured a lot during his career. His latest injury involved some 500 stitches, the consequence of running through a sliding-glass door he mistakenly thought was open.

The final competitor to join Johnny Musso was Steve Bisceglia, a junior college transfer from Fresno, California. Bisceglia was a 5-foot-11, 185-pounder who played for Fresno Community College after starring at Bullard High in the same city. Assistant coach Kenny Martin, another California boy who had played for the Tide in the mid-sixties, recruited him. Bisceglia had been a UCLA and Stanford fan when he was growing up. He was familiar with Coach Bryant and the Alabama tradition, but he was not like the kids who lived there. He recalled, "it was a big culture shock. In California all you ever heard about was the peace movement in response to the Vietnam War. When I went to Alabama, all I ever heard was we needed to bomb them [North Vietnam] back to the stone-age. There was a big difference in opinions."[94]

David Bailey caught 111 passes during the 1969 and 1970 seasons for over 1,500 yards and scored eight touchdowns in the drop-back pass-oriented offense. He set many Crimson Tide individual receiving records that included a number of catches during a season (56), catches during a game (12), and passes caught during a career (111). Many Tide fans at the time thought Bailey to be the greatest receiver in their long and storied history. He played for Bob Tyler at Meridian High in Mississippi. Bryant came with Ken Donahue unexpectedly after one of Bailey's basketball games for a visit. This meeting sold Bailey, who signed immediately.[95]

A couple of other capable split ends, Wayne Wheeler and Dexter Wood, were behind the venerable Bailey. Wheeler was the same height as Bailey but weighed about 15 pounds less. He also had better speed. Wheeler had been red-shirted in 1970 and was looking forward to this first real season with the varsity. Like Bailey, he ran excellent pass routes and had extremely soft hands. Wood, at 6-foot-4 and 202 pounds, was taller and heavier than both Bailey and Wheeler, but he knew how to get open in the secondary and catch the ball. Wood was expecting to be red-shirted during the 1970 season, but he was needed and played quite a bit during the last half of the year.

The other wide receiver/backfield position was the flanker, who also had several strong candidates. Going into spring practice, A. B. "Bubba" Sawyer was the leading contender for the position. He was the smallest man on the Alabama squad at 5-foot-9 and 170 pounds, but he possessed excellent speed, good hands, and a big heart. This Fairhope, Alabama, native was a starter his sophomore season in 1969 and caught eighteen passes for 371 yards. That was over 20 yards a catch, the best on the team. He also scored two touchdowns and had an average of 21.2 yards in kickoff returns. Bubba had a number of injuries that limited his playing time in 1970, but he was expected to rebound for his senior year. Dexter Wood could also play this position as well as the split end, which was his more natural spot. Other candidates included Wilbur Jackson and Jerry Cash. Jackson had great natural ability and size (6-foot-1, 197 pounds) and would get a real look in the spring practice. Pat Dye thought he could be as good as or better than Terry Beasley, the All-American receiver at cross-state rival Auburn. Jerry Cash was much smaller at 5-foot-10, 170 pounds but played a great deal the year before and had a 100-yard dash speed less than ten seconds. Cash had a great knack for making things happen when he touched the ball; he caught three passes during the 1970 season, all for touchdowns. In addition he carried the ball twice, once for a touchdown and another time for a successful 2-point conversion.

The tight-end position was an area that worried Paul Bryant. "We are only average at this position," claimed Bryant before spring training got under way.[96] Randy Moore and Jim Simmons were the two top candidates for the job, and both had played a great deal during the previous season. Moore was a 6-foot-2, 205-pounder from Montgomery who played for three state championships at Montgomery's Lee High School. He was a capable blocker and had decent hands. Moore could also be used as a backup kicker. Jim Simmons hailed from Yazoo City, Mississippi, and had been the starter in the opening game against USC the year before in Birmingham. He had tremendous size at 6-foot-5, 230 pounds and was expected to do great things. After the humiliating 42-21 loss to the larger and faster Trojans in Birmingham, Coach Bryant was livid and told the already demoralized squad that the practices were going to be like they were in Junction, Texas, and they were going to find out who wants to play. Simmons did not think that he wanted any part of this and decided on Sunday to return home to Yazoo City, perhaps transferring somewhere else to finish his football career.

> By the time that I got home, my father was waiting at the door and already heard the sports from the Jackson [Mississippi] station stating that I had left the team at Alabama. We had a short discussion about what I was going to do. I told my parents that I was going to transfer to Troy State to play my last two years of football. My dad asked me how I thought that I was going to get to Troy State. My response was the same way I had gotten home from Tuscaloosa, in that Chevy out there in the driveway. He told me in no uncertain terms that car was registered in his name and I was not going to drive it anywhere except to Tuscaloosa, Alabama. Coach Donahue had also called my father and told them that Coach Bryant might take me back if I met with him when he came to his office the next morning. That was exactly what I did.... I got back to Tuscaloosa at about 2:00 in the morning and stayed in the Holiday Inn out by the interstate. I called Robin who had also quit and told him what I had found out and we were waiting on the coliseum's steps at

five o'clock in the morning when Coach Bryant came rolling up in his university-issued Chevrolet. He did not say one word to us and walked up the steps and right past us. He then unlocked the door and went in and came right back out to say to us that he figured that we were there to see him. We followed him upstairs to his office. It was not a pretty sight when we got there. He called us everything bad imaginable... For me, I did the worst and best things in my life within a twenty-four-hour period.[97]

The quarterback is the most important position on the offense. He is the field general and like a coach on the field. Bryant gave his quarterbacks a great deal of discretion on the field and wanted them to take charge. During the last three seasons of Alabama football, the quarterbacking position had been in the capable hands of Scott Hunter. While Hunter was a very good passer and the offense scored many points, the team was clearly in decline. That was not to suggest that the deterioration was entirely Hunter's, but often quarterbacks get a good deal of the blame because of their position. The team faced numerous other problems as previously mentioned, but now the issue at hand was Hunter's replacement.

Terry Davis, Billy Sexton, and Benny Rippetoe were the leading candidates to replace Hunter. Butch Hobson and Gary Rutledge would also get good looks, but Davis was the front-runner for the quarterback slot. Davis was a 6-foot, 170-pound sprint-out-style quarterback who was a much better runner than he was a passer. Terry had been red-shirted in 1969 because he wanted to play quarterback. He had been given the opportunity to convert to a defensive back and in that position he probably would have gotten some playing time that season, but he decided that he really did not want to hit people as much as the defensive players have to. Davis admitted that the prior season was difficult for him and his style of play: "The few times that I did play, I did okay, but I never felt comfortable in that offense. I never did develop a feel for having to stand there and having people run at me and throw like that."[98]

Junior Billy Sexton and red-shirt senior Benny Rippetoe would be Davis's likely challengers in the spring. Sexton and Rippetoe were much more of the Hunter mold, because both were dropback passers and both had strong arms. Sexton was a native of Tallahassee, Florida, and made All-State as a senior at Leon High. He received more publicity than the others and was thought to be the heir apparent to Hunter, given Alabama's particular type of offense. At 6-foot-2, 187 pounds Sexton was plenty big enough to stand in the pocket and take the heat from the opposing defense. Rippetoe was also 6-foot-2, weighed 215 pounds, and was in his fifth year of football at the Capstone. He hailed from Greeneville, Tennessee, an hour northeast of Knoxville and the University of Tennessee. However, the last four years of playing had not been kind to Rippetoe. His career was up and down, the most serious injury a broken shoulder on his passing arm. In the meantime he had gained about 10 pounds a season and now weighed nearly 215 pounds. Rippetoe expected to compete for the quarterback position in a meaningful way now that his shoulder was completely healed. He recalled, "This was my fifth year and I had not played very much, but I was going to give it my best shot, because it was going to be my last shot."[99]

The offensive line would be one of those problem areas Paul Bryant anticipated going into the spring training. Even though three of the five starters were coming back for the 1971 season, Bryant believed that clearly there would to be a great deal of improvement if the Crimson Tide were to be competitive in the Southeastern Conference or nationally. In an interview with Bill Clark of the *Orlando Sentinel* conducted before spring practice, the esteemed head coach identified some of the questions that needed to be answered: "We have only one winner back on the offensive line and one who we think is going to be a big one in the future. Jimmy Rosser is a winner and John Hannah is definitely one that we think can be. Both of these players are tackles. The rest of our interior line is suspect. Our tight ends are average. We are going to have to find some people to play in the middle of the line. At this point, we don't have winners in those positions."[100]

Jimmy Rosser was a two-year starter from Jones Valley High in Birmingham who had come to the University of Alabama for two reasons: to get an education and to have the opportunity to play for a championship football team. This former All-State and All-American was a quiet and studious type who was mature beyond his years, a quick study who usually had to be shown how to do something only once. Rosser was a quiet leader on this team and probably would have gotten more individual recognition had John Hannah not been the other tackle on this squad. He was looking forward to his senior season: "We had lost too many games in the past couple of years and were determined to be better for my final season."[101]

John Hannah was one of the biggest players ever to play for the University of Alabama. At 6-foot-3 and 275 pounds, this Albertville native often played much heavier during the season without losing any quickness. Before Hannah came to the Capstone, his father Herb Hannah and uncle Bill Hannah had already played for the Crimson Tide. John had played at Chattanooga Baylor during his first three years in high school and finished up at Albertville his senior season. He was All-State in both football and wrestling. In addition, he set numerous school records in the shot put. Hannah also competed in wrestling and was undefeated during his freshman year until he lost in the NCAA championships. This fine athlete was certainly one Bryant thought could be the best offensive lineman ever to play for the University of Alabama.

Don Cokely, Gary Reynolds, Rick Rogers, and Allen Cox were also considered to get some valuable playing time by backing up the two starting tackles. Cokely was 3 inches taller than Rosser and played at the same weight. He was a junior college transfer who played a great deal in 1970 and could be counted on for more playing time in 1971. Reynolds and Rogers were two of the starters on the undefeated freshman team. Reynolds was probably the strongest player on the team and at 6-foot-2, 232 pounds was one of the promising freshmen that could be counted to help a great deal in the fall. Rogers, another strong sophomore-to-be at 6-foot-2, 220 pounds, hailed from Boise, Idaho. The last of the tackles was Allen Cox, who was from Mobile and was a three-sport athlete at Satsuma University Military. He was red-shirted in 1970 and looking for his opportunity to perform. Cox was nearly 6-foot-3, and weighed 215 pounds.

The center position was open, with Jimmy Grammer and Pat Raines fighting for the job. Grammer had been the starter in the first game against USC last season and suffered a season-ending injury in the second quarter of that infamous Alabama loss. His older brother Richard was an outstanding offensive lineman at Alabama. He was two years older and had starred in the 1967–1969 seasons. Richard died tragically in a fishing accident before the Liberty Bowl game against Colorado at the end of the 1969 season. Jimmy was fully healed heading into practice and anticipated a great spring for his last season. While only 5-foot-11 and 200 pounds, Grammer was extremely quick, had great blocking techniques, and played much bigger than his natural size. However, he almost quit two and a half years earlier: "These two-a-day practices were killing me, and I was going home. I hitchhiked on Highway 82 and had about five different rides before I got home. By the time I got home, my daddy had gotten the news and was waiting for me. He told me that you could go one or two places: you can get in the car with me and go back to Tuscaloosa, or you can go to the Army Recruiting Center."[102]

Pat Raines had shared the starting position with Cary Varnado after Grammer went down with the knee injury. Varnado was also expected to compete for the center's job, but he quit the squad just before spring practice to concentrate on his studies. At the time, a controversy arose over why Varnado left the team. *The Crimson-White* reported in its March 12 issue that sources in the athletics department attributed the cause partly to the excess regimentation and the hair-length policy. In its next day's edition the paper retracted the story, perhaps due to Varnado's prodding. In any case, Carey's absence would thin the depth at the center position. Raines was a little bigger than Grammer at 6-foot-2, 215 pounds but was not quite as quick as his pesky counterpart. Raines was another of those fine Montgomery players who played on three state championship teams at Sidney Lanier. Mike, his younger brother, would be a sophomore and a promising defensive lineman for the Tide in 1971.

The guard positions were wide open because the prior season's starters, Reid Drinkard and Mike Hand, had graduated. The contenders included Jack White, Mike Eckenrod, Buddy Brown, and Marvin Barron. White was a 5-foot-11, 208-pound senior who had not played a great deal during his career, but he had a great attitude and did not realize he was not very good; he played as if he were a great athlete and much larger than his 5-foot-11 frame. He was the last guy to sign a scholarship in 1968 and almost ended up without a place to play football. When White checked into the dorm nobody knew who he was, but that soon changed.[103]

Mike Eckenrod was another of those players, like Jack White, whose size was more suited to the early- though mid-60s era. Six feet tall and only 195 pounds soaking wet, Mike would have to be able to block people 30 or 40 pounds heavier than he was, as the college game had gotten bigger. "Eck," as his friends called him, was one of those linemen who was interchangeable and could play either guard positions or the center, depending upon the team's need. He was the younger brother of Pat Eckenrod, the starting center on the University of Kentucky football team. Eck committed after his junior year and believes that if he had waited until his senior year he would have never received a scholarship because he was too small.[104]

Buddy Brown and Marvin Barron were the other contenders for the starting guard positions going into spring 1971. Both of these linemen were bigger and stronger than White and Eckenrod and could play either way. Brown was red-shirted in 1970. Barron was a part-time starter at defensive tackle during the 1970 campaign and would play wherever the coaches wanted him to. He recalled why he came to the Capstone: "I came here to be part of a championship program. There were a lot of other places I could have gone if I just wanted to play football, but I wanted to play for a winner and Coach Bryant."[105]

QUESTION MARKS FOR THE KICKING GAME

The kicking game was another area that was unproven but appeared to have adequate athletes. Frank Mann and Richard Cienmy had graduated but the cupboard was not bare. Returning varsity athletes Randy Moore and Steve Wade played other positions but could help if pressed. Moore could kick off or kick extra points, while Wade had done the short punting the year before. Wade had been the regular punter on the 1969 freshman squad and had a 37.4-yard average. Bill Davis and Greg Gantt handled the kicking duties on the undefeated freshman team and both had great legs. Gantt was a proven punter who could consistently punt a long way, but he had had some problems getting the ball off quickly enough. He could also kick off and usually got the ball in the end zone. Davis handled the extra points and field goals admirably as freshman. His older brothers, Tim and Steve, had been kickers for the Crimson Tide during the sixties. If Davis progressed as the coaches thought he would, there would not be any problems with this area of the game.

"DEFENSE IS OUR KIND OF FOOTBALL"

Bryant believed that defense was the most important part of winning football games. In *Building a Championship Football Team*, the veteran head coach was quite emphatic about defense:

As a matter of fact, we work on defense more than we do on offense. We feel if we do not permit the opposition to score, we will not lose the football game. While in reality most teams actually score on us, we still try to sell our players on the idea that if the opposition does not score we will not lose. If you expect to have a good defensive team, you must sell your players on the importance of defensive football. Our players are enthusiastic about defensive football. I believe we do a good job of teaching defensive football because the staff and players are sold on what we are trying to do. Defense is our kind of football.[106]

In the previous couple of seasons, either the coaching staff had not sold the players on the importance of playing defense or there had not been enough talented players to execute the staff's plans. In any case, the suffering defense had been losing games by the scores of 42-21 and 48-23. Bryant felt that the defense in 1971 would be much better than it had been in the last few years. He thought that in each position on the defensive side of the football the players were "stronger, faster, and had at least one winner." Nine starters and fifteen lettermen would be returning as well as several talented sophomores, like Chuck Strickland and David McMakin, who were expected to contribute to the varsity immediately. Bryant believed that part of the problem in the past had been that not enough players were willing to sacrifice and pay the price necessary to win. [107]

THE DEFENSE

In the 1971 press guide, University of Alabama assistant sports information director Kirk McNair wrote of the defense that "Bama has a total of nine players who have shown the potential and ability to be all-star candidates. Five of these players were on the defensive side of the football: On defense, linebacker Jeff Rouzie, end Robin Parkhouse, tackle Terry Rowell, free safety Lanny Norris and halfback Steve Higginbotham all rate nominations for honors."[108]

Alabama's standard defensive set included three linebackers, four defensive lineman, and four defensive backs. The defensive ends could play like ends or stand up like linebackers, depending on the formation. The defensive players who usually made the most tackles were the linebackers. Jeff Rouzie, Bama's best linebacker in this set, played on the strong side of the football. He grew up in Jacksonville, Florida, and prepped at Wolfson High. He was heavily recruited by all the major schools in the South and was leaning toward Florida or Tennessee until Alabama appeared:

My dad went to Florida and so did my dad's brothers.... Florida had been putting a lot of pressure on me and there was also a lot of pressure on me from my hometown that wanted me to stay in the state. It's about

10:30 at night, I'm asleep, and my mom wakes me up says, "It's real important; Coach Bryant is on the phone." I said, "Oh God, what have I done?" He said "Jeff, I am sorry for calling you so late, but I'm making plans for the next four years, and I need to know whether I can count on you or not." I said, "Yes sir." My dad is trying to tell me in the background while I am talking to Coach Bryant. He tells me, "You know what you're doing, son?" I said, "Yes sir; do you want to talk to him?" He said no, that it was my decision. I stuck with it. It was the best decision in my life.[109]

Rouzie was now 6-foot-1, weighed 235 pounds, and was one of the strongest guys on the team. He had been a starter for the entire 1970 season and was third on the team in tackles with forty tackles, thirty-six assists, and two broken-up passes. Rouzie was the most valuable player in the 1970 Astro-Bluebonnet Bowl in which the Crimson Tide tied Oklahoma 24-24. He would have a lot of help at the linebacker position as this area had some depth.

Jim Krapf, another starting linebacker, would provide Alabama additional help in 1971. He played in the middle and was first on the team in tackles with thirty-five tackles and fifty-seven assists. Krapf and Rouzie were nearly identical in size except that Krapf was 1 inch shorter. A three-time national prep heavyweight-wrestling champion from Newark, Delaware, Krapf was quick for his size and also played football as fullback and linebacker. He would be pressed by Chuck Strickland and Wayne Hall for the middle linebacker position.

Strickland was the same height as Rouzie and Kraft but was some 30 pounds lighter. Chuck came from Chattanooga, Tennessee, and East Ridge High. Chattanooga is geographically situated near the Alabama-Georgia state line. All of the major schools in the three-state area, among others, recruited Strickland, but he originally wanted to go to Auburn because his father had graduated from there. Like a lot of the kids from this era, however, Strickland ended up at Alabama because he wanted to play for a winner.[110]

Wayne Hall, the other middle linebacker candidate, was thought to challenge for the starting position in 1971. He was slightly taller at 6-foot-3 and weighed 210 pounds. He was red-shirted in 1970 and had already suffered some knee injuries that had fully healed going into spring practice. He hailed from Huntsville High and, like Chuck Strickland, was leaning toward Auburn because both of his parents wanted him to go there. Hall was intimidated by Coach Bryant, but that allure made him want to play for him even more.[111]

The other linebacker position was on the weak side of the football. A weakside linebacker has to be a little quicker than the other two. He is often counted on to cover running backs out of the backfield on passing routes. Tom Surlas was the leading aspirant for this job. Hailing from Mount Pleasant, Pennsylvania, about an hour's drive southeast from Pittsburgh, he had been a part-time starter the prior season and had been hampered by injuries in the first half but finished strong. A couple other members of last year's squad would push him hard to play at this position. Andy Cross, another of those fullback-linebacker types, had played both ways at Ensley High in Birmingham. Cross played much bigger than his 5-foot-10 frame. Steve Root, the other linebacker expected to compete for the weak-side position, had been playing with the first team until a knee injury in the first game against Southern California cost him the entire season. Like Surlas, Root was a junior college transfer who came from the small community of Indio, California, where he played both at the high school and junior college levels. His journey to the South and the University of Alabama was a memorable one for both himself and the famous head coach:

> I had been recruited to play football by some of the Pac-10 teams out here, but I figured my best shot was in baseball. I get a phone call my last semester in junior college from Bear Bryant. I had heard the name and knew he was a famous coach, but outside of that, I didn't know about him or Alabama. He offered me a scholarship to play football at the University of Alabama. I asked him how serious he was. He was somewhat taken aback. I told him that until I see some scholarship papers to sign, I was not that interested. There was short pause on the line and said he was giving his word and that was enough. I let him know that that was not enough for me and lots of my friends had been offered scholarships to play at different schools, but when it came down to it, they did not get anything. He came out here and met my mother and I signed with Alabama. Needless to say, I had never been outside of California, and the South was a new experience to me, but everybody was nice to me and very helpful and I came to like it a great deal.[112]

The entire defensive line would be back for 1971, and Robin Parkhouse would lead it. Parkhouse was a two-year varsity athlete who at the end of the last season had been considered by many in the

Southeastern Conference to be the best defensive end in the league. He missed four games after the USC fiasco due to a suspension for temporarily leaving the squad for a day. Parkhouse unexpectedly returned in 1970 as a starter for the Tennessee game and was the leading tackler in the Tide's 24-0 loss to the Volunteers. He recalls, "I had no idea that I was even going to play in the game but when Coach Bryant read my name on the starting defense right before we went out on the field, I was dumbfounded. I was so fired up and had a good game. That game was a turning point for me and it propelled me to play at a high level for the rest of the year."[113] Parkhouse led the team in tackles from the Tennessee game until the end of the season. He was a free spirit from Orlando, Florida, whose cultural frame of reference was much different from most of the other players from the South. He had been exposed much more to the outside world. His father was competitive fighter at Malvern College in England. Most of his teammates thought that Parkhouse the toughest guy on the team due to his genes and experience in the broader environment. His flaming red hair and fair skin caused his teammates to dub him the "Pink Panther." Parkhouse was ready for his last spring training, much more so than many others on the team. "I knew that was going to be my last time around and I expected it to be the best. I was very motivated and there was going to be no give in me. I knew that it was up to me and the seniors to expect no less from the other players."[114]

Ed Hines was the other defensive end who had been a starter in the previous season. He was a quite a surprise and performed admirably for the Crimson Tide. The 6-foot-2, 200-pounder grew up in Auburn's backyard in Lafayette, Alabama, some 22 miles north from the university on the plains. Tommy Lusk, John Mitchell, David Watkins, and oft-injured John Croyle were competing for the other defensive end position. Lusk had started for the four games Parkhouse did not play and did a fine job in the defensive leader's absence. Although somewhat undersized at 6-foot-1, 190 pounds, Lusk had great speed and had been the Tennessee state high hurdles champion his senior year at Clarksville High. This speed often allowed him to go around the larger and bulkier offensive tackles before they had a chance to get a good lick on him. In the meantime, Tommy had put on 20 pounds in the off-season and was up to 210 pounds. In addition to playing defensive end, Lusk would get a look at the weakside linebacker spot.

John Mitchell had been a junior college All-American at Eastern Arizona and could have gone to a number of different schools but chose his native Alabama. The off-season conditioning program had been the hardest ordeal he had ever been through and he hoped the spring training would be better. Mitchell hoped to be competitive and get a chance to be a starter at the other defensive end position across from Parkhouse. Coach Bryant had assured him that he would be treated just like anybody else and would have the same opportunity.

The last two candidates for defensive end were sophomores. John Croyle was the tallest player on the team and potentially one of its best athletes, if he could stay healthy. He was 6-foot-6, weighed 205 pounds, and had good quickness and speed. When recruited for the University of Alabama, Coach Bryant told him that he could play both football and basketball. Unfortunately, a knee injury before the freshmen season of 1969 killed his chance to play basketball. He hoped that this spring training would be injury-free. David Watkins, the other sophomore defensive end, hailed from Rome, Georgia, where he excelled in three sports: football, basketball, and baseball. He was an All-State defensive lineman his senior season and had more than 100 tackles at West Rome High. Watkins knew about tough practices and conditioning from his high school experience: "Coach [Nick] Hyder was extremely demanding and would get everything he could out of you. When I came to Alabama, Coach Bryant was just the same, the difference being there was a lot more talent there than I had in high school."[115] Watkins thought he was ready and would get his real opportunity in spring 1971.

Terry Rowell and Jeff Beard were the returning starters at defensive tackle and both of these linemen were expected to have big seasons during their senior campaigns. Rowell was extremely quick at nose tackle and weighed only 195 pounds. He was closing in on a 100-tackle season until a mix-up on the practice schedule caused him to be late and as a result he was suspended for the last two regular season games. He returned for the Bluebonnet Bowl and performed admirably. Rowell was one of those players who played much bigger than his size and was usually so quick that no one could block him. A lot would be expected of Rowell in 1971 because he clearly had real all-star potential. Jeff Beard was the other starting defensive tackle who was returning for his final season. He played high school football in Hueytown along with Tide defensive back Steve Higginbotham. His older brother Ken had played football for the Tide a decade earlier and Jeff's peers expected him to do the same. Beard was another one of those players who almost went to Auburn but went to Alabama in the end.[116] At 235 pounds he was much heavier than his counterpart at defensive tackle but he had quick feet. He put on 35 pounds in the off-season between his freshmen and sophomore squads since the Crimson Tide caoches had plans for him on the defensive line they moved him to the defensive line. Things worked out fine for him, as he lettered in both his sophomore and junior seasons.

If he stayed on the defense, Marvin Barron could be the first defensive lineman to give Beard and Rowell a breather. He was on the defense during the 1970 season but probably would get more snaps on the offensive line this spring. If Barron moved to offense permanently, senior Jim Patterson would most likely be the first backup. Hearty sophomores like Mike Raines and Skip Kubelius would get some extra looks on the defensive. Both of these sophomores were over 6-foot-3 and weighed over 240 pounds as defensive tackles. Patterson was a fifth-year senior from Annandale, Virginia, who had a series of injuries that limited his playing time. Patterson's older brother, Mike, played with the Crimson Tide in the late sixties, while his younger brother Steve was an up-and-coming sophomore offensive lineman. At 6-foot-3, 252 pounds, he certainly had the size to compete for the position if he could keep his health. Patterson played high school football in Omaha, Nebraska, and was heavily recruited by the Nebraska Cornhuskers. He came to Alabama after watching the Tide demolish the Cornhuskers in the televised Orange and Sugar Bowls after the 1965 and 1966 seasons. "I figured that Alabama was the place for me, especially after those two games. My brother had gone there and I thought it was the school to go to win a national championship. I even told Bob Devaney [head coach of Nebraska] that when he came to my house to recruit me."[117]

Cornerback Steve "Higgs" Higginbotham led a battle-tested defensive secondary that returned three starters. The only difference in the secondary rotation was that three-year starting safety Tommy Wade had graduated. Higginbotham was just a little over 6 feet tall and weighed only 170 pounds, but he played like a larger man. The Hueytown native was the second in his family to play football for the Crimson Tide. Older brother Robert had been a varsity athlete in '67 and '68 and had served as a graduate assistant during the past two seasons. A number of schools in the South recruited Higginbotham, but there was no doubt where he would go. As he puts it, "None of those other schools mattered, because I just wanted to go to Alabama." During the last season Higgs had intercepted four passes, one for a touchdown in the last couple of minutes against highly-ranked Houston at the Astrodome. "A lot of seniors on the defense grew up quite a bit and were looking for bigger and better things for our final year." Higginbotham was hoping that what they learned after the Tennessee shutout of last season would carry over to 1971.[118]

Steve Williams was the fastest player on the Alabama squad and manned the other cornerback position. He would be running track in the spring and would miss spring practice. His best time was 9.6 seconds in the 100-yard dash. He was a part-time starter in 1969 and had been a full-time starter the previous season. Williams was named the defensive most valuable player for Alabama in the 1969 Liberty Bowl game. He hailed from Moline, Illinois, but had roots in the South, as his mother was from Mississippi. A number of Big Ten schools recruited Williams to play football, while several smaller colleges wanted him to play basketball. Williams essentially recruited himself to play for the Crimson Tide.[119]

Lanny Norris had been a starter at free safety during the last season and would have been the year before if not for a broken arm. Lucky for Norris, he was able to red-shirt and would only be a junior in football terms. He had his best game against the Houston Cougars where he had nine tackles, five assists, and one interception. In the previous season Norris had also returned an interception for a touchdown against Miami. The 6-footer had put on some 30 pounds since coming to Alabama and now weighed 192 pounds.

The other secondary position of free safety would be up for grabs but was not without some capable performers. Junior Steve Wade and sophomore David McMakin would be the likely candidates for the last starting spot on the defense. Wade was the younger brother of Tommy Wade and played a great deal during the 1970 season. He could play a number of positions like running back, punter, wide receiver, or even quarterback in a pinch: he was taller than the other defensive backs at 6-foot-3, with good range and mobility. David McMakin was a sophomore and had the same body type as Wade. They were about the same height but McMakin outweighed Wade by 23 pounds. McMakin's older brother was the starting tight end at Clemson. Along with Chuck Strickland, McMakin was the defensive leader of the undefeated freshman team. Like Strickland he would be counted on to contribute immediately, and the spring practice would be his first opportunity to prove his worth.

A couple of Alabama natives would also get some serious attention in the secondary that spring. Wayne Adkinson and David Knapp both played quite a bit during the season and would compete for starting positions in the defensive backfield. While both of these players had played defense during the last season, they would also be receivers on the offensive side of the football. Adkinson would get some repetitions at flanker, while Knapp would see some action at halfback. This would not be much of a stretch for either of these players because they went both ways in high school. Adkinson was a teammate of the Wade brothers at Dothan, while Knapp prepped at Birmingham Ramsey.

WEEK ONE

"Mother Nature" smiled favorably on Thomas Field that first day of spring practice. The weather was sunny and the temperature in the low 70s, an ideal day for the normal 2-hour drill. Nothing spectacular occurred in this March 31 practice, but more fans attended than usual. Granted, some of the fans were there because they wanted to get the first look at the Crimson Tide, but a good many more were hoping to catch a glimpse of Joe Namath. They were disappointed to find out he was not there because he was in New York taping *The Tonight Show*.

Billy Sexton and Lanny Norris were the only players mentioned who did not practice that first day. Buddy Brown had injured his hand in practice and was being evaluated day-to-day, but it was not yet apparent how serious the injury was. Norris had hurt his back in the off-season conditioning program and was unsure when he would return. Rick Rogers and Bobby Stanford would miss the entire spring. Rogers was out with mononucleosis, while Stanford was still recuperating from a couple of knee injuries. Bryant was circumspect in his assessment of the beginning of spring drills when he said, "We've got a big squad—a good-looking squad. It was a routine day. I can't tell much about anyone yet. We had so many in drills and switched so many people around on teams that you can't see each of them enough to say much…. We'll have each of them learning a little more about what they are doing in the next two or three days and at the same we'll know a little more about personnel."[120]

The second day saw a continuation of good weather with temperatures in the mid-70s. There were a number of areas of improvement over the first day's practice. These included the offensive backfield and the kicking game. Buddy Brown's injured hand kept him out of Thursday's preparations, but he was expected back for the next day's practice. Skip Kubelius suffered a neck injury and spent the night in the hospital for observation. The extent of the injury was undetermined.

The first Friday in April included some rain showers in Tuscaloosa, but not enough to hamper football practice or the baseball doubleheader between the Crimson Tide and the Ole Miss Rebels, which was being played at Sewell Field. While the two squads were splitting the double-header, the football team was having a few hits of their own just a few yards away. A number of new faces marked the top offensive and defensive units at this Friday session. John Mitchell was sharing time with Robin Parkhouse and Ed Hines at defensive ends, and Tom Surlas joined Jeff Blitz at weakside linebacker. Blitz, who had missed the last season because of mononucleosis, was becoming one of spring's early pleasant surprises. The Montgomery native had been a defensive back exclusively and had done well at the linebacking spot. The team was already counting on Surlas for good things on the defense. On offense, Billy Sexton shared quarterback duties with Davis and made a number of good throws downfield. Wilbur Jackson ran a little with the red team at flanker and showed that some of his great speed was returning after the leg injury had slowed him during his freshman season.

Saturday's practice was moved to Denny Stadium because the Alabama relays were being held at Thomas Field. Two players Bryant had been counting on for the upcoming season sustained knee injuries that day. The previous season Jimmy Grammer had injured his knee during the first half of the opening game against Southern California and had missed the entire 1970 campaign. On this fourth day of spring practice, he reinjured the same knee he had had surgically repaired the previous September. The extent of the damage was unknown. Wayne Hall, another Huntsville native, hurt both knees and was further evaluated over the weekend. Despite this, Bryant still had reason for optimism:

> We've improved the four practices we've had. We've had some good hitting, but we've been handicapped by key injuries to key people. Hall was beginning to look like a football player. He'll be out for awhile....On defense, the most improved player is Jim Patterson. Jeff Beard has also improved a lot. Terry Rowell has also improved some. Robin Parkhouse and Ed Hines looked real good today. Higginbotham has been doing well all along.... We think Mitchell [John] has some ability and Chuck Strickland is doing real well—he likes to get in front of the football. David McMakin is coming along all right. [2]

Monday's practice was the fifth day and then the team would be off for nine days of spring break. Monday would also be the first scrimmage of the spring practice, albeit a controlled one. The offense was pitted against the defense in certain specialized situations and allowed a certain number of plays in which to advance the ball. The players worked in the middle of the field and backed up near their own goal line or ten yards from the goal line, depending upon what the coaches wanted to see. On the down side, team doctors decided that Wayne Hall would have surgery on both knees on Tuesday morning and would be lost for the rest of the spring. On the positive side, Jimmy Grammer's injury was not as bad as originally thought and he was expected to be back at full speed after the break. In addition, the injury to Skip Kubelius's neck was not as serious as once feared and he too would return to practice after the break. Paul Bryant believed that his squad was making significant progress in a number of aspects of the game. Paul Crane helped with the linebackers as he made his first appearance of the spring. The ex-Tide All-American intended to be on hand for the rest of the spring to assist in any way Coach Bryant needed him.

WEEK TWO

On Tuesday, April 13, students returned from spring break. The football team did not practice that day but would start again on Wednesday. Bryant stated that there was no need to change plans on the practice schedule. The second week would go four days in a row and end on Saturday.

The big news about the practice on the first day back concerned Joe Namath. He was present for the first time. More spectators than usual filled the practice area and outside the fences hoping to see the famous signal caller, who was also testing the right wrist. In addition, Jets head coach Weeb Ewbank attended Wednesday's session. Ewbank was optimistic in his appraisal after seeing Namath throw for the first time in five months after the injury: "Golly, for the first day he looked really great.... He fought his way back from the knee trouble and he'll be back after this thing. Joe loves to play, and he'll be ready."[122]

Meanwhile, the football squad got back to work amidst the carnival atmosphere that had taken over the practice field. Coach Bryant was quite happy with the overall level of play, particularly his defense. He singled out a number of defenders who caught his eye: "Steve Wade, Jeff Rouzie, and Johnny Sharpless looked good, and Jeff Blitz, Terry Rowell, and Tom Lusk have been doing well. Ed Hines and Robin Parkhouse had some good licks. So did John Mitchell."[123] Joe Labue and Ronny Robertson missed practice with injuries. Jimmy Rosser was excused from practice to go home and be with his father, who was having surgery.

The first full-scale game scrimmage was on Thursday. Terry Davis and Billy Sexton led the Red offense, while Benny Rippetoe (playing on both sides) and Rick Pitalo quarterbacked the Whites in this intra-squad battle. It clearly was one in which the defense dominated, and the Whites won the game 12-9. The game was relatively even until the Whites scored in the final two minutes, as Rippetoe hit Dexter Wood with a 20-yard pass for the game-winning touchdown. Bobby McKinney made a 63-yard punt return in the second quarter for the Reds' only touchdown. John Dorough also kicked a 43-yard field goal for the Whites in the second period. In the final quarter Buddy Brown tackled Rippetoe for a safety for the Whites before the winning touchdown. Benny Rippetoe performed the best among the quarterbacks and was the top passer during the scrimmage. The Greeneville, Tennessee, native was 7 for 13 for 85 yards. The Reds' David Bailey and Phil Murphy had three catches apiece, while Wilbur Jackson and Wood caught two passes for the Whites. Paul Spivey and Richard Bryan were the leading rushers, as Spivey gained 61 yards in nineteen carries for the Reds while Bryan gained 54 yards in nine carries for the Whites. Greg Gantt was one of the bright spots during the game, for he had a number of good punts averaging 44.5 yards in nine attempts.

This scrimmage had been a real head-knocker. Many of the younger players were surprised by the intensity of the action. Steve Sprayberry recalled his thoughts as the team rode back from the stadium to the dressing room: "I remember being exhausted from that first scrimmage. The players were sitting two to a seat and Wilbur Jackson was beside me. We were just laying on each other trying not to fall in the floor. We were just two guys trying to hold each other up. It made me think about all the fuss about integration that had been going on before we got here. I was white and he was black, but we were the same. It really didn't matter to me."[124] This was another sign that where race was concerned, the young athletes on the football squad were more progressive than many of the state's polititians. The act of Wilbur Jackson laying his head on Steave Sprayberry's shoulder may seem innocuous, but this symbolizes the tone Bryant set for his team amid the racial tensions of that era. The fact that a black player would even touch a white player shows the positive atmosphere Bryant created for his players—one devoid of outside politics.

In the next practice, the team tried to regain their legs. It was a learning practice in which the squad attempted to make up for the previous day's lackluster play. Saturday was another story, however, when the veteran head coach took his team back to Denny Stadium for a controlled scrimmage. Bryant was much happier with the team's performance than he had been on the previous days' efforts. He singled out the quarterbacks for praise: "Terry Davis did real well all afternoon and Billy Sexton made some nice plays. Joe [Namath] noticed that our quarterbacks hadn't been getting back far enough in the passing pocket and that if they did, they sometimes moved back up too close to the line. We had seen that, too, but we're glad Joe spotted them and it'll help us.[125]

A number of visitors saw Saturday's practice. John Brodie, quarterback of the San Francisco 49ers, came up from Pensacola, Florida, where he was playing in a Pro-Am golf tournament. "I just wanted to come up and see the place and of course, I wanted to see John David [Crow, a former teammate]," he said. Several ex-Tide players were on hand, including Steve Bowman, Tom Somerville, Wayne Owens, and Johnny Moseley. A couple of future Bama players were also viewing the scrimmage. Dennis Durance and Gary Yelvington had signed football scholarships and would join the University of Alabama in the fall.[126]

Some bad news also came out of Saturday's practice. Reid Underwood, a junior offensive lineman from Dothan, and Mike Harder, a sophomore running back from Shreveport, Louisiana, quit the team. Harder was the third leading rusher on the undefeated freshmen team and simply had decided he did not want to play football anymore. On the other hand, Underwood's leaving the team was a mystery. Coach Bryant talked with Harder but not with Underwood. Bryant stated that the practice schedule was not set, but he'd just "play it by ear" as to when the next session would be.[127] Most likely the third week of spring practice would begin on Monday or Tuesday.

WEEKS THREE AND FOUR

Paul Bryant left practice early on Monday for a speaking engagement in Anniston, and Sam Bailey took over the coaching duties in his absence. After practice, Bailey told the media it was "a typical learning session. We've got so many people crippled up, particularly in the middle of the defensive line, but I certainly think we got something out of it, though. We'll take Tuesday off and try to play some kind of game on Wednesday."[128]

A notable visitor was seen on Thomas Field at Monday's practice. Howard Schnellenberger, a former Kentucky player under Bryant and former Alabama assistant coach returned to Tuscaloosa with a number of observations. Schnellenberger was now a professional assistant for Don Shula of the Miami Dolphins. He had been an offensive coach for the Crimson Tide for five seasons from 1961–1965, and during that stretch Bama had won three national championships. Schnellenberger is generally credited with getting Coach Bryant to adjust his offensive scheme by using the pass more often. He commented to the *Tuscaloosa News* regarding the current Tide squad along with the difference in coaching in the professional ranks: "It looks like there are more of those gifted players here this year. They look bigger and more talented in recent years and I think Alabama will be getting back on top soon… Yeah, you're a lot closer to athletes as a college coach and you have a direct bearing on what they do. You have a big influence on their life and help set their habits for the future."[129]

Sophomore strong safety Jeff Blitz was one defensive Alabama player Paul Bryant prominently mentioned several times during the halfway mark of spring practice. Blitz was a former quarterback from Montgomery who had led Sidney Lanier High to two state championships and a 33-1 record in his three years on the varsity. He had been red-shirted the previous season when he contracted mono at the beginning of fall practice. He was not very big at 5-foot-11, 170 pounds but plays much bigger. "He doesn't have particularly good speed, but he loves to hit people and is an extremely intelligent football player," Bryant mused. Jeff had been playing with the first team the entire spring.[130]

On Wednesday's practice, another starting safety appeared for the first time. Lonny Norris had been hurt the entire spring and thought he would miss all of spring practice. He got to see his first action in the eleventh session of the spring. Norris only got in on a few plays, but was glad to be back. Some other news also came out of Wednesday's practice, as reserve quarterback Rick Pitalo left the team. "We talked it over and Rick would like to transfer. And considering his situation, I think it's the best thing for him," said Bryant.[131] It was not readily apparent where the fourth-string signal caller would end up, but the veteran head coach wished him the best.

Injuries were beginning to take their toll on the Crimson Tide. There were at least eight players who were hurt; all of them were either starters or first line replacements, including Terry Rowell, Ed Hines, Steve Biscelgia, Johnny Musso, Jeff Beard, Richard Bryan, Jimmy Grammer, and Skip Kubelius. Lanny Norris was attempting to practice his way back after missing half of the spring session. Cloudy skies marred Friday's workout, but it was not the weather that most disturbed Coach Bryant. He was more concerned with the lack of players. "We had hoped to play some type of scrimmage Saturday, but it looks a little doubtful now. We're so crippled that it's hard to get a good picture of things. I guess we'll have some sort of controlled workout now."[132]

Even though the Tide did not get to scrimmage on Saturday, they were still able to accomplish some things. The footballers worked on their quickness and fundamentals. Overall, Bryant was much more charitable in his assessment than he had been in the past few practices, especially with his defense: "Yes, I think that we've made some good progress there so far [on the defense]. We've still got some crippled folks there and we really haven't had a good test yet, but I feel considerably better now than I did this time a year ago."[133]

Monday was another off day for the football team, giving the injured another day to rest. On Tuesday there was some scrimmaging, but still the injured players affected how much the coaching staff could achieve. Coach Bryant saw some good and bad: "We did a little bit of everything. We did some things very well. However, we weren't consistent and we also did some things very poorly."[134]

On Tuesday the big news coming out of Tuscaloosa was the announcement of the A-Day rosters. Johnny Musso would captain the Red team, while Steve Higginbotham would lead the White squad in this intra-squad tilt on Saturday.

Wednesday was the last practice for the Tide before the Saturday A-Day game. In a spirited two-hour affair, the head coach was cautious in summing up the workout to reporters: "There was a lack of consistency. We did a little bit of everything and did some real well. First of all, I was highly pleased with Gary Rutledge and I thought Rippetoe and Davis had some good throws. Labue, Biscelgia and Spivey all ran the ball well, but we didn't use Johnny [Musso] because he was getting some honors Jason's and ODK at the school's Honor's Day programs]."[135]

A-DAY GAME

Sam Bailey, Ken Donahue, and Clem Gryska accompanied Bryant in the press box to view Saturday's game. The coaches were announced for the upcoming A-Day battle: John David Crow would lead the Red team while Richard Williamson would direct the White squad. The game started at 3 P.M., airing live across the state on the Alabama Educational Television Network. Frank Blodgett of the network broadcasted the game, assisted by Ray Perkins, who, after working with the receivers for the past few weeks, did the color commentary.

Crow's associates were comprised of the following coaches: Dude Hennessey, Jack Rutledge, Bob Tyler, Bill Oliver, Jim Tanara, Danny Ford, Richard Cinemy, and Joe Namath. Ford and Cinemy were graduate assistants. Ford played his last season in 1969, while Cinemy had played for the prior year's team. Tanara had been the wrestling coach and also helped on the football field. Williamson's assistants included Kenny Martin, Jimmy Sharpe, Pat Dye, Mal Moore, Robert Higginbotham, Tommy Brooker, Perry Willis, and Paul Crane. Higginbotham and Willis were former players who were lending a hand as graduate assistant coaches.

Between 15,000 and 20,000 fans were expected for the afternoon kickoff. Eighteen college scouts from five of Alabama's 1971 opponents were also attending the intra-squad game. Four scouts were from Southern Mississippi, six from Ole Miss, five from Tennessee, two from cross-state rival Auburn, and one from Vanderbilt.[136]

A "sun-baked" crowd of 15,043 saw the underdog Whites defeat the Reds 21-15. Steve Dean, the red-shirt sophomore tailback from Orlando, was the star of the White team's victory. Dean gained 86 yards in sixteen carries and won the inaugural Dixie Howell award for the most valuable player of the spring game. Dean served notice to Bama fans that Johnny Musso might not be the only star in the Tide's 1971 backfield. Musso had a workmanlike performance, gaining 70 yards on fourteen carries and catching two passes for 55 yards. Bryant was quite pleased with the play of all the running backs: "We both [Bryant and John David Crow] thought all of our running backs played well. Steve Dean had an exceptional day—just a terrific day and Johnny [Musso] played well though he had that fumble early in the game. Paul Spivey, Ellis Beck, Joe Labue, Steve Bisceglia, and little Phil Murphy all did well."[137]

One of the biggest surprises of the day was the play of quarterback Gary Rutledge. Thought to be red-shirted in the fall, he threw himself back into the quarterback sweepstakes by leading the Whites to two touchdowns. Bryant was quite pleased with the slender sophomore's performance: "Gary Rutledge took his team 99 yards and two feet for one touchdown. I thought he was the outstanding quarterback out here today. We're gonna take some more good looks at Gary."[138]

Terry Davis, generally thought to have the inside track on the starting quarterback position, had some good and bad plays in the intrasquad game. He completed six of twelve passes for 109 yards for a touchdown but had two passes intercepted. Davis also showed his running ability when he gained 28 yards on ten carries.

It was the defense, however, that most caught Bryant's eye. Except for the past two seasons, the hallmark of success during his reign at the Capstone had been the defense. Robin Parkhouse had an excellent game, leading both sides with thirteen tackles. White captain Steve Higginbotham also performed well, ranking second with twelve tackles. The Bear did not offer many comments about his defense after the game but changed his tune after viewing the film:

> I thought that the Whites had a lot of leadership. Robin Parkhouse played real well and he was always around the football. John Mitchell played pretty well, too. So did Jeff Rouzie, Jim Krapf, Chuck Strickland, Tom Surlas and Steve Root at the linebacking places. I thought Terry Rowell did well and Jeff Beard and Jim Patterson did well some of the time. Steve Higginbotham played real well. He made some good plays in the secondary and made several big tackles. Robby Rowan and Steve Wade did well, too.[139]

Two big interceptions in the game led to White touchdowns. Robin Cary picked off a Terry Davis pass and went 18 yards for a touchdown early in the second quarter. Steve Wade picked off another Davis pass late in the third quarter at the Red 37 and returned it 32 yards to the 5, setting up another touchdown.

Paul Bryant thought his defense was more physical and combative this entire spring game and Saturday's game was no different. The defensive secondary was an area of concern before practice started, but it would be one of strong points by the time the season rolled around in the fall. The veteran head coach was quite pleased when he made this appraisal. "The film showed the defensive secondary to be more aggressive than it has been around here lately and their sudden change was good, too. You saw that by the way they ran back those interceptions."[140]

Currently the Crimson Tide has given its players seven awards, including six named for men who played for Bryant in the 1960s. Those six were Lee Roy Jordan, Jerry Duncan, Billy Neighbors, Paul Crane, Ray Perkins, and Bobby Johns. The seventh was named for Dixie Howell, who played with the Bear in the 1930s. In 1971 all of these former players except Howell, who had died recently, attended and/or assisted in various parts of the spring practice.

THE FINAL WEEK

After the spring game the Crimson Tide had four practices remaining. The first of these was held on the Monday after the game. It was one of those typical "learning practices," as Coach Bryant liked to call them. The team did not scrimmage or do a lot of hitting. "We were just trying to learn our assignments offensively and we didn't do any of the full-speed stuff on either side," claimed Bryant as he left practice. Bryant wanted to use the last week to focus on a few problem areas. He spoke plainly when describing them: "Our offensive line has a ways to go. We've got to do better. We're going to concentrate on our kicking game and give our quarterbacks all the work in pressure situations we can." Two of the final three practices would work in game-type situations.[141]

Terry Davis sat out the scrimmage but observed it from the sideline. Benny Rippetoe and Butch Hobson quarterbacked the Red squad over the Whites, who Gary Rutledge and Billy Sexton led by a score of 31-21. Rippetoe completed eight of eleven passes for 113 yards and two touchdowns. One of the touchdown passes went to Pete Pappas, who caught six balls in the game scrimmage. Paul Spivey was running with great abandon, gaining 167 yards in twenty-four carries. Bryant was pleased with the exhibition.

The next-to-last practice, another "learning session," was on Thursday. Very little contact work was done. Coach Bryant wanted the players to "brush up on things" and get ready for the final scrimmage and practice of the spring on Friday afternoon. The last session featured the No. 1 offense against the No. 2 defense and the No. 2 offense against the No. 1 defense. Mal Moore handled one of the teams while Pat Dye took the other.[142]

Several big plays marked Friday afternoon's last practice at Denny Stadium. One guest in attendance was former Tide All-American and Dallas Cowboy linebacker Lee Roy Jordan, who watched the scrimmage with Coach Bryant from the press box. The offense had their share of the glory as the Reds defeated the Whites 37-21. The action included a 53-yard touchdown pass from Billy Sexton to Pete Pappas, a 27-yard run by Rod Steakley, a 19-yarder by Ron Richardson, a 15-yard run by Phil Murphy, and four runs of more than 10 yards by Ellis Beck. Wilbur Jackson and Bobby McKinney ran back punts for touchdowns. Jackson turned on the speed for 71 yards, and McKinney sped down the field for 83 yards. Also, David McMakin, a sophomore defensive standout, intercepted a pass and ran it back for a 96-yard touchdown.

Statistically, Phil Murphy led all runners with 74 yards on fifteen carries, while Beck added 67 on ten carries and Rod Steakley contributed 56 yards on seven attempts. Terry Davis completed ten of thirteen passes for 83 yards, leading the Reds to victory. Backup quarterback Billy Sexton was three of four passes for 89 yards for the victors. On the other side, Butch Hobson was five of six for 63 yards for the losing Whites. Gary Rutledge was effective for the Whites, completing seven of eleven passes for 52 yards in the loss. Steve Dean had four catches for 42 yards, and Pete Pappas caught three for 60 yards as the most prolific receivers.

Bryant was generous with his praise on the final practice. Players from both sides of the ball won the accolades of the Alabama chieftain: "We had a lot of people with big plays. I'm sure there are some I missed, but you couldn't help see Tom Lusk and Robin Parkhouse. And John Mitchell blocked a punt. Lanny Norris and David McMakin had some big plays, and we had good sudden change on McMakin's interception. Offensively, Ellis Beck ran well and so did Rod Steakley. Pete Pappas made that fine catch and he's been doing that all spring. All the quarterbacks had big plays. Overall, the defense whipped the offense. The kicking game was the deciding factor."[143]

Paul Bryant's Alabama teams of the 1960s had won games this way. The defense would stop the offense, while their offense was able to run the ball effectively and make some big plays. The kicking game was often the deciding factor in close games. Maybe this formula for success could be replicated in the fall. While there were no formal practices in the summer, the players were expected to run, lift weights, and be in top condition when they reported in August. Less than four weeks later, the Tide would travel to Los Angeles and begin the 1971 season. However, the experienced head coach had a lot of things to do before that could happen.

BRYANT'S MOMENT OF DECISION

ONE OF THE FIRST THINGS PAUL BRYANT DID AFTER RETURNING
to the University of Alabama was come up with a plan to upgrade the
school's physical facilities. An avid planner, one of his initial priorities
was to improve his athletes' living conditions. The Bear saw that air-conditioning was installed in Friedman Hall, which was then the athletic
dormitory. After the success of the 1959 and 1960 seasons, he had cam-
paigned for a new athletic dorm that would be the envy of the college
football world. Young Boozer, his old sidekick from his playing days at the
Capstone, aided him in this effort. Boozer had been one of Bryant's best
friends over the years and was happy to lead the fund-raising offensive to
build a new athletic dorm. After the Crimson Tide rolled through the
1961 season and won the national championship, the money seemed to
pour in from everywhere. The result was a "Taj Mahal" to house the athletes, accomplished without any public monies.

BRYANT HALL

Paul W. Bryant Hall was built in 1963 as the athletic dormitory for
football and basketball players. The dormitory was not originally named
for Bryant. A long-standing law on the books in Alabama prohibited
public buildings on college campuses from being named for living persons. In summer 1965, after Bryant won his second national

championship, the law was amended and thereafter the dorm has been known as Paul W. Bryant Hall. Often referred to as the "Bear Bryant Hilton," at the time it was generally considered to be the most modern athletic dorm in the country. This was another recruiting advantage Bryant could point to when entertaining prospective athletes. He wanted recruits to know that if they came to the University of Alabama to play football, they would be treated better than anywhere else on campus or any place in the country.

The facilities could house 136 athletes, two to a room, and contained all the up-to-date conveniences of the day. It had central heating and air-conditioning, two dining rooms, a color television room, four guest rooms, apartments for live-in coaches, a large recreation room, and several large meeting rooms that were also used as study halls. The rooms were equipped with 7-foot-long beds, dressers, lavatories, desks, bookshelves, and large closets. In 1970, telephones were installed in the rooms. Three meals were served daily, followed by a late snack usually served between 9:30 and 10:00 at night. In addition, a backyard patio with a number of grills was available for those who wished to cook out on special occasions. Gary White became director of the dorm in 1964 and lived there with his wife.

GARY WHITE

White knew that Paul Bryant would often do things in an unorthodox manner and the veteran head coach was not afraid of change. He had been with Coach Bryant since 1958 when he was a student manager on the football team. He came to the University of Alabama in fall 1957 and was on a manager's scholarship during the last year of the Whitworth regime. White had been a huge Tide fan while he was growing up in northeastern Alabama. When Bryant called a meeting of the student managers in early January, just after being hired by Texas A&M, White did not know what to expect. He barely knew who the new coach was. He found out quickly that this was a man who did things his own way:

> I was a freshman at the time. He called all the managers in there. There were about of twenty of us. A lot of them I had never seen before. They were political appointees that Coach Whitworth had on board. They were on scholarship and were assigned to big alumni around the state. I

know now what it was, but not at the time. It was a thing put in place to kinda appease the big money people in the state that had contributed to keep the fires put out. Coach Bryant came in and called all the managers over. He said, "All but the head manager, I'm going to let go. You're welcomed to get out there and work and the ones who work will help us in the fall." I did not know what I was in for. I had earned this scholarship and worked hard to keep it. Then Coach Bryant comes in here and takes it all away.[144]

The youngster from Gadsden knew he did not want to go back home and work in the Goodyear plant where his father had worked for thirty years. White had watched his father come home from that kind of work over the years and did not want the same for himself. He talked his father into paying for the spring semester and promised that he would be back on scholarship in the fall. White and the head manager were the only managers who were retained in fall 1958. He would later become be the head manager himself for three years. After graduating in spring 1963, he did scouting work for the Dallas Cowboys. In fall 1964, he moved back into Paul W. Bryant Hall as dorm director.

Things were highly structured in those days, and White had specific plans for managing the dorm. Gene Stallings, who was an assistant coach at the time, put together the dorm rules while on the staff from 1958–1964. White was given a copy of the rules and regulations and was expected to implement them. He knew from his days as a student manager what expectations the head coach had for him. "Coach Bryant was not the type to stand over your back—period. He expected you to do your job, and he expected you to work. I understood that," said White.[145]

Times were difficult during that period. Students all over the country were demanding more freedom on college campuses, and it was no different at the University of Alabama. The spring semester even ended a few days early due to campus unrest after the 1970 Kent State shootings. Even though the football players were somewhat insulated by their daily programs and schedules, they were not completely immune to the conflict. The players wanted to be treated as individuals, not just cogs in a machine. Gary White spoke on these changes and how they impacted his last couple of years as director of Bryant Hall:

Well, those were turbulent times. The thing was the deal over the long hair and the hippies or beatniks... The Vietnam War was going on.

There was a change of attitude all over the nation. I think that it got here down in the South a lot later. But we were faced with it and struggled with it. He [Bryant] made certain adjustments on things like hair length, but he did not change his fundamental philosophy. He told the players that "if you want to play, you're going to play the way that I want you too. I know how to coach and I know how to win." This would never change.[146]

Now, nearly seven years later, White was experiencing more changes. Bryant had reassigned him to head academic affairs. In addition, he would also become Sam Bailey's administrative assistant, as Bailey was overwhelmed by the new paperwork the NCAA had begun to require of its member institutions. Bob Tyler, who also doubled as the receivers' coach, would replace White as dorm director.

BOB TYLER

Bob Tyler had only been on the staff since the first of February. A few weeks later, at 2 in the afternoon, he got a phone call from Bryant outlining his new responsibilities. The head coach told Tyler that he wanted him to be the new dorm director because he was transferring Gary White to another position. Tyler was shocked:

I asked him when he wanted me to move in. I thought that I would have a few weeks since we were just now getting settled into a townhouse across the river. I then asked him when he wanted me to move in, and he replied, "Tonight after supper." That was the way he did things. We moved in that night. Luckily, everything was furnished and it was not that difficult. Coach Bryant did not give me any guidelines on how he wanted the dorm run. He only said that he wanted me to move in and supervise the boys. I had a great deal of freedom to run it like I saw fit.[147]

This particular move may seem inconsistent given that Bryant loved to talk about how a player's family and religion were more important than football. Bob Tyler could have seen it this way, but he did not. One's career often came first in those days, especially for men. There were times when everybody had to make sacrifices for the greater good, in this case the greater good being the welfare of the football team.

Unfortunately, the new dorm director encountered a small problem. The apartment had only two bedrooms. Bob and his wife Dale had three young boys and needed another bedroom. To solve this problem, the oldest son Breck was allowed to have one of the guestrooms. These rooms were made available for use on special occasions for visitors; sometimes Coach Bryant would stay there himself. It was a small tradeoff but gave Breck the privilege of having his own room, completely separate from the family, with the added thrill of interaction with the athletes.

Early on a few players told Bob Tyler that he did things a little differently than his predecessor. That did not mean he was overlooking some of his responsibilities, but suggested rather that his personality and reactions were a little different. He came to coach the receivers for the Crimson Tide and to learn from one of the greats in football history; the additional responsibility of running the dorm did not change this.

> Coach Vaught [at Ole Miss] had a heart attack during the 1970 season. There was a time after the season in which he thought he was going to the new athletics director and I would be the head coach. It did not work out that way. I called Coach Bryant's office and talked to his secretary. He called me back from a coach's convention in New Orleans and told me to come down here to talk to him about a job. He hired me there. He did not say anything about running the dorm.... When he did ask me to do it, of course I said yes. I don't know how to describe how [my wife Dale and I] did it. We were a little more laid back. They [the players] felt a little looser and freer than they had been in the past. Several players told us that. We were a little more laid back in how we did things there. I respected the kids and I think that they respected me. Once in a while we had some problems and had to correct them, but that was all part of it.[148]

The fact that Bryant did not give the new dorm director any significant advice on how he wanted the dorm operated speaks volumes about his ability to adjust to the times. Coach Bryant was well aware of the changes in the wider culture. He also knew that he could control some things but not others. He wanted his players to feel at home in the dorm, but these players were there to play to football and get an education. If they wanted to do other things on campus, Bryant was not necessarily opposed as long as they kept their priorities straight. Bryant thought that priorities had been lacking in the past few years. Too many of his players had been trying to do too many things other than play football and get an education. He also believed that to be winners players had to sacrifice, both on and off the field. He understood what it meant to be a student and be heavily influenced by one's peers, but not everyone who attended the University of Alabama could play football for the Crimson Tide.

Paul Bryant was completely involved in all aspects of his football team's organization. This included how the dorm functioned. The Bear would usually assign one of his married graduate assistant coaches to move into the dorm. This graduate assistant would have no primary responsibilities in the dorm itself but was another set of eyes and ears for the head coach. The assistant essentially served as a liaison between Bryant and the players. Danny Ford, one of Bryant's former players and a current graduate assistant, moved into the dorm in 1971 to help Tyler. In operating the dorm, the head coach knew that he needed someone who understood the players and their needs. This did not mean that Gary White did not understand the players while Bob Tyler did. Sometimes outside events have a life of their own and force changes upon organizations; the athletics department at the University of Alabama was no exception. It is always easier for a manager or leader to look for answers within an organization, rather than going outside of it. White had certain skills that were needed elsewhere in the athletics department but he could not run the dorm if he performed other tasks. Bob Tyler was Bryant's choice to replace Gary White. In making this change, Bryant limited Tyler's recruiting responsibilities in order to free more time for the new director of Bryant Hall.

PLAYERS LEAVING FOR THE SUMMER

At the end of the spring semester, the football players could not just go home for summer break like the other students. With certain procedures in place, they had to complete a checklist before leaving the university. One task was to list three prospective roommates in rank order for the fall semester. The dorm director would forward these to Coach Bryant and discuss the various possibilities of living arrangements. Bryant would always make the final decision. Another item on the players' list was to turn in their books to the athletics department; if they lost one, they had to pay for it. After turning in their books, the players had to meet personally with Coach Bryant. This meeting would usually last anywhere from ten to thirty minutes at a time while the coach reflected on the particular player and what expectations that he had for him. After the meeting was over, Bryant would sign a form that gave the player permission to leave the campus. At the first of June, the player would receive in the mail the specific goals he needed to accomplish over the summer, such as the specific weight he needed to be and the time he was required to run a mile. These requirements were not negotiable. They were another example of the sacrifice Paul Bryant expected of his players.

WHAT WERE THE COACHES DOING?

Meanwhile, the coaching staff had other matters at hand. They continued with their recruiting responsibilities. The NCAA did not limit the number of scholarships member institutions could offer during this period, but at the time the SEC had a limit of forty-five. The coaches met with prospective recruits at their high schools before the end of the school year in May. During these very crucial times the coaches continued to build relationships with the senior-to-be prospects, as it was nearly impossible to begin recruiting a player during his senior season without any prior relationship. In addition the coaches were available for public appearances in various communities throughout the state. This usually continued until the beginning of July. Bryant reserved the first two weeks of July for his assistants to take their vacations. By the middle of July, the coaches began holding meetings for the upcoming fall practice, which would begin in about three weeks. All of the coaching staff participated in recruiting. In general, they were assigned particular geographical areas but were not limited to those regions. Some cross-checking ensured a broader assessment of the athlete's abilities. The coaches and geographical zones were as follows:

Mal Moore—Montgomery
Jack Rutledge—northeastern Alabama
Clem Gryska (coordinator)—anywhere in the country
Dude Hennessey—border states
Ken Donahue—western Alabama and Mississippi
Jimmy Sharpe—Mobile area
Pat Dye—below Montgomery and southern Georgia
Bill Oliver—northern Georgia and Atlanta area
John David Crow—Birmingham
Richard Williamson—between Birmingham and Montgomery

Bob Tyler—Richard Todd, a quarterback from Mobile who had already
committed to Auburn, was Tyler's only recruit
Kenny Martin—Florida[149]

BRYANT SETTLES THE QUESTION

While the coaching staff was hard at work recruiting prospective college athletes and building goodwill among the Alabama faithful, Bryant
was troubled. He was very uncertain about the offense and whether they
were good enough to win using the existing scheme. The 1969 and 1970
squads were categorized not by too little offense; quite the reverse was
the case. They scored a lot of points but could not consistently stop the
opposition from scoring. Coming out of spring practice Bryant felt that he
was going to have a strong defense, but the same could not be said for his
offense.

What Bryant did know about his offense was that he had a lot of
running backs and receivers and very few good offensive linemen. The
quarterback situation was up in the air. Johnny Musso led the running
backs and was considered by the head coach to be the best runner in the
country. Bryant needed an offense that could showcase the Birmingham
native's many talents. Musso could run, block, catch, and even occasionally throw the football well. David Bailey had caught 132 passes over the
past two years and was arguably the best receiver in Alabama football history. Jimmy Rosser and John Hannah led the offensive line at the tackle
positions but left question marks at the guards and tight end positions.
The center position was unsettled, as otherwise number-one Jimmy
Grammer awaited recovery from his knee injury. He had missed nearly
the entire previous season. Jim Simmons and Randy Moore were adequate at tight end. The quarterback battle was far from being settled.
Terry Davis was listed as the number one but had not distinguished himself enough to have a lock on that position. Benny Rippetoe and Billy
Sexton were better passers and much more comfortable in the pro-style
passing offense. They had both had some practices in the spring and had
challenged Davis for the starting position. He was a good runner with
quick feet and could throw the short and medium passes, but he lacked
the arm strength of Scott Hunter or Joe Namath. In fact, some of the
new twists in the spring offense complemented Davis's natural skills. Mal
Moore had already been experimenting with him, trying some additional
plays that better fit his style. Bryant asked Bob Tyler to show the other

offensive coaches some of the things Ole Miss had done the past few seasons with Archie Manning and help determine whether some of these tactics could be replicated by the Alabama offense. Some sprint-out passes and sprint draws were added to take advantage of Davis's speed around the corner. These helped Davis to be more effective, but the offense was still quite inconsistent as a whole. What could Bryant do to get the most out of his existing offensive personnel? An idea had been brewing in Bryant's head since the first of the year. The head coach decided to call upon one of his best friends in the coaching profession for some guidance.

THE TEXAS CONNECTION

On the previous New Year's Eve, the Crimson Tide had tied the Oklahoma Sooners 24-24 in the Astro-Bluebonnet Bowl in Houston. During the 1970 season, Oklahoma had resorted to the wishbone offense, which they had learned from the University of Texas coaching staff. As the team flew back home the following day, something happened on the plane ride that would later have major ramifications for the Alabama football program. Coach Bryant usually rode in the last row of seats. On this particular ride, however, he sat in the middle of the plane. Kirk McNair, who was assistant sports information director at the time, sat across the aisle from Bryant. McNair recalled the ride home: "I was not talking to him and was just minding my business when he started diagramming some plays. I did not give any thought at the time, but remembered it at the beginning of fall practice. Coach starting drawing up the wishbone."[150]

Paul Bryant had a few close friends who were also college football coaches. Darrell Royal from Texas, John McKay at Southern California, and Charlie McClendon from LSU were often mentioned as being his closest contemporaries. They were also the three Bryant alluded to when he had almost taken the Dolphins job a year and a half earlier. These friendships had evolved over a number of years. It was sometime in June when Paul Bryant called Darrell Royal, his old buddy in Austin, Texas. Royal was eager to accommodate his old friend. Bryant wanted to come out to meet him and learn about his wishbone offense. As the Bear was flying out to Austin, Darrell thought about the first time he met the famous head coach: "It was in 1950, right after I had graduated from the University of Oklahoma. We were in spring practice and Coach [Bud]

Wilkinson wanted me to show [Bryant] around. Coach Bryant was at Kentucky then. He was visiting the University of Oklahoma to observe the split-T offense and how we did things here…."[151]

After Bryant arrived, the old friends talked as they drove to the hotel. Earlier Royal had offered the Bear use of the athletics department facilities at the University of Texas, but Bryant scoffed at the offer because he thought there would be a chance of the press coming around and asking why he was there. With film and projector in hand, the two coaches went up to Bryant's hotel suite to view the training film the Texas coaching staff had put together to teach the intricacies of the wishbone offense.

Before viewing the films, Royal explained that this offense was the brainchild of Emory Bellard, who was Royal's offensive coordinator at the time. Bellard created it in his own backyard while playing football with his sons. Royal explained why the wishbone was such a great offense: "For one thing it was much faster around the ends than the split-T. It was nearly 5 yards faster around the end. The backs were lined up with their weight forward. In order to move sideways, you had to turn more to get moving in that direction. The backs had to come out of a stance to move right or left, depending on what you were going to run. You were lined up a lot tighter to the line of scrimmage. You had to bow back. In the wishbone, you were set inside of that and in an upright position."[152]

Paul Bryant at the White House in the mid-60s with President Lyndon Johnson and his coaching friends. Darrell Royal with LBJ in front. Looking on are Bud Wilkinson, Jake Gaither, Bryant, Tonto Coleman, Duffy Daughtery. (Paul W. Bryant Museum)

Less than three years earlier, in autumn 1968, Darrell Royal had made the decision that his Texas Longhorns would switch to this offense. They made the changes less than two weeks before their first game of the season. Royal explained how they had been able to do it in such a short period of time: "There were so many things about the alignment that fit into the same things that we were running about the backfield with the split-T, and we did not have to change that much. It was an offense that we could run pretty easily if we were successful in teaching it. We installed it in about a week and half before our first game in fall 1968 and experimented with the quarterback running the triple-option."[153] The initial success was less than glamorous for Texas, as they lost and tied their first two games. Many observers thought that Darrell Royal had lost his mind. Royal told them to be patient and the Longhorns won thirty games in a row with back-to-back national championships in 1969 and 1970.

The tapes were broken down into the offense, defense, kicking game, running game, and passing game. It did not take the Alabama head coach long to make the decision to switch to this offense. Royal recalled watching play after play with Bryant until his friend from Alabama asked how much of the practice Royal devoted to pass protection. When Royal replied, "None," an incredulous Byrant decided firmly that Alabama would be spending the vast majority of its practice on offense as well.[154] The two visited a little longer then Bryant returned the next day to Tuscaloosa, excited about the prospects of running this new offense.

RETURN TO ALABAMA

Within a couple of days after Bryant returned to the Capstone, he called a meeting of his offensive coaches. He told them about his meeting with Texas and his decision to switch to the wishbone. None of the offensive coaches were really happy with the progress of their offense, but, conversely, none wanted to make a switch without having a lot more lead time. There was no cheering among the coaches about this change. John David Crow, on the other hand, recalled it a little differently:

I remembered the first meeting with the offensive coaches during summer 1971. Coach Bryant was pretty sure that we were going to make the switch to the wishbone. I was ecstatic. I knew that we had to have an offense that featured Johnny Musso and this was it. I knew in my heart that this was what was needed. The offense would fire out and hit the opponent straight ahead. This fit him [Bryant] much better. Coach Bryant was a fire-out and knock-them-in-the-nose type of coach. His strategy was to keep hitting them until the fourth quarter and by then they will throw in the towel. What we had been doing with the passing game was out of his element. It went against everything that he was about.[155]

There is some dispute as to whether or not there was a vote among the coaches. Clem Gryska remembers one in which almost all of the assistants voted against any change in the offense, while most of the other assistant coaches were either unsure or do not remember a vote. It really does not matter because the head coach had already made the decision to do it and it was up to his underlings to follow through. All of the offensive coaches were present for this meeting and would later view the training films and break them down. Mal Moore and Jimmy Sharpe went to Coach Bryant a few days later and told him they needed some additional help if they were going to be successful in this new endeavor. Moore had been a quarterback himself but had been coaching the defensive secondary the last few years. He needed more talking points to work with before he felt comfortable teaching the new strategy. While there was no official offensive coordinator at the time, Jimmy Sharpe was the de facto leader. Sharpe reminisced about this exciting summer meeting and what it meant to him:

> Darrell Royal had told Coach Bryant about the overview on how to run the wishbone. The Lord had implanted in me that if I did not understand it completely, then I could not teach it. I was like a sponge just trying to soak it up with as much information as possible. It was fascinating. It was basically Mal and myself who spent the most time with the films. We flew out to Austin for a few days and met with the Texas coaching staff, breaking down the films. Emory Bellard took the lead in explaining it to us. We came back with a lot better understanding of the concept of the wishbone offense. It was now up to us to be able to implement it and teach the kids how it will work for them.[156]

Another meeting between Bryant and the offensive coaches took place about a month later in late July. This was a couple of days before the high school coaching clinic was scheduled to come to Tuscaloosa. In his autobiography, Bryant recalls telling his assistants, "Three springs ago, when I knew that we couldn't win with what we had, doing what we were doing, I told our coaches. What we could win with was the old split T. We may be dull as hell, but we can win."[157] Mal Moore remembered a few more details of this address: "He told us that 'we were going to open the season in the Coliseum in Los Angeles against Southern California, and we're going to end it in Legion Field in Birmingham against Auburn. We were not going back to our old offense three or four games into the season like some others have tried.' He gave us no way out. We had no playbooks. We had nobody who had played it and had no one who had been involved in it. There was no resistance to it. He made his decision and we knew what we had to do."[158] The case was now closed. None of the coaches left the room. They had spent the previous few weeks studying the wishbone and going through the different scenarios the defense would counter. The coaches now felt a little better about the new offense.

COACHES CLINIC

At the end of July the University of Alabama athletics department sponsored an annual coaching clinic for high school coaches around the state. Over 1,000 high school coaches attended the event. Also scheduled was the high school all-star game held at Denny Stadium between the top senior players chosen throughout the state to play their last contest at this level. During the week the featured college coaches held seminars with their high school counterparts. The speaker for the banquet at the end of the week was Darrell Royal, who fondly remembered, "Bear said that he wanted me to come to speak to the high school coaches. He wanted me to bring my offensive coaches with me. He told me that he wanted them to lecture to the clinic. You and I don't have to do a damn thing, but play golf. That is what we did. Our staff visited with their staff. He had already told about the secrecy of switching offenses. We certainly did not mention that Alabama was going to use this offense or anything like that."[159]

During the clinic the Alabama coaches met with the Texas coaches at the Stafford Hotel to discuss different strategies concerning the operation of the wishbone offense. In an interview with Clyde Bolton of the *Birmingham News* conducted during that week, Royal debunked some of the myths surrounding the wishbone and what kind of team would be best served by using this offense:

It doesn't take super athletes above what it takes to win in any formation. You've got to have good athletes to win in any formation. I don't say if you want to throw the ball to get into the Wishbone. I say you have passing opportunities, though, because of what the defense has to do to stop the running game. You've got to have confidence in it before you go into it. Some teams tried it and then, the first time something went wrong, they went back to something they had confidence in. The same thing happened when the Split-T came out. A lot of teams junked it because they didn't have the patience to stay with the basic attack.[160]

Paul Bryant had confidence in the formation of this new offense. He also thought he had the kind of athletes that could be successful in this offense. Once Bryant got something in his head, it took a great deal of evidence to convince him otherwise. Now he had to persuade his football players that this was what was needed to return to the winning ways of the past.

It was now well into the second summer session. The quarterbacks, running backs, and centers were taking class and practicing on the new formation in their shorts and tee shirts in the basement of the coliseum. They knew about the switch about a week earlier than the other players and were sworn to secrecy. The Crimson Tide offensive coaching staff knew that the beginning of fall practice was just around the corner. The assistants were not sure what was going to happen. What they did know was that they had better learn this offense backwards and forwards if they were to be successful in teaching it.

RETURN TO GREATNESS
OR MORE OF THE SAME?

DURING THE FINAL WEEKEND BEFORE HIS TEAM WAS TO REPORT for fall practice, Paul Bryant was a busy man. He appeared at the Friday-night "Football Spectacular" in Birmingham to sign autographs at the Western Hills Mall. Thousands of Crimson Tide fans were on hand to see the famous head coach, who was getting ready for his fourteenth season at the Capstone. He seemed confident that this season would be much different from the mediocre seasons of the recent past: "We've had some great teams at Alabama, but the past couple years haven't been that good. We're going to have another great team at Alabama one of these days. One of these days could be right away, much sooner than people think. In fact, the beginning could be Monday morning….the beginning of a Return to Greatness."[161]

JOHN VAUGHT DAY

The next day Bryant traveled to Jackson, Mississippi, to attend a tribute to John Vaught of the Ole Miss Rebels, a long-time friend and competitor. Vaught had been the head coach of the Rebels for the past twenty-four seasons until a heart attack forced him into retirement after the 1970 season. His teams won six SEC championships and ranked in the top ten nationally ten times during his tenure. At the time of his premature retirement, his overall record was 185-58-12, which placed him second only to the Bear among active coaches at the time. The former Ole Miss skipper was seeing Bryant for the second time that summer. Earlier the two had played golf at the July "Bear Bryant Golf Classic," which Bryant hosted in Tuscaloosa. Acknowledgements came in from all over the South, as all the schools from the Southeastern Conference sent representatives to honor the great coach. Bryant had a lifetime 7-6-1 record against Vaught and was quite gracious in his remarks, which summed up what everyone at the event already knew: "Johnny was always a gentleman in victory or defeat."[162]

RETURN TO GREATNESS?

On the Sunday afternoon of August 15, the players were supposed to report to Bryant Hall for their room assignments, weigh-ins, and football gear. At 5:45 P.M. they would have their first dinner together at the dorm. After the evening meal they would meet with the coaches for an address by Coach Bryant. First, Bryant would address the incoming freshmen and welcome them to campus. At this meeting the head coach was all business and surprised many of the new players. Ray Maxwell, a freshmen lineman, recalled what occurred next. "Coach Bryant was short and to the point with us. He told us that he, not us, was going to win a national championship in the next four years, with or without us."[163] After that he walked out of the room. Most of the players were just shaking their heads and wondering what just happened.

The Bear next addressed the varsity separately in the projection room. These meetings usually lasted only five or ten minutes and consisted of welcoming the players back to campus, much as he had done with the freshmen. This meeting was quite different. It was at this assembly that Alabama football would be changed forever.

Coach Bryant briefly welcomed back the players and made some general comments about the upcoming season, as he had always done in these types of settings, but he then shifted gears and got specific about the state of affairs of Alabama football. The meeting lasted about thirty minutes and he did not waste any time getting to the point. Rod Steakley, a reserve flanker and fifth-year senior from Huntsville, recalled this speech:

He [Bryant] highlighted his career as a football player and a coach. What he basically did was talk about learning how to be a champion.... He had rebuilt the championship traditions at Alabama, and he had allowed for termites to get into the woodwork. Termites had eaten at the foundation and he took full responsibility... "I've allowed it to happen, and I take full responsibility for it, but we have gotten away from championship football. We had gotten to the point where we had a number of blue-chip athletes who were good enough to make good plays, and we would win ball games. But I know that's not the way to win championships. You can't win on athletic ability alone. You've got to have that mix of players who are disciplined, have a work ethic, and a desire to be some-thing. We have come to this. What I have done is I have taken myself out to Texas and have learned the wishbone offense from Darrell Royal and his team. We have decided we are going to run the wishbone offense. We have taken what they have taught us, and we have affected it and tweaked it. We think that we have the best wishbone offense in the country. That's what we are going to line up and play Southern Cal with. We are going to sink or swim with the wishbone." He then told us that he was going to close all the practices, and we were not to discuss this change with anyone and that includes our family, our girlfriends, the media—no one.[164]

Bryant next went to the chalkboard, drew up a series of offensive for-mations, and proceeded to explain them. He drew the I-formation, the split-T, the veer, and the wishbone formation and made brief points on what makes these offenses effective. When he came to the wishbone, Bryant went into a much more substantive discussion on its strong points. He explained to the players that the key to making this offense work was the credible threat of the fullback running the football. In order for the fullback to do this, two things had to occur. First, the guards were the most important offensive linemen in this sequence, for they had to be able to clear out the middle of the defensive line. If they were able to complete this task, this would give the fullback the opportunity to run the ball up the middle for good yardage. Second, the quarterback had to have the wherewithal to read the defense and decide whether to give it to the fullback, keep the ball and run it himself, or run to the corners and option the ball to the trailing halfbacks. These things were imperative if the offense was to succeed. Finally, the veteran head coach turned to his star running back, Johnny Musso, and asked him to come to the black-board and essentially repeat to the team what he just said. Bill Oliver, a former Bryant player and now defensive coach, was amazed at what happened next:

> What he did was much like he did to us coaches in staff meetings. He would make some key points on the blackboard and ask one of the assistants to now come up and explain what he said. He expected his assistant coaches to be good listeners. He did not repeat himself. Coach Bryant was now asking a player to do this. He asked Musso to come up before the chalkboard and explain what he just said. Johnny went up there and recited almost verbatim what he had just gone over and knew everything from A to Z. The reason that he called on Johnny [was] because he knew Johnny was smart and it would leave a strong impression on the players about this switch to the wishbone.[165]

Paul Bryant showed a short training film on the wishbone and dismissed the team after the film was over. There was not a lot of discussion among the players as they left the projection room and headed back to their rooms. Picture day was in the morning, while the mile run and physicals were on schedule for the afternoon and two-a-days were just around the corner.

SHOW AND TELL

Picture day on the practice field at the University of Alabama signified the beginning of fall practice. The players would dress up in their game uniforms and have the photographers from across the state snap their pictures in various poses. This would usually last a couple of hours then the players would change clothes and go back to the dorm for lunch. After the midday meal they would get a couple of hours of rest before taking their physicals, weighing in, and running the mile. Linebackers, receivers, and backs were supposed to run the mile in under six minutes, whereas linemen had six-and-a-half minutes. Linemen could either run the mile from start to finish or have it broken up into four 440-yard runs, with a one-minute break in between. This adjustment had been made the previous year because some of the larger linemen (John Hannah in particular) had great difficulty making the time, even though they were in great physical condition. If the players failed on their weight or the mile, they were digging themselves into a hole that was often difficult to get out. They would be required to complete additional running, which would be extremely difficult given that two-a-day practices would begin on Tuesday. These practices left the players depleted physically. The twice-daily drills would normally last a week to ten days leading up to the beginning of the fall semester.

This was also the time the press would begin previewing the team according to the expectations that normally accompany the beginning of the fall practice. The Crimson Tide had twenty-nine practices to complete before they would debut the 1971 season on September 10; they had three and a half weeks left. Expectations were high among the press across the state despite the two previous "off" seasons. Bill Lumpkin, sports editor of the *Birmingham Post-Herald*, wrote an example of this: "Talent is here in sufficient number this year to return those better days. There's depth to complement the front ranks. Spirit, determination, and respect are plentiful for the red jersey, which stands for tradition and designates the players who play the best and hardest."[166] Sportswriters in many of the state's major newspapers echoed much the same.

MUSSO STEALS THE DAY

Almost every story began with a discussion of the team's prospects and a feature on its star player, Johnny Musso. He was a pre-season for All-American in a number of sports publications, and he was on pace to break almost the entire career rushing records at the University of Alabama and the Southeastern Conference. While the individual glory was fine for the senior tailback, Musso did not come to play for the Crimson Tide because he wanted personal achievements. He came there because he wanted to compete for the national championship. Musso believed that after the Houston game in 1970 this team started to wake up. He also believed that the team's defense would set this team apart from the previous squads. In an interview with Delbert Reed of the *Tuscaloosa News* conducted in late July 1971, the star running back noted, "I think the thing that's going to help this year is that our defense is going to be able to play. That is the thing that wins, and I'm convinced that the defense is going to be ready."[167]

Musso had spent all but three weeks of the summer in his native Birmingham working as a stockbroker and training for his final season at the University of Alabama. He, along with Stan Maulding of Texas, Rocky Long of New Mexico, and Lydell Mitchell of Penn State, spent twenty days visiting South Vietnam, courtesy of the United States

Department of Defense. This encounter broadened his horizons and gave him greater perspective going into his senior season.

> I didn't think I wanted to visit the hospitals, but it was the most rewarding thing about the trip. I saw one boy from Birmingham, Tommy Morton, who had just had a leg amputated. The only thing he was worried about was if his mother knew he was all right. His courage was really an inspiration to me.... The men we visited at the fire-bases out in the jungle were bored to death. They were glad to see anybody. I thought they might be resentful because we were college boys and they were over there, but that wasn't the case at all.... Over 90% of the country are farmers. All they want to do is farm their rice fields. They don't know who the United States is. They could care less whether the communists or whoever runs the country. [168]

Picture day went off without a hitch as the photographers took still shots of the Alabama football team.

The Bear on the sidelines talking to his star player of the 1971 squad, Johnny Musso.
(Paul W. Bryant Museum)

BACK TO WORK

In the afternoon, when the players reported for their physicals and the mile run, all the players reporting were physically fit except for Ed Hines and Bubba Sawyer. Hines's knee had required surgery in July, and Sawyer had had an emergency hernia surgery the same month. It was unclear whether either of these players would be ready to participate in the 1971 season. Steve Root had not yet reported because his younger brother had just been killed in a tragic car wreck, but he would report later in the week. Jim Simmons and Steve Williams had gone to summer school and were now both eligible academically to participate in the fall practices. All the players made their times on the mile, and Bryant was pleased with the outcome.

The NCAA mandated that the first three days of fall practice had to be non-contact and completed without pads. The players practiced in shorts and concentrated on conditioning and learning. Normally there was not a lot of fanfare or news during these first few sessions. The first fall practice day of 1971, however, was an exception. Five players unexpectedly quit the team: Carl Tayloe, Woody Flowers, Frank Lary, Jr., Gary Reynolds, and Mitchell Weaver. Reynolds's quitting was a shock to everybody because they knew he was expected to contribute a great deal that fall. He was the strongest player on the team and had been the top offensive lineman on last year's freshman squad. Wilbur Jackson recalled how Reynolds's departure affected him: "There were some days during the two-a-day period of 1971 that I did not know whether or not I could go on. The practices were so tough. Gary Reynolds had quit the team. He was the toughest guy out of our freshman squad. If he quit, I sure did not know where it left me. I was just out here fighting for my life with the rest of the players."[169] The other players would have competed for positions but were not listed with the first two teams on the depth chart. Tayloe, Flowers, and Lary notified the head coach while Reynolds and Weaver did not. Bryant was livid with this development but appeared more upbeat about the first-day's action. "Several decided not to play. We had two who weren't at practice. They didn't have the courtesy to say goodbye. I guess they've quit. I know they have. I really think they lost their guts, if they ever had any. Anyway, I'm glad they quit now rather than wait until they got into a game. They are Mitchell Weaver and Gary Reynolds.... On the other hand, I think we had a good practice. We worked on conditioning and rehearsed our offense and defense. They are quite alert. I thought we did some things pretty well for the first day."[170]

Over the next two days of practice, the players and coaches got back into their regular rhythm. The only injury was a mild hamstring strain to Paul Spivey. He was expected to be back at full speed within a few days. A couple of position changes also merited attention. One involved moving David Bailey from wide receiver to tight end for a number of snaps. The other concerned transferring John Hannah from tackle to guard. Bailey would play both positions, depending on the formation. These changes were made in order to accommodate the wishbone offensive formation. The guard was a more crucial position in this particular scheme, and Hannah was an ideal choice given his size and strength. The Bear was generally pleased with these practices and was highly complimentary, particularly of Terry Davis and the entire defensive secondary. "Terry is doing real well. He was zipping the ball to receivers Thursday, and they were catching well, too. The defensive secondary is quite improved, and they were bouncing around the ball in good shape. Steve Williams intercepted a couple passes Thursday with good speed and quickness, and Wayne Adkinson made some good plays."[171]

Another development between practices on Wednesday blindsided Paul Bryant: Steve Dean quit the team. This case came as quite shock to the head coach, for he was counting on the Orlando sophomore to be one of his top running backs alongside Johnny Musso. The tailback was expected to be a starter this season after having a great spring in which he won the Dixie Howell award as the most valuable player at the A-Day game. Bryant remarked, "Steve came to me and we had a long conversation. His decision to leave the squad surprised me. He's a solid citizen."[172] Bryant refused to say anything else to the press concerning this issue. This was the way that he did things. Coach Bryant treated his team as his family, and, as with family, when there is pain and conflict one protects the privacy of those involved. Dean recalls that he suffered a great deal of personal anguish during this period of his life and had decided to give up football:

> Three bad things happened: being messed up with a girlfriend and homesick, being red-shirted, and my brother being killed in Vietnam. When he was killed, I had some real intellectual things going on in my head. I had won the most valuable player in the spring game. I came back for two days and my heart was not in it. I thought I should have been the other halfback behind Musso. What I really wanted was for somebody to talk me into staying. I was so messed up. Practice to me was like hard labor. Not from the physical aspect, but my heart was not

in it. I was miserable. I didn't know if I wanted to play football anymore. I went in to see Coach Bryant. When I told him that my heart wasn't in it and maybe it was best that I just leave the team, he was taking a big draw on that Chesterfield and he almost choked when I told him this. He said that he "was sorry that I felt that way." He did not do a hard-sell job. It was just that way. I guess he figured if you don't want to do it, you don't want to do it.[173]

On Thursday Paul Bryant had to deal with another player-related issue. Between practices he had a meeting with Steve Williams, who was distraught because he had not been listed on the depth chart during the first days of practice. The senior was the fastest player on the squad and had been a two-year starter at cornerback. At the end of the spring semester Williams had had a disagreement with Coach Donahue over some conditioning. He had also had some academic problems by not earning enough credit hours to be eligible for the fall, even though his overall grade point average was fine. Williams enrolled in the second session of summer school but had become disenchanted and almost gave up on the class and the football team. In late July he had received a call from his mother while vacationing in Atlanta with his girlfriend. The phone call had gotten his attention and put into motion a string of events that led to this early fall meeting with Coach Bryant:

It was then when my mother called me from Tuscaloosa and asked me, "Steve, what are you doing? Coach Rutledge has called me and has arranged with your finance professor to take your final exam in five days." A light went off in my head. I got a haircut and hitchhiked back to Tuscaloosa. I spent the next four days cramming for that exam. I barely made it with a D. That allowed me to be eligible. I had to do some extra running for Coach Donahue and had run the night before the mile run. My legs felt like lead and I did not think that I would make the time. I almost quit about halfway through, but I sucked it up and finished with the best time of anyone. During the picture day, Coach Bryant did not let me get my picture taken with the defensive backs was really putting pressure on me to do something.... I go to his office and asked him if he was not going to put me on the depth chart, that he should release me and let me transfer to another school so I could finish my career somewhere else. He let me know that "he would not hurt another school like that by recommending me." I told him that I was a big boy and I could take it if he wanted to kick me off the team, but it would kill my father. He had taken up and moved his family from Illinois to Alabama so he could be near me. I remembered how Coach Bryant had given us a speech back in 1969 about "winning one for the papas." I then asked him, "What about my papa?" He leaned back in his chair and didn't say anything for several seconds, which seemed like an eternity to me. I knew that had him thinking about it. He then told me that he was going to give me one more chance, and I would be back on the depth chart for the next practice. I knew right then that I was going to have a good season.[174]

BRYANT'S FIRST-WEEK ASSESSMENT

The first day in pads for the 1971 squad was an extremely productive one. The team scrimmaged in particular situations and in full contact, but this was usually limited to the circumstances. Bryant was pleasantly surprised with the work of his offense, which had been behind the defense in terms of development all spring and during the first week of fall drills. "The offense got some full speed work, but the defense didn't get any contact except on punts.... Really, the highlight was Terry Davis's performance at quarterback. His passing was excellent. Every pass he threw was on target, and all of our people were catching well, particularly Dexter Wood. Danny Taylor caught a long one and Wayne Wheeler and Wilbur Jackson also did well."[175]

Saturday's morning workout was more of the same, with a great deal of learning and conditioning. The afternoon practice was a spirited one, cut short by the rain. There had been no major changes in the depth chart. Coach Bryant was uncharacteristically happy after the first week of practice. In an interview with Alf Van Hoose after Saturday's afternoon session, Bryant reflected on what the team had accomplished and where they were headed: "I've enjoyed this week. It's fun putting together the pieces again, though we're not sure they're in the right places yet and probably won't be sure for some time. Yes sir, you can say it. I'm optimistic about this team. That doesn't mean it has the greatest ability in the world, particularly speed afoot, but it's showing some other qualities, which could overcome that."[176]

Often at this time of the year Paul Bryant would be complaining loudly about his team being slow, not tough enough, and the like. That the veteran head coach lavished his team with praise might be a good omen of things to come. On the other hand, the wily coach might be overly encouraging them before turning on them during the second week of practice. He was always challenging his players and coaches to stay on their toes. Many times they did not know how to take him, but they would learn soon enough as they rested over the weekend and tried to regain their legs for Monday's morning workout.

Before Monday's workout Paul Bryant had a visit from Allen Cox, an offensive lineman. Cox had come to meet with the head coach's office staff to discuss his future with the Crimson Tide. Cox believed that the switch to the wishbone had killed his chances to be an effective lineman. Bryant offered to move him to tight end, but Cox did not think he had the speed for that position. Paul Bryant met this situation the same way as with any other player. He was honest with Cox and may have agreed with him, but it was what he thought was best for the team that counted. Though Cox would acknowledge this three decades later, he was mad at the time. Unfortunately he just had to deal with it.

"GROWLING" COMES BACK

After a week of praise, on Monday the Bear came out growling at his squad. His offensive team came under particular criticism. "The offense was terrible. Today, we saw every kind of fumble known to man. There was very little leadership, explosive speed, and very little second effort." The defense did not come under the same type of scrutiny. "The defense did pretty well, especially Chuck Strickland, who did a very good job of tackling."[177] Strickland had been battling Jim Krapf for the starting middle linebacker position. Krapf had been a starter most of the last season and had made the All-SEC sophomore squad. Strickland was really pushing Krapf for this position, and both were listed as first-team on the depth chart for Monday's practice. Strickland was the leading tackler on the undefeated 1970 freshman team and he was beginning to make his presence felt on the varsity. Strickland knew why he was improving: "I think the main thing that helped me as far as becoming a better player happened to me as a freshman. We were on the scout team for the first offense varsity. I had to line up everyday in front of John Hannah. You either get better or die. You learned how to take on the blocks or get away from them. This helped a lot of us to grow up quick."[178]

A sign of the times appeared outside every entrance to the practice field. The signboards declared that practices would be closed until further notice. Not even visitors with special passes were allowed to witness practice in preparation for the early September contest with Southern California. Coach Bryant had told the team a week earlier that he was going to close practices, but he had waited a week to act on his promise. Vinyl tarps were wrapped along the fence outside of Thomas Field to shield the practice fields inside from public view. It had been several years since Coach Bryant had done this, and he was extremely serious about the task.

Tuesday's practices signified a number of things. First, this was the last of the two-a-day practices. Second, it was the beginning of registration for the fall semester, which would begin on Thursday. Thirdly, and perhaps most importantly, there were a number of position changes. Jimmy Rosser moved from tackle to guard on the offensive line. This move might have been anticipated since John Hannah had made a similar move toward the end of the prior week's practice. Rosser and Hannah were generally considered the best offensive linemen. Since the end of spring training, on a number of occasions Bryant had called Rosser "the best offensive lineman that we have."[179] This was quite a compliment given that John Hannah had been heralded as the best offensive line prospect since the Bear's return to Tuscaloosa and had been on a number of pre-season All-SEC teams. Jim Krapf moved to offensive tackle, and Rosser moved to guard. Krapf had great athletic ability but had not played on the offensive line since high school. This move would be a challenge for the Delaware star but was one Bryant thought necessary. He felt that, with the exception of Rosser and Hannah, there was too much inconsistency on the offensive line. Krapf shared the first team position with Marvin Barron. The final placement switch involved David Knapp. Knapp, a junior defensive back who had lettered as a sophomore and had played a great deal during the previous season, moved to the halfback position on offense. Since the Huntsville junior had experimented in that position during the spring, it was not an entirely new experience for him.

There was more grumbling from the head coach as the Tide finished their two-a-day practices. They were at the halfway mark in terms of preparation time for the season opener with USC, and the next two weeks would be critical. Bryant was extremely cautious about the task ahead. "We've got to regroup and get ready to play Southern California. The next few days are awfully important as far who's going to be doing the playing." However, Bryant did have some praise for a couple of sophomores, Chuck Strickland and Rick Rogers. "Strickland has been doing well all along, but we expected him to. Rick is doing well, considering that he missed part of last season and all of the spring. We sure wish now we had had him during spring training."[180] Rogers had missed the spring because he was sidelined with mononucleosis.

The big news out of Wednesday's practice was that Montgomery sophomore Paul Spivey hurt his shoulder in a full-contact drill while blocking a defensive player on the corner. Spivey's injury was serious and he would probably be out for three to four weeks. Most observers thought that the running back position was to be one of the strongest for the Crimson Tide when they started fall practice. Yet in less than ten days it was depleted by the loss of Steve Dean and now Paul Spivey. David Knapp's move to the offense the day before was looking even more important now with Spivey's injury.

Thursday marked the beginning of the fall term at the University of Alabama. The football squad went through a spirited two-hour workout, which pleased Paul Bryant. This was a departure from the previous three day's worth of practices. "We've got better execution out of our backs and wide people today." In addition, the head coach singled out a number of offensive linemen for praise. "I think the interior line is doing better every day. Doing a particularly good job are John Hannah, Jimmy Rosser, Buddy Brown, and Marvin Barron."[181]

DEFENSE CONTINUES AHEAD OF OFFENSE

Defense ruled the day, as it had throughout the spring and early fall, in the first full-contact scrimmage on Friday afternoon. Bryant did not play his first team offensive backfield, as he did not want any further injuries. The first team backfield included Terry Davis, Ellis Beck, Johnny Musso, and Joe Labue. Davis was solidifying his grip on the first team quarterback. Beck was running first team fullback, while Musso and Labue were listed as the first team halfbacks. The Bear had nothing but approving words for the defense: "All the linebackers played well. We scrimmaged Wayne Hall a little for the first time. He did pretty well. All in all, I think the defense had some fun. The defense whipped the offense badly."[182]

Bryant made another position change towards the end of the scrimmage to improve the already thin offensive line. Steve Sprayberry had been playing defensive tackle but moved back to offensive tackle during this practice. With two weeks to go before the Crimson Tide traveled to

Los Angeles, Paul Bryant continued to sing the praises of his defense. This was quite a change for him. The last two season's defensive teams had finished in the bottom half of the SEC in total defense and scoring defense. The improvement on this side of the football was imperative for Bama to return to the top of the conference, where they had been for most of the sixties, and become national contenders.

Saturday's practice drained most of the players. It lasted three-and-a-half hours, with the temperature hovering in the mid-90s. The heat on the artificial turf was often 15 to 20 degrees higher. As had been the pattern, Coach Bryant continued to lavish compliments on the defense: "I think we've made quite a bit of progress in some areas. I think that we have improved defensively. We're not blessed with a whole lot of speed and quickness, but we're beginning to hit with more authority. Parkhouse, Mitchell—really all that front group have looked good. The linebackers have all done well. In the secondary, Steve Wade has improved a lot, and Steve Williams is coming along well after having missed spring training for track."[183]

Much of this improvement was due to eight returning starters, most of them seniors. Robin Parkhouse was the leader of the defense. Since his return to the starting lineup the previous year against Tennessee, he had been playing like a man on a mission. In the spring he had won the Lee Roy Jordan Headhunter award for the most outstanding defensive player. In the first two weeks of fall practice, he proceeded to take things up another notch. The Orlando senior knew that his group's time had arrived. He recounted his feelings during the two weeks before the first game of the 1971 season: "This was our senior year. We knew that this is what we will be remembered for."[184]

As the Tide went into their second full-scale scrimmage the defense was so far ahead of the offense that Paul Bryant would not play his first offense against them. Bryant was beginning to feel concerned ten days before they went to Los Angeles, and there were only nine practices left after Monday's scrimmage. He gave a mixed evaluation of the second scrimmage: "Time is running out on us if we don't get some speed and quickness. I wish we were playing the freshmen; we move the ball well on them. We tried a little bit of everything today. We worked on a little of everything, and we scrimmaged the offense against a weak defense."[185]

There was some good news on the offensive side of the football. Bubba Sawyer, the senior flanker from Mobile, came to practice for the first time since his hernia surgery several weeks earlier. He would not be ready immediately and perhaps not for several more weeks, but his presence alone brought a smile to Coach Bryant's face. The coach was the first person to greet Bubba as he trotted out onto the field.

Tuesday and Wednesday's practices were tough grind-it-out workouts, and the offense did pick up a bit. Bryant seemed happier with the offensive line but hollered for the players to give some help to Musso in the backfield. The final scrimmage before the trip west was on Thursday afternoon. The defense carried the day again, and Coach Bryant was beginning to sound like a broken record:

> They were more aggressive and more oneness than the offense. The offense didn't get 11 players doing the same thing often enough. One person would break down. We also had several penalties on offense. You can't move the ball that way. I saw Mike Raines on defense make some good plays for the first time.... On offense; there was no one on the offensive line who was not getting whipped occasionally. I don't think John Hannah got whipped much, though. Musso played well, as he always does, but not many others did. I don't think that we are ready to play a game.[186]

The Tide needed to get ready to play because the first game was only a week away. Paul Bryant knew that with only eight practices remaining time was of the essence, and the USC Trojans would certainly be ready. Only time would tell if Bear Bryant could get the Crimson Tide ready to perform on Friday night in Los Angeles.

IT CAN BE DONE

PAUL BRYANT AND HIS COACHES VIEWED THE FILM OF THURSDAY'S scrimmage and began making their preliminary evaluations. Thursday was the last day of full-contact work as the Crimson Tide continued their full preparation for USC. On Friday there was a lot of dummy work, more conditioning, and limited hitting. The players needed to regain their leg strength, as they were only one week away from their first game.

The 1971 version of the Alabama football team included its first two scholarship African-American players, Wilbur Jackson and John Mitchell. When commentators discuss this period of Alabama football, they often refer to these two as "firsts." Their backgrounds, personalities, and experiences were different but their fierce determinations to be successful at the South's premier football program were the same. Jackson was the first of his race to sign a football scholarship in 1970 and was one of the game captains of the undefeated (5-0) freshman squad that same year. Mitchell would become the first black starter in 1971 and the first black captain the following year. Both of these players would be making the trip to Los Angeles to play USC.

WILBUR JACKSON

Wilbur Jackson grew up in Ozark, Alabama, some 75 miles southeast of Montgomery and less than an hour's drive from the Florida state line.

He was one of four children of Melvin Jackson, who spent more than forty years working with the railroad while his mother kept house. He loved sports and played all the major ones in their respective seasons. Jackson fondly remembers those Sunday afternoons in the fall from 4 to 6 P.M. when he would watch the *Bear Bryant Show* and the *Shug Jordan Show*, wondering whether he would get the opportunity to play football at either university.

Jackson was also familiar with the problem of race. He was in junior high school during the first attempt at integration, but the "freedom of choice" his school system used were essentially measures to maintain the status quo in the schools. Under this arrangement, parents would sign off on what school their kids wanted to attend the next year. Almost all students, both white and black, would choose to attend the school they had attended the year before. Only a few black students attended white schools and no whites in Ozark attended the all-black schools. Jackson did not understand people's attitudes about race during this formative period in his life, and he still has problems understanding it today. Mostly, blacks associated with blacks and whites did likewise. However, there was some intermingling of the younger generation during summer and recreational league sports. It was not until summer 1969 that the school board in Ozark completely integrated the school system. This took place between Jackson's junior and senior years in high school. During his first three years of high school he attended D. A. Smith (an all-black school) and he spent his final year at John Carroll, previously an all-white school.

Jackson played all three sports in high school and he excelled at football; in his senior year at Carroll, he caught forty-two passes and scored seventeen touchdowns in a pro-style offense. His performance earned him All-State honors at the flanker position. Yet Jackson was not widely recruited. Tuskegee College offered him a football scholarship and a few schools in the Midwest, such as Iowa State and Minnesota, recruited him. With the exception of Alabama, none of the Southeastern Conference schools actively recruited the speedy wide receiver. The year before, two players from Carroll High had received scholarships from the Crimson Tide: Ellis Beck, a fullback, and Dexter Wood, a flanker. Jackson knew both of these students but had not played with either of them. His high school coach was Tom McClendon, who was generally regarded by area recruiters as having strong Auburn ties.

After Alabama offered Wilbur the scholarship, Auburn made a last-minute effort by offering a grant-in-aid proposal, but their effort was to no avail. Wilbur Jackson would play for the Crimson Tide. At the time he did not think much about it and guessed he was "a little naïve" on the significance of being the first scholarship black football player to play at the Capstone. Jackson said, "It really did not hit me. The leaving home was the biggest thing that I had to deal with. It just went over my head."[187]

A NEW EXPERIENCE

Jackson broke his ankle playing baseball in spring 1970, and it slowed him when he first reported for practice in August of that same year. He had been favorably compared to Terry Beasley but was bigger, stronger, and faster. In fact, Pat Dye commented on the scouting report that he would be better than the Auburn All-American. The report indicated that Jackson ran a 4.6-seconds 40-yard dash. In his autobiography some twenty-plus years later, Coach Dye said that Jackson could run the 40 in 4.4 seconds. Jackson said the time was about 4.5 seconds.[188] The exact time was academic; what Alabama coaches, and later their opponents, would come to know was that Jackson was fast and hard to catch.

In August Jackson reported with the other Crimson Tide players for the beginning of fall drills. At that time freshmen practiced and played together except in a few periodic drills with the varsity, coached by Clem Gryska. In the 1970 season the Baby Tiders were undefeated with wins over Mississippi State, Vanderbilt, Ole Miss, Tennessee, and archrival Auburn. Jackson did have a successful freshman season, but he did not contribute significantly in the game statistics. He caught three passes, rushed the ball once, and ran back two kickoffs and one punt.

Jackson's social life was not that memorable. Outside of football he was a member of the Afro-American Student Association and usually attended their meetings on campus. Of the approximately 15,000 total students enrolled, Jackson was one of some 400 African-American students at the University of Alabama. Football was an all-consuming activity at the Capstone, and Jackson ate and slept football as did most of the players from that period. He also attended all the varsity football games that were played in Birmingham and Tuscaloosa. The lives of football players were highly structured, and this was fine for Jackson:

> Our schedules were tight. We ate breakfast at the dorm. We went to class and ate lunch at the dorm. We went to practice, ate dinner at the

dorm, and had lights out at 11 p.m. Whenever anyone would ask you where you lived on campus, and you said, "Bryant Hall," people would look back at you like "Wow" and "You must be really something to live there." Nobody was going to mess with you if they knew that you lived there. Coach Bryant told me if I had a problem, racial or otherwise, to come to him first and we would work it out. Luckily for me, I never had to do that.... I did not feel isolated. I had the type of personality that I never did feel isolated. For example, I had a lot of friends in high school, but I rarely went to parties. I did basically the same thing at Alabama that I did in high school. I was pretty much a homebody.[189]

JOHN MITCHELL

John Mitchell, Jr., grew up in the bay area of Mobile, Alabama. He had one brother and three sisters. His father was in the Coast Guard and his mother was a housewife. At Williamson High School in Mobile, Mitchell played both football and basketball. The school stood right in the shadow of Ladd Stadium, the site of the annual Senior Bowl college football all-star game. Mitchell recalled these early years: "Growing up in Mobile in the 1960s, Alabama had won three national championships. I listened to Alabama and Auburn games on the radio on Saturday afternoons and would listen to LSU at night on WWL [a clear-channel 100,000-watt AM station from New Orleans], because they went everywhere. You had names like Lee Roy Jordan and Joe Namath and everybody knew them. It was a time that for a black kid growing up in Alabama, there were only two places you wanted to go and it was Auburn or Alabama. However, they were not recruiting black athletes at the time."[190]

During his senior year in high school, Mitchell, along with four other students from his school, competed in the local science fair at Bates Field in Mobile. They won this competition and were invited to participate in the state contest in Montgomery. The group from Mobile won the statewide meet and competed in the nationals at Columbia, South Carolina, finishing third in the nation. All five of the students received academic scholarship offers from a number of colleges and universities, including Alabama and Auburn. Mitchell wanted to play "big-time college football," but he was 6-foot-3 and weighed only 185 pounds. He received scholarship offers from other schools, including black college powers such as Grambling University and Tennessee State University.

Mitchell chose another route and enrolled in a junior college before giving up his dream of playing Division I football.

Mitchell enrolled at Eastern Arizona State College on a football scholarship. A couple of friends from his high school had gone there and liked it. The junior college was considered a good feeder program for the big football schools of the West, such as Arizona State, UCLA, and Southern California. Mitchell had a very successful career, playing both offensive and defensive ends, and became a junior college All-American. He thought he was best noted for his defensive abilities. He even put on 35 pounds of muscle without any loss of appreciable speed. The USC coaches were recruiting a number of players from Western Arizona, Eastern's biggest rival. In fact, three of the four players from the famous "Wild Bunch" defense were from Western, and Mitchell had his best games of the season against Western Arizona. He received scholarship offers from a number of other schools but originally committed to USC. After the 1970 season, Coach McKay and Coach Bryant got together over cocktails in Houston to discuss their teams and what McKay and Bryant expected to do in the off-season. Bryant had brought along an old friend from his days at Texas A&M, a fellow by the name of Johnny Mitchell. Bryant recalled the conversation and its outcome:

> I had a list of prospects on the West Coast that I was asking McKay about. I knew that I could not beat him if he wanted any of them bad enough, but I was checking anyway. Finally he laughed and said, "Well hell, Paul, the best one out there isn't even on your list, and he's got the same name as him"—and pointed to Johnny Mitchell—"and he's from Mobile, Alabama. And I want him." I excused myself after a minute or two and went into another room and called my office to find out who this Mitchell was. It was all checked out—John Mitchell, an end from Mobile, then in junior college at East Arizona State. It so happened that Johnny was home vacationing at the time. Two hours later, my recruiter in the area [Hayden Riley] had him in a motel room in Mobile, and I talked with him long distance from Houston. He was very receptive.[91]

A week after the meeting, Mitchell and his parents traveled to Tuscaloosa to meet with Coach Bryant and discuss the possibilities. Bobby Jackson, who was Bryant's first quarterback when he returned to the Capstone and who was then a successful businessman, accompanied the Mitchells on their trip to the university. Mitchell vividly recalled this meeting: "My family and I are sitting in his office, and Bobby Jackson is there.… We're all sitting around in his office and Coach Bryant is saying that if you come up here, you might have some problems, but I promise you if you come to me and not go to the press, I'll take care of it. You are gonna be treated like anybody else. I don't have black players, white players, I have just players."[192]

SURPRISES

Before Friday's afternoon practice Bryant addressed his troops. He told them he did not know who was going to make the California trip after yesterday's scrimmage, but he knew two players who were going. Both of these players were surprised when he mentioned their names because they were just fighting to move off the scout teams. "These guys might not be worth a crap, but I am going to reward them for busting their butts yesterday. I can tell you two players that are going to go on the trip to Southern Cal. They are Rod Steakley and Glenn Woodruff."[193] Both players were overjoyed to hear this.

Steakley was the smallest player on the squad at 5-foot-10, 160 pounds and had been feeling a bit left out in his fifth year as a member of the Crimson Tide. He had been moving up and down the depth chart and really did not know whether he had a future. Because of an earlier meeting with Bryant, Steakley did not know whether he would still be playing. He remembered the moments he poured out his heart to the head coach:

> I went to Coach Bryant's office and knocked on his door, almost trembling. He invited me in and I sat on that couch looking up at him. In that environment, he looks bigger than life. I told him that this was the hardest thing that I had to do in my life was to walk into this room, but I believe that God has a plan. I don't want to glamorize it because I hope you know that I am not a quitter, that I am not here because I am gutting out or that I have lost my courage. I want more than anything else to continue to play, but I really believe God is calling me to do something else. He said, "Rod, I'll tell you what, I'll make a deal with you. You're a fifth-year senior, I know you are not a player. I don't think you are here because you lost your courage or anything else." He said, "It's Monday. If you still feel that the same way you do on Friday afternoon after practice, I'll look into making you a graduate assistant and keep you on scholarship and letting you do what you need to do." Needless to

say, after he called my name out, I decided that I had gotten the message that I needed.[194]

Glenn Woodruff came to the University of Alabama as a quarterback. He had played a number of positions during his career without a great deal of success. In the spring Woodruff had played baseball as the starting catcher and was now without a position. He also had been playing linebacker during the fall practice and was not making any headway, given the number of good linebackers that were ahead of him. Coach Dye approached him about switching positions to tight end, and Woodruff told him that he did not care where he played as long as it was somewhere. He was very excited when Bryant called his name after the last scrimmage: "After the scrimmage, Coach had me listed on the Red [first offense] team with Jim Simmons. I was overjoyed at this new situation."[195]

Just before the players left the team meeting to go out to practice, Coach Bryant told them that he had one more thing to say. He announced that Robin Parkhouse and Steve Higginbotham would be the defensive captains, and Johnny Musso and Rod Steakley would be the offensive captains for the Southern California game. When Steakley heard his name, he thought he had not heard the head coach correctly. He turned to Jerry Cash, who had been sitting beside him in the meeting, and as they were leaving the room asked him who the offensive captains were. Cash smiled at him and said, "He called your name." Steakley said in return, "I don't believe it." Cash told his friend, "Well, I am not so sure that I believe it either."[196] Steakley knew he could always depend on Cash to bring him back down to earth. Needless to say, Steakley did not think he needed to meet with Coach Bryant about what he intended to do. He had already been shown what to do.

SEC SKYWRITERS TOUR VISITS ALABAMA

In late summer before the football season begins, sportswriters from around the Southeast visit all of the campuses of the Southeastern Conference and evaluate their football teams. On the last Saturday before the opening kickoff of the 1971 season, thirty-eight writers from the region visited Tuscaloosa and observed practice. Several of the writers had been on campus earlier in the week talking to players, coaches, and those closely involved with the program. Bryant had cautioned his players before the practice not to mention anything about running the wishbone, and security had been extremely tight during the week. Jack White recalled how things were during those practices leading up the Southern California game: "I think that it was right before the Skywriters came in. Coach Bryant had campus security and the Tuscaloosa police checking out those apartments across the street from the practice field. He looked from his tower and thought there was someone spying on us. The police did not find anyone spying on us, but he did clear the roofs of the apartments of the fans or students who were watching from there."[197] Alabama would run the old offense throughout the practice for the benefit of the visiting press. The Bear allowed only four Crimson Tide players—Johnny Musso, Jimmy Rosser, Robin Parkhouse, and John Mitchell—to talk to the media, and he advised them to be very cautious and humble when doing so. He did not want any "bulletin board material" to be available to the Tide opposition.

At the beginning of fall practice Charley Thornton and Kirk McNair from the sports information department briefed the working sports press in the state of Alabama. He advised them not to write about the switch to the wishbone if they wanted optimum access to the football program. None of them directly mentioned it but some made veiled hints, such as running the option more, running the wishbone in certain situations, and sprinting out more by the quarterback and such. Delbert Reed, the sports editor of the *Tuscaloosa News*, tells an interesting story of an event that occurred toward the beginning of fall practice. Reed had been on vacation during the first week of practice, and Charles Land, the former sports editor, filled in during this period. When he came back to work, Reed learned some interesting things and relayed them to Coach Bryant:

I went to practice from the time they went onto the field until the time they went off and then went off to write. I'm out there watching, watching, and watching... They had everything blocked off and were very secretive about putting in the Wishbone.... I remember one day coming out of the stadium after a scrimmage, and I am walking around with Coach Bryant and listening to him. I was getting some quotes and talking to him. I also told him that [South Carolina's coach] McKay had ordered to the paper to check on the progress of the Crimson Tide in fall practice. In addition, I told him that I haven't mentioned the name "wishbone" in my stories, but it looks like we're running the wishbone and lot of other stuff. He puts his arm around me and proceeds to tell me a few things. "Delbert, I wouldn't ever tell you what to write. But the way I feel, you're either with us or against us." I got the message. I said, "Okay, Coach!" I understood exactly what he meant.[198]

Delbert Reed was not going to be the Alabama sportswriter who broke the story of the Crimson Tide's switch to the wishbone offense and betray the Bear's trust. If someone broke that story, that person would have to live with the consequences. This journalistic style was much different than that in some parts of the country at the time. Sports journalists in major markets were much more combative and did not always back the home team, but in much of the South it was not that way. Reporters would risk losing access to the team they covered and had to be very discrete about what they said in print.

At the end of the practice, the sportswriters gathered in one of the conference rooms and asked Paul Bryant a series of questions concerning his football team. Fred Girard of the *St. Petersburg Times* did not feel as encumbered as the Alabama beat writers, as he asked the cunning head coach about switching to the wishbone. Bryant went to the chalkboard, drew a series of offensive formations, and compared and contrasted each of them. He then stated the player's lineup in the wishbone in goal-line formations and he had done for the past couple of seasons. Girard was persistent and told Bryant that he had heard a different story from the players. Bryant wanted to know which players were stating this to reporters. Girard replied that Morris Hunt was one of the players who had told him. Bryant brushed aside the question but was furious. The Bear finished the news conference and would deal with this problem later, but not in front of the press.[199]

PREDICTIONS AND MORE PREDICTIONS

A number of predictions about the approaching college football season were released over the weekend. In the Associated Press poll, Southern California ranked fifth while Alabama ranked sixteenth in their pre-season forecasts. USC ranked fourth in the United Press International (UPI) poll and the Crimson Tide ranked eleventh. These were respectable rankings for Alabama, given where the program had been the past two seasons. Tennessee, Auburn, and LSU were the three Southeastern Conference teams that ranked ahead of the Red Elephants. The various newspapers around the state also published their pre-season football editions on this weekend. All of the papers in the state predicted that the Tide would be vastly improved but wondered how much the team's record would actually improve, given that they were scheduled to play the toughest schedule—seven top-20 teams—in the conference.

The Skywriters Poll of SEC writers came out on Monday. This poll was not as generous as some of the other prognostications. It ranked Alabama fifth in the conference with LSU, Tennessee, Auburn, and Georgia ranked ahead of the Crimson Tide. Florida, Mississippi State, Ole Miss, Kentucky, and Vanderbilt ranked beneath them.[200] Kirk McNair and the sports information department were incensed. McNair called a number of writers and chastised them for such a low pre-season prediction for the Tide. "It really upset us because we were good enough to have four players on the all-conference team, the best running back in the country and the best coach in the country, and all they could say was fifth place in the SEC. We wondered where they had been these last few months. They certainly were not watching this team practice."[201] Johnny Musso, John Hannah, Jimmy Grammer, and Robin Parkhouse were all expected to make All-SEC according to the skywriters.

TROJAN WEEK

At the beginning of Monday's practice, as the players sat on one knee listening to Coach Bryant's pre-practice remarks, there was some apprehension. The players never knew what the coach was going to say or what kind of mood he was in. Bryant always kept them off balance, and he was straight to the point about what he wanted to say. Reserve guard Morris Hunt remembered what happened next:

> The writer from the *St. Petersburg Times* came to the dorm and talked to a number of us about practice and different things. He asked me a number of questions. I was very naïve and very young. He asked me if we ran the wishbone, of which I said, "yes," and I answered it as honestly as I could. The next day at practice, when he blows the whistle and we came around for his comments. He said, "Where is Morris Hunt?" I did not know why he was singling me out. I thought that I had been doing well in practice and had no idea why he called my name. He said something to the effect of "What is some third-string turd who is talking to the press and the media about the wishbone?" I told that I did not know what he was talking about. He then asked me if I told him we were running the wishbone exclusively, of which I responded, "No sir! From what I recall from the incident, I think that I told him that we were

running the wishbone in goal-line situations. I certainly do not remember telling him that we ran it in the middle of the field or all the time." I denied it. He grumbled a little bit, but I never had any repercussions from this.[202]

All of the players interviewed recalled something about this conversation. The players had mixed feelings in their response at the time. Most of the other players felt some sympathy for Hunt's situation, but at the same time they were mad at him for leaking the information to the press.

In the next two practices the Crimson Tide went over their game plans and further honed in on Southern California. Compared to previous practices in the fall, these were considered light workouts. On Monday, Bryant announced the game captains to the press and travel squad. On Tuesday, the four game captains talked to the press. They knew that they were going into the fight of their lives with USC and were ready for it. These four all remembered last year's calamity and were desperate not to repeat it. Johnny Musso recalled the speed and quickness of their defense. "The thing that struck me was how well they pursued the football, especially the defensive ends. I was surprised how big and fast they were. They had a lot of people who tackled well." Rod Steakley chimed in stating that this is a different Alabama squad. "Last season we didn't know what to expect. When things started out so badly, we had many people who had not played before who let it get to them. This year we should be able to execute better and do a better job." Steve Higginbotham remembered that he actually had a good game last year, even though USC did not go to his side of the field that much: "They were splitting a man out real wide and running to the other side or up the middle. With us playing a man-to-man defense—me on the wide man— I don't think that I made but three or four tackles." Finally, Robin Parkhouse recollected the game as a blur. "I remember their running around me. I think we all were surprised how well they did. This year is a different year, and we will be ready."[203]

On Tuesday, Musso and several other senior players met with Coach Bryant to discuss the issue of leaving Jimmy Horton, a senior defensive end, off the travel squad. They did not think it was fair to exclude a senior player like Horton, who practiced so hard, and thought he should be rewarded. Amazingly, Bryant agreed with the players and put Horton on the travel squad. Horton recalled the predicament:

I had worked hard in the summer and came back in good shape. I only weighted 190 pounds. I had really worked hard enough to get myself on the traveling squad… the thing I remember is that Musso and a couple of other players went to Coach Bryant… They talked him to taking not just me but several other guys who had worked hard that fall in getting the offense together and putting everything together for the wishbone.[204]

Besides the additon of these players, Alabama had another advantage, Jimmy Sharpe, an offensive assistant coach and former Alabama player, had had a series of conversations with a contact out in Southern California:

We had a former player named Dennis Dixon [tight end in 1967 and 1968] who I had recruited from a junior college in California. He was now a high school coach in the Los Angeles area… I called Dennis and asked him how close to the USC practices was he and he told me only about fifteen minutes away… Coach Bryant had instilled in us that we were not going to buy players and we were not going to cheat. We did not think that [Dennis] going to practice and only telling us whether their defense was preparing for the wishbone was cheating. I did not want to know anything else about their practices. Their practices were open to the public. This went on everyday for two weeks. The last time I talked to him on Tuesday before the game, he told me that they were not preparing for the wishbone. That was one of those dark secrets of something that went on that we did not talk about, but it was a fact.[205]

Wednesday's practice was held at 8:00 P.M. in order to simulate the Friday's night game. It started at approximately the same time the pep rally was beginning on campus at the quad in front of Gorgas Library and behind Denny Chimes. Over 4,000 students attended the pep rally. The rally went on for about thirty minutes and started to move across the University of Alabama campus like a wave heading toward Thomas Field. As the cheering crowd approached, Coach Bryant summoned security to open the gates and watch the practice. It was the most spirited practice of the entire fall as the lively gathering cheered on their heroes. Bryant personally thanked the crowd, and he thought their presence would help the players get ready for the trip west: "I thought we had a real fine practice. We had a lot of pep and lot of zip. We were certainly helped by the presence of thousands of students who came over. We're deeply grateful for them coming out. The team looked very quick.… We're taking quite a few kids. We're taking a lot of them because it's a good trip and they

119

IT CAN BE DONE

helped us get ready for it, especially the non-scholarship boys."[206] Meanwhile defensive coach Richard Williamson did not attend Wednesday's practice because of the death of his father. It was uncertain at the time whether he would be available for the Friday night clash.

Paul Bryant always assigned an assistant coach to help draw up the game plan and scout the opposing team. John David Crow was given this task for the game against the Southern California Trojans; he had gone to their spring game in May and came away quite impressed. His scouting report provided a good overview of what Alabama was going to be up against.

> This year's University of Southern California football team is bigger and better than last year's, and I think every Alabama follower knows that they were great in every way in 1970. They've got a stable of fine running backs including Sam Cunningham, who gained more than a first down every time he carried the ball against us last year... Jimmy Jones is going to hold just about every USC record when he gets through and he's being pushed by Mike Rae, so you know they are in good shape at quarterback. They've got two great receivers in Mike Morgan and Lynn Swann... John Grant will be at one defensive end post this year. Willie Hall, an All-American, was supposed to be the other, but Coach McKay has moved him to linebacker... The defensive backfield has a great deal of potential, including returning starter Bruce Dyer, and a super prospect, Skip Thomas. Artimus Parker, Al Pekarcik, Steve Fate, and Pat Collins could play for just about anybody. It's obviously another great USC team. It'll take all we can give to play with them.[207]

This Southern California team had a great deal of talent, and it was the same team that had trounced Alabama in Legion Field the year before. Their season's record was comparable to the Crimson Tide at 6-4-1, but there were a couple of big differences. They tied eventual national champion Nebraska and defeated Notre Dame, who ended up being the runner-up to the Cornhuskers in the final polls of the 1970 season. It was clear that the University of Alabama was going to have its hands full when it got to Los Angeles.

In the Wednesday, September 8 edition of the *St. Petersburg Times*, two days before the Crimson Tide opened against the Trojans, Fred Girard wrote a big story on the first page of the sports section that previewed the 1971 Alabama football season. Girard was quite explicit both in his predictions for the Tide offense in the upcoming season and in revealing the evidence he had used to make these bold assertions:

> Bryant at first denied it, then downplayed it before the writers of the Skywriters Tour, but the Crimson Tide will run the wishbone offense made famous by Darrell Royal at the University of Texas. A week before, when I was at the University of Kentucky, Head Coach John Ray discussed his own offense and said, "We'll be running a variety of things, including for the first time this year some formations from the wishbone. I've talked to a lot of other coaches about this offense and I know Bear Bryant, for instance, will be using the wishbone. I don't know if I'm supposed to say that.".... Morris Hunt, an offensive lineman from Orlando at the University of Alabama told me later that week "we've been practicing nothing but the wishbone. It's just the total picture of our personnel that makes it the best offense. I don't know if I am supposed to be saying that."[208]

Picked up on the Associated Press wire, the story ran nationally in a number of newspapers around the country. One of those papers included the *Los Angeles Times*. On the day before the game, above a story written by Dwight Chapin, the headline in the *Times* read "Bama May Spring Wishbone T Attack Against Wary Trojans." Four Alabama players were quoted in the article, the same four that Bryant had allowed to talk to the Skywriters. While Chapin did not mention the AP story, he did give some insight as to what the Southern California football team was thinking about. John McKay had said earlier in the week that he thought the Alabama defense had "improved 200 percent." Chapin wrote that John McKay had talked to him and others the weekend before about Alabama maybe running the wishbone, but to what degree was uncertain. McKay was quoted at the beginning of the article, referring to the wishbone offense as "fumble football."[209] It was clear that he did not have a lot of respect for it. On the other hand, it was uncertain whether the Trojans had been preparing for this. Given what Dennis Dixon had observed at their practices, this certainly did not appear to be the case.

ON TO LOS ANGELES

Crimson Tide fans received good news on Thursday as the team flew to Los Angeles. The headline in the *Birmingham News* read "Tide to have Spivey-Musso available for USC." The dislocated shoulder that had troubled the Montgomery speedster for the past two weeks had not completely healed, but holding him out three to four more weeks would not heal it either. Alf Van Hoose wrote about the prospect of having Spivey in the lineup:

> Spivey has been bugging Paul Bryant for a week that he can play. The doctors have assured the head coach that time is no longer a factor in Spivey's healing progress, that his shoulder could pop out with six weeks more rest as easily as it could now, and that there is no cause for alarm as to permanent damage. "We'll play it by ear," Bryant summed up Spivey's game-action prospects. "He'll be suited up. There could arise a situation where we might stick him in there."[210]

On Thursday everything was going according to schedule until the Tide reached their hotel destination, the Sheraton West on Wilshire Boulevard. A mix-up at the hotel meant that only a handful of rooms were immediately available for the football squad. Bryant, David Mathews, and a few of the other coaches took these rooms. The majority of the players had to wait several hours to get into their rooms. The hotel had the rooms reserved for the San Francisco 49ers, who were playing that night in the Coliseum in an exhibition game against the Los Angeles Rams. Tom Siler, sports editor of the *Knoxville News Sentinel,* reported the following concerning the incident. "Management had thoughtlessly sold the rooms to the San Fransciso 49ers, who were not releasing them until close of the dinner hour. Chaos, it was, and Coach Bryant was less than enchanted."[211] This debacle was not reported in the Alabama newspapers.

The practice went much smoother and according to plans. The workout lasted a little over an hour. The offense ran the old formations and used hand signals to tell where they were actually going to run or block. This was done in case the Trojans had spies at the Alabama practice. Defensive back Lanny Norris recalled the atmosphere of the pre-game trip in California: "I can remember everywhere we traveled we were on the bus. People would come up to us and ask who we were and what we were doing here. It seemed that no one that we ran into knew that we were playing Southern California that weekend. Everyone out there seemed surprised that we were here. In Alabama, that was the only thing going on and we were counting the days to go out there. Those were big differences."[212] This was a perfect example of the difference between the cultures of Southern California and the state of Alabama.

College football was like a religion in Alabama, while in Los Angeles it was just another means of entertainment.

After dinner the team attended a movie. John Croyle recalled seeing something strange on the street after the movie: "There was a big black limousine and two black guys with fur coats on got out and had an ocelot on a leash. The cat was sitting there and it hopped out of the car. We had never seen anything like that. It was like 'Leroy' coming to town.[213]

After the movie the players had an hour or so to kill. Most of the guys stayed around the hotel until they met for the late night snack. Joe Labue was not one of them. It was his first visit to California, as was the case with all of the players except Steve Root, Steve Biscelgia, and John Mitchell. Root and Biscelgia had been born and raised in California. Mitchell had made several recruiting trips there while at Arizona playing junior college football. Labue decided to venture outside the hotel for the hour or so before the snack period. He remembered how he and a few teammates got their first taste of Hollywood:

> Here we are out here on Sunset Strip and Hollywood Boulevard. We are just a bunch of little Alabama boys. I was sitting and watching the movie, and I thought I might do a little exploring. I talked to the manager of the theater, and he is telling this and that. He told us that the Chinese Theater is right down there. So here I go. I jumped up and ran down there. It was only four or five blocks away. Man, I was looking at John Wayne, Marilyn Monroe, and Clark Gable handprints on the sidewalk. All of the movie stars that I grew up with and watched on television... It was another world out there.[214]

Jim Murray, long-time Bryant critic and sports editor of *The Los Angeles Times*, compared the Crimson Tide football team to the army of the old Austro-Hungarian Empire and George Armstrong Custer, who was massacred by the Indians at Little Big Horn. They might have looked good, but they were only paper tigers when it came to producing.

> When coach Bear Bryant and the University of Alabama football team agreed to play the USC Trojans in Birmingham last September 12, the news must have run through the gridiron world like the electrifying word run through the Indian tribes in 1876, "Custer is coming out!" When an elite, but heretofore sheltered, force joins the battle, the repercussions can be seismic.... The wipeout last September would have been as total as Custer's except USC, in effect, took pity and took prisoners. You see, Alabama was like those...armies. It looked good in parades and it looked

good on paper. All those dancing uniforms with the satin stripes on the side and fur hats. But it was a peppermint candy army, good for jumping hedges and chasing broomstick armies back in the mountains only. They never met anybody who got their plumes dirty. Then, they entered in the slogging wars of trenches, barbed wire, vermin, railroad cannon, gas, land mines and tanks. And all those chocolate soldiers melted.... So Custer wants a rematch.[215]

This enraged the Alabama football team—they had been insulted by one of the best-known sportswriters in the country. The team was not alone in feeling this slight. 7,300 Crimson Tide fans had chartered nineteen planes in order to be with their team in Los Angeles. The team had enough on their minds and did not need any external motivation to psych them up for the game. Jimmy Sharpe, previously an offensive lineman and now an assistant coach, knew this only added fuel to an already lit flame. Jimmy Rosser recalled how Sharpe challenged them: "We were in our group meetings on Friday and Coach Sharpe read this to us. We were outraged. He kept reading it to us. The linemen took this to heart and were determined to show the people out here on the West Coast that we knew something about football. We were loaded for bear when we hit the field."[216]

Plenty of the Alabama players had felt the sting from the prior year's loss to the Trojans. Among these players were John Hannah, Jeff Beard, Jimmy Grammer, and Terry Rowell. John Hannah recalled the game and how it affected his feelings in 1971:

> I was scared to death. I had to block Tody Smith, who was Bubba Smith's [All-Pro defensive end for the Baltimore Colts] younger brother during the game. I also remember Sam Cunningham running all over and us getting trounced...I loved the wishbone. I was happy about the switch to it. I would much more like being the attacker than being attacked. The running game suits me fine. I remember flying out to LA and practicing in the coliseum in our old formations. We did the same in the warm-ups before the game. We did not get in the wishbone. In a way, it built us up because we knew that they did not know about it and it gave us a mental edge.[217]

Jeff Beard felt that the Tide had been humiliated the previous year. There were many differences between the 1970 and 1971 teams, but preparation and leadership were among the biggest. He reminisced about the Alabama squad's attitude on the eve of the Friday night battle with

Southern California: "We knew before we played Southern Cal that we had a good defense. We had practiced much harder and were much better prepared than we were for last year's game."[218]

Jimmy Grammer would tear up his knee in the second quarter of the game and would not play again the entire season. He was not upset about the lick he received *per se* but how it cost him a whole year's worth of eligibility. What he especially remembered was a conversation with roommate Terry Rowell on this subject:

> Terry was probably the meanest player on the team and I was probably the shyest on the team... When Terry opened up to you, he was serious and meant what he said. Tears rolled up in his eyes and said: "You know Jim, those SOBs laughed at me last year; by God they're not gonna do it this time." I remember when we were lining up for the coin-toss before the game, I looked over at Terry and I could see those same tears in his eyes. I knew that things were going to be different this time around.[219]

As the team traveled from the hotel to the coliseum for the game, the bus was extremely quiet. This was a business trip for the Alabama football team and the business at hand was the Southern California Trojans. The players knew what they needed to do.

PUT UP OR SHUT UP

AFTER THE PRE-GAME MEAL, MOST OF THE PLAYERS GOT TAPED at the hotel before the ride to the coliseum. Trainer Jim Goosetree and assistant trainer Sang Lyda were extremely busy because they had brought only one student trainer to California. They were almost overrun at the hotel and worked feverishly to make up for the lack of manpower. Several players had to get taped in the locker room before the game, which was almost never the case.

The Trojans of Southern California were 12-point favorites over the Crimson Tide. Earlier in the week the oddsmakers had had them as high as 14 points and as low as 11 points. Twenty-two sportswriters from Alabama attended the game; almost all of them agreed that the Tide would be vastly improved, but very few actually thought they would win the football game. Nine of the eleven "guessperts" of the *Birmingham News* picked USC. Frank McGowan and J. D. Ferguson were the two prognosticators from the state's largest newspaper who picked Alabama.[220] Delbert Reed of the *Tuscaloosa News* also went with the Tide. Reed's prediction was 23-18, in favor of Bama.[221]

The game began at 8:00 P.M. Pacific daylight time, two hours behind Alabama time. At this hour most people in Alabama would usually be engaged in their normal evening activities such as coming home from a high school football game, watching the ten o'clock news, or getting ready for bed. This was not the case on this particular September night.

Alabamans stayed up listening to the radio telecast of their beloved Crimson Tide as they invaded the Los Angeles Coliseum. There was no television coverage of the game but it was broadcast on the Armed Forces Radio Network to more than 400 stations across the country and the world.

INTIMIDATION TACTICS

As the Alabama players exited the bus for the dressing rooms, they met their USC opponents as the two teams literally had to walk past each other. This phenomenon was clear to the smaller players on the Crimson Tide. Wayne Adkinson, being only 5-foot-10, 175 pounds, noticed the differences in size as well as what the Trojan players were trying to do:

> They came right up beside us and it was like "Look at us." They wanted us to see them. I think it was right as we're going in the locker room, and we had to go by them. We were just shocked. I know there was a lot of "Did you see that guy?" Again, this was before we were on the field when both teams were arriving. They tried to intimidate us. They tried you every way you could. Coach Bryant was scared to death. I don't know why. I mean he seemed more uptight at that game than any other I can remember. He really did. He talked to us constantly about it, [saying] "You gotta be ready. It's going to be hot there. They're gonna be noisy."[222]

These tactics did not scare the Bama players; it only hardened their resolve. They had waited a year for this moment and were not going to fold up and run before the game began.

As the team prepared for the game, Richard Williamson was inside the locker room getting ready. The former Tide player and now assistant coach had been with his family at a Montgomery hospital where his father lay dying. John Mitchell was both shocked and impressed by this: "His father was near death Wednesday before the game on Friday night. I did not think he would be back for the game; I looked up in the dressing room before the game and there he was. That showed me what kind of man that he was."[223]

In the pre-game warm-ups the Alabama offensive warmed up in the old offense. They refused to show the opponent their hand until they had to. As the players from both squads met at midfield for the coin toss, one of the Trojan players engaged in even more posturing. Rod Steakley, one of the offensive captains, remembered what happened just before opening kickoff as the players went to their various teams: "One of their captains was a guy named John Vella, who turned out to be an All-Pro for a number of years with the Oakland Raiders. In fact, one of the ironies of the game when we shook hands at midfield [was] he looked down at me. He's about 6-foot-4 and 280. He looked down at me when he shook my hand and kind of grinned and said, "This is a good day for a hog killing. We're gonna get some little porkers like you."[224]

Just as the team ran onto the field before the coin-toss, Chuck Strickland was visibly moved by the importance of the game. The sophomore linebacker recalled how his emotions got the best of him: "It was amazing. You hear about the coliseum. You've always heard about the coliseum, but to actually be there. We went out and warmed up and it was not any big deal. We went back to the dressing room. Then, as we were about to come out, I realized what was about to happen. This was my first game as a member of the Alabama Crimson Tide, and look where we were. I started crying. I was so emotionally worked up. I've got to hit somebody to do something to get calmed down."[225]

Southern California won the coin-toss and elected to receive the ball at the beginning of the second half. The Crimson Tide would receive the opening kickoff.

THE STARTING LINEUPS

Alabama Offense

David Bailey	Split End	6'1"	193
Jim Krapf	Quick Tackle	6'0"	235
Jimmy Rosser	Quick Guard	6'0"	225
Jimmy Grammer	Center	5'11"	202
John Hannah	Strong Guard	6'3"	274
Buddy Brown	Strong Tackle	6'2"	235
Terry Davis	Quarterback	6'0"	178
Johnny Musso	Halfback	5'11"	196
Ellis Beck	Fullback	5'11"	196
Joe Labue	Halfback	6'0"	195

Alabama Defense

Robin Parkhouse	Left End	6'3"	205
Terry Rowell	Left Tackle	5'11"	193
Jeff Beard	Right Tackle	6'2"	235

John Mitchell	Right End	6'3"	230
Jeff Rouzie	Strongside Linebacker	6'1"	231
Chuck Strickland	Middle Linebacker	6'1"	215
Jim Simmons	Tight End	6'5"	230
Tom Surlas	Weakside Linebacker	5'11"	198
Steve Higginbotham	Left Cornerback	6'1"	178
Steve Williams	Right Cornerback	5'11"	175
David McMakin	Strong Safety	6'3"	204
Steve Wade	Free Safety	6'2"	181

Southern California Defense

John Grant	Left End	6'5"	229
Mike McGirr	Left Tackle	6'5"	265
Mike Hancock	Right Tackle	6'3"	241
John Skiles	Right End	6'3"	220
Willie Hall	Strongside Linebacker	6'3"	214
John Papdakis	Middle Linebacker	6'0"	235
Kent Carter	Weakside Linebacker	6'3"	216
Skip Thomas	Left Cornerback	6'2"	205
Bruce Dyer	Right Cornerback	5'11"	184
Steve Fate	Rover	6'2"	193
Artimus Parker	Safety	6'4"	207

Southern California Offense

Charles Young	Tight End	6'4"	213
John Vella	Strong Tackle	6'4"	266
Allan Graf	Strong Guard	6'0"	246
David Brown	Center	6'0"	228
Mike Ryan	Weak Guard	6'2"	235
Pete Adams	Weak Tackle	6'3"	235
Mike Morgan	Split End	6'1"	182
Jimmy Jones	Quarterback	6'1"	192
Sam Cunningham	Fullback	6'3"	212
Lou Harris	Tailback	5'10"	205
Lynn Swann	Flanker	6'0"	180

THE FIRST HALF

Bobby McKinney took the opening kickoff at the Alabama 8-yard line and returned it 33 yards to the 41-yard line. The 9.7-second sprinter from Mobile looked like he was "shot out of a cannon" on this return. The first play from scrimmage saw the Crimson Tide in a shift out of the wishbone, with the right halfback going to the flanker position. This was not unexpected, but Johnny Musso lined up in the fullback position with Joe Labue to the left behind him. The Southern Cal defense was yelling, "Musso at fullback, Musso at fullback," when Johnny Musso went right up the middle for 7 yards.[226] On the next play, the Tide got into the wishbone and stayed there the rest of the night. Ellis Beck explained, "Coach Crow told me that I was not going to start the game because it was my first varsity game, and they did not want to put any pressure on me. They did not want me fumbling the ball. I came in on the second play. In addition, by putting Johnny Musso at fullback, it started messing with their defense right off the bat."[227]

Two plays later, Terry Davis optioned on the right side of the line and ran 19 yards to the Southern California 32-yard line. After two plays, Davis hooked up with Jim Simmons on a 16-yard reception to put the ball at the USC 13-yard line. From there it only took one play for Johnny Musso to score, as he went around the right end. In doing this, the senior tailback outran Willie Hall and Kent Carter to the end zone. Bill Davis kicked the extra point and, in less than three minutes, Alabama led 7-0.

Greg Gantt kicked off to the Trojans as Charles Hinton ran it back 23 yards to the USC 27-yard line. Sam Cunningham carried the ball the first two plays for only 5 yards and was hit by three defenders on both occasions. The Southern California offense was a balanced one. Jimmy Jones showed this by mixing in a few passes along with a couple of good runs by Lou Harris, and the Trojans were at Alabama's 29-yard line. Jones went back to pass and tried to hit Mike Morgan inside the 10-yard line. Steve Williams was closely guarding Morgan as Jones threw toward the receiver. Steve Wade intercepted the football, running it back 22 yards to the Alabama 32-yard line. Wade recalled how being in the right place helped him on this interception. "Coach Oliver had shown us that when their receiver made a certain move to the inside, they would throw to him almost all of the time. I saw the move and got in front of the play like a centerfielder, and the quarterback threw it right in my area. I don't think he even saw me."[228]

Alabama started their second drive on their own 27 as a result of a 5-yard penalty on the runback of the interception. With this, Terry Davis went back to work and ran the triple-option to near perfection. All of the backfield ran with reckless abandon on this drive, which stalled at the Southern California 20. Joe Labue's 24-yard run on the left side was the highlight of the drive, as the offensive line blew away the larger and confused the Trojan defensive line. Still, pictures from the first quarter showed the dominance of the offensive line in the first few series of this game. All of the offensive linemen were blowing off the line of scrimmage like a well-oiled machine. There was only one problem, as Jimmy Rosser described: "They had just moved Jim Krapf from linebacker to tackle just a couple of weeks before we played Southern Cal. Jim played the tackle right beside of me. We were driving and Krapf could not remember the snap count. He kept asking me the snap count and who he was supposed to block."[229] The Alabama players certainly did not resemble those "chocolate men" melting before the larger and faster Southern California defense. In fact, the Trojan defense was on its heels most of the first half. Alabama's offensive linemen were 3 yards down the line before the Southern Cal defense could respond. Bill Davis kicked a 37-yard field goal to make it 10-0 with 1:59 left in the first period.

As the first quarter came to a close, with the Crimson Tide leading 10-0, long-time Alabama broadcaster Doug Layton told what occurred as each team switched sides of the field. Layton and John Forney, the play-by-play announcer, had gotten together earlier on Thursday and exchanged notes on the tendencies of each team. Layton recounted what came next: "Our booths were side-to-side in the press box. In between the first two quarters, one of their announcers was hanging outside the press box and waving to us and trying to get our attention. They were asking us about the wishbone. We acted like we did not know anything about it. We just played dumb. Of course, we had been sworn to secrecy by Coach Bryant concerning mentioning the switch to the wishbone and were not going to go against his wishes."[230]

The Alabama defense held Southern California on four plays and the Trojans were forced to punt. Steve Williams nearly blocked the punt that rolled down to the Alabama 9-yard line. The Southern Cal defense thought they had the Crimson Tide where they wanted them, backed up inside their own 10-yard line. Twelve plays later, Johnny Musso went over from the 8-yard line to increase Bama's lead to 16 points. Bill Davis kicked the extra point to make the score 17-0 with 9:54 remaining before halftime. Eleven of the twelve plays were running plays. The one pass was a completion from Davis to David Bailey for 15 yards. It was now clear that the Southern California defense did not know what hit them.

It would be up to the Trojan offense to get back into the game. They certainly had a number of weapons. USC again started their offensive drive at their own 27-yard line. Jimmy Jones was a multidimensional player who had a good throwing arm and good running speed. Jones led the men of Troy down the field in thirteen plays to cut the score to 17-7 with 3:46 remaining in the half. He completed a 7-yard touchdown pass to Charles Young in front of Lanny Norris, who had good position, but slipped just as Jones threw the ball. Jones and Lou Harris were the offensive stalwarts during this drive. Jones completed two passes for 19 yards and ran for 13 more. Harris ran five times for 27 yards. There was one bright spot for the Crimson Tide on this drive when, on the second play of the drive, Sam Cunningham went wide to the right side of the field and Steve Higginbotham took him head-on, tackling him for a 1-yard loss. Higgy weighed some 44 pounds less and was 2 inches shorter, but he was strong enough to take down the powerful fullback. Cunningham had run wild on the Tide defenders last year and had some good runs in the first half, but usually was hit by at least three defensive players when he had the football.

The final time the Crimson Tide had the ball in the first half was more of the same. Terry Davis led the offense over the midfield with a couple of first downs. David Knapp came in for this series to give Labue some rest, and he carried the ball twice for 6 yards. The drive was interrupted, however, as Davis threw an interception with forty-seven seconds left before the half. Bruce Dyer intercepted Davis's pass and returned to the Alabama 45-yard line. Jimmy Jones completed a couple of passes, one to Mike Morgan and the other to Lynn Swann, which put the Trojans on the 19-yard line with seven seconds left in the half. Mike Rae came in and kicked a 36-yard field goal to cut the score to 17-10 at halftime.

HALFTIME STATISTICS

	Alabama	Southern California
First Downs	13	10
Yards Rushing	195	104
Yards Passing	40	57
Total Yards	235	161
Turnovers	1	2
Score	17	10

SECOND HALF

Southern California came out for the second half energized by their second-quarter finish. They scored their 10 points in the last seven minutes and narrowed the gap on the visitors from Alabama 17-10. They clearly had some momentum going into the third quarter as they received the second-half kickoff. It would be up to the defense of the Crimson Tide if they were going to hold back the Trojans. It has often been said that the first five minutes of the second half are extremely important in deciding the fate of a football game, and this game would be no exception.

The Trojans started their first offensive series of the second half at their own 21-yard line. They were moving the football with a couple of good runs by Harris and Cunningham and a pass completion from Jimmy Jones to Mike Morgan. They had made three first downs in this drive and were at the Alabama 37-yard line when Jones dropped back to pass. He faked a pass as Parkhouse jumped high to block the ball and continued rolling to his right with Parkhouse in hot pursuit. As Jones was passing the football downfield, his tackle John Vella blindsided Parkhouse with a crushing block. Steve Higginbotham intercepted the pass at the 19-yard line and ran it back for a couple of yards. The Tide stopped the drive and took over the football. Paul Bryant called the lick by Vella on his defensive end "the hardest lick I have ever seen in a football game. I did not know if he was going to get up after that hit."[231] He was temporarily unconscious about 5 yards from the Alabama sideline. As the gutsy Parkhouse lay on the ground, Paul Bryant, Jim Goosetree, and Dr. Brock cautiously approached him. His legs were twitching on the ground as he was beginning to regain consciousness. His head was foggy, but he remembered the blow:

> On the particular play, I had blown by Vella and was chasing Jimmy Jones. I could see that he [Vella] was catching up on me. I was running wide open, and I saw him out of the corner of my eye almost in the same instance that he hit me. I was laying on the ground in front of Coach Bryant, and I think I heard him say to one of the other coaches that it was the hardest lick that he had ever seen. I was just numb on the ground. I kinda started moving my leg, and he was standing over me. In my mind, the only thing that I remember is screaming at myself, "Get up, Get up," and I must have willed myself to get up. I looked at him [Bryant] and said that was all you [Vella] got, that ain't good enough. It was going to take more than that to keep me down....My dad had been

a boxer, and I had been in a lot of fights in my life. But on that play, I had taken a shot. He knocked me cold and numb, but not out.[232]

This particular sequence symbolized the resoluteness of the Alabama defense, a defense that had been much maligned in past seasons. Players like Robin Parkhouse were going to see that this would not be the case in 1971. Parkhouse had the heart of a lion and showed it throughout this game. He regained his composure on the sideline and went back into the game for the next defensive series without missing a play. His display of leadership was not lost on the Alabama players, especially the defense. This was the type of player Bryant thought would bring the Crimson Tide back to national prominence, and certainly Parkhouse did not let his head coach down.

The first time Alabama got the ball in the second half, they did not do anything with it. They ran only four offensive plays before Greg Gantt entered the game for his first punt. He was a sophomore with the strongest leg of all of the kickers, and he had beaten out Steve Wade for the starting punting position. His first kick of the game Friday went only 17 yards, which put the Trojans in good field position.

Southern California started their second series of the half at the Alabama 42-yard line. Two quick bursts by tailback Lou Harris put the Trojans at the Tide 19. Sam Cunningham took the pitch from Jones on the next play as USC ran their favorite play of "student body right," in which the runner has several blockers pulling and going in front of him on the right side of the field to form a protective wall. Cunningham had a number of blockers in front of him as he took the pitch at the 24-yard line and flew behind the wall until he was hit at the 12 and fumbled. Bama's Steve Williams recovered the ball at the 8-yard line to stop another Southern Cal drive.

The second series for the Crimson Tide was much like the first, as they bogged down after four offensive plays and had to punt the ball again. This time Gantt did much better, punting it 37-yards downfield. USC started their third offensive series at their own 39-yard line. On this occasion, the Alabama defense was much more forceful in their efforts; it was three plays and out for the Trojans.

Steve Higginbotham took the punt and returned it 37 yards to the Southern Cal 39-yard line, putting the Bama offense in great field position. Alabama fumbled a great offensive opportunity on the first play. Terry Davis's pitch to Musso was tipped and recovered by USC's Kent

Carter. A penalty moved the ball back to the Southern California 15-yard line, where they began their next offensive series.

Mike Rae replaced Jimmy Jones at quarterback for the next set of plays. Both of these quarterbacks had been running neck-and-neck in the fall practice when Jones barely beat out the upstart Rae for the starting position. John McKay had indicated before the game that both quarterbacks would play, but Jones would be the starter. McKay explained this move after the game by saying that it was not a demotion, but rather provided his starter a different place to observe the Alabama defense.

Rae was not very effective in his first appearance in the game. After a 9-yard gain by Sam Cunningham, Rae tried a little "razzle-dazzle" with an end-around with Charlie Young. The play lost 2 yards as Parkhouse and David Watkins stopped the big tight end. Rae's first pass was ruined thanks to another great effort by the Tide secondary. Lanny Norris made a great play by tipping the ball right as the it was about to enter Young's hands. The Trojans were forced to punt again.

With less than two minutes to go in the third quarter, Alabama started in good field position at their own 47. They did much on this series by relying on their "bread and butter." In the first three Tide possessions in the third quarter, Johnny Musso had not carried the ball. This time it changed as Musso carried the ball four times for 22 yards before the drive stalled at the Trojan 31-yard line. Bryant decided to punt the ball and try to push the opposition back even further. Gantt's punt sailed into the end zone where Southern California would take over at the 20-yard line.

Jimmy Jones came back in as quarterback for USC with less than thirteen minutes left in the game. He did not do any better than Mike Rae. The big play was a 14-yard sack loss by none other than Robin Parkhouse. Southern California was forced to punt the ball away from their own 14-yard line.

The USC defense rose to the occasion by stopping the Alabama offense after six running plays. Greg Gantt had to punt the ball away this time to Lynn Swann. Swann received the punt at his own 15-yard line and proceeded to evade Crimson Tide tacklers 57 yards before David Bailey made a game-saving tackle by tripping the speedster.

Now the Trojans had their chance. With less than eight minutes remaining in the game, Mike Rae came back in at quarterback for Southern California. After a couple of running plays for short yardage, another big play occurred. Lou Harris gained 7 yards on a strong run that gave USC an apparent first down at the Tide 16-yard line. A 15-yard penalty was called against the Trojans for a personal foul on John Vella, who was thrown out of the game for slugging Alabama linebacker Tom Surlas; Surlas was temporarily knocked unconscious on the play. This backed the Trojans to the 33-yard line for a crucial third-down play. Rae attempted to hit Swann over the middle of the field, could not do so, and the pass fell incomplete at the 22-yard line. Robin Parkhouse's defensive pressure made Rae throw the ball earlier than he wanted. On fourth down, another great defensive surge by the Tide forced Rae out of the pocket as he tried to scramble for the first down. He was not successful, as Parkhouse and Jeff Beard chased him down at the 21-yard line.

With less than six minutes to go in the game, the Crimson Tide needed to hold on to the ball and, wanting better field position, they turned to the "Italian Stallion." Johnny Musso ran for 19 yards to get Bama a first down and out of a hole. It was not enough, however, as Gantt was forced once again to punt the ball to the dangerous Swann. This time the punt coverage team did its job; Marvin Barron and Musso stopped him as soon as he caught the ball.

Jimmy Jones came back in at quarterback for the Trojans with three minutes remaining in the game and 94 yards ahead of him for a score. After three plays the Trojans were at their own 43-yard line. In the next play Jones was sacked for a 3-yard loss by Terry Rowell and Robin Parkhouse. He tried another bomb on the subsequent play and narrowly missed Edsel Garrison downfield inside the 15-yard line. Mitchell almost took his head off on that play. On third down, Jones dropped back again to throw downfield. This time Parkhouse stripped the Southern Cal quarterback of the football, and Tide teammate Rowell recovered the fumble on the USC 36-yard line.

The game clock in the end zone of the coliseum showed 1:52 left as the Crimson Tide got the ball for what they hoped would be the last time. All they needed to do was make one first down and run out the clock, but this was easier said than done. Terry Davis ran the first play to the right for 3 yards. Ellis Beck ran it up the middle for 4 yards. It was now third down and 3 yards to go. The Trojan defense stopped Musso for a 1-yard gain. This set up a fourth down and 2. Johnny Musso rose to the occasion, as he was hit behind at the line of scrimmage and carried several Trojan tacklers with him to the 24-yard line, which was more than enough for the first down. Davis went to one knee for the final play of the game.

ANALYSIS AND SIGNIFICANCE

On this September night in Los Angeles Paul Bryant won his 200th game. He joined only five other college coaches who had won that many games, achieving this at the beginning of his twenty-sixth season in college football. This was a wonderful birthday present for the head coach, who turned 58 on September 11. With the time difference, the victory occurred on his birthday. Bryant briefly spoke with Darrell Royal on the phone before addressing his team, and Johnny Musso presented Bryant with the game ball to celebrate the occasion. The Bear had nothing but good things to say about his victorious squad: "I've been around better teams, but I've never been prouder of one than this one. I don't know how well we played, but I know that everyone played as hard as he could. The fact it meant so much to them to win, you sense that on the bench. We had to be pretty lucky on some turnovers. But we made some great plays on turnovers, too. When they got the ball deep in our territory late, I sent word in to suck em up one more time and hold em. They held them."[233]

The Bear was even more reflective as he talked to reporters at the hotel on Saturday morning. He modestly complained that too much emphasis was being placed on him and not on the players who had won the game. There were also some things the veteran head coach was not able to accomplish in the 17-10 upset:"We weren't a good football team last night, but I think that we can be a top team if we work at it enough. I think winning this game opened the boys' eyes. The big thing about the entire game and the way it came out is the players themselves now know they're capable and that they can get better and better. I wish that I could have been able to play more people, but we stuck with our plan."[234]

Alabama was able to win the football game because of three things. First, they had a better game plan and clearly out-coached the more talented Southern California team. Next, they were able to control the football and line of scrimmage with just a couple of turnovers. Lastly, the Crimson Tide made big defensive plays throughout the game. By being able to keep the wishbone secret, the Tide added an element of surprise. At nearly fifty-eight years old, Paul Bryant was ready to roll the dice one more time. He made this huge change at a time in his career when many coaches are lining up their retirement packages. John McKay claimed he knew the Tide might run the wishbone, but this did not concern him much because he thought his players' talent levels were more than sufficient to offset any surprise by the opposition. Tide assistant John David Crow, in charge of the game plan, was surprised by the outcome:

> We did not know what was going to happen. We never ran the first offense against the first defense for any period because we were afraid that we would get people hurt. I had no idea what was going to happen when we got the opening kickoff. We got 17-0 on USC. I was on the sidelines in shock. I could not believe it. They came back and made it close, but our defense hung on. I remember the last time that we had the football, and Johnny Musso made a superhuman effort. I don't know how he did it.[235]

Alabama was able to run the football and control the line of scrimmage. They did so with just one fumble and one interception. This was within the context of running a new offense with a new quarterback. Terry Davis did a masterful job in his first start at quarterback, completing five of six passes with one interception. Davis said this game brought back a lot of good memories:

> Our attitude was so different than the last year. We had the incentive. Our job was to show them that the South still had some good football players. Our offensive line controlled the line of scrimmage. The whole first half, USC was on their heels. The second half was different. I threw that interception before the half, and they got a field goal out of it. That scared Coach Bryant a bit. We did go more conservative the second half. Our defense was playing so good and we did not move the ball as well as we did in the first half. This was pure vanilla wishbone and we had only a handful of plays. We did have some variations to try to change it up, but not a lot in this game. We had only three or four option plays, but every play had three plays in it itself. We had only three or four passing plays to go along with the wishbone. The offense worked beautifully. I was so damn scared that first series. That series set the tone for us and it put us 7-0. After being up 10-0, we got the ball on our own 9-yard line and drove it 91 yards for a touchdown. We were able to sustain a drive, going twelve or thirteen plays and make no mistakes. That drive was impressive, and it certainly was a confidence builder. I don't know what happened in the second half. They did some adjusting, and we got more conservative. It was a crazy night.[236]

In addition to Davis's excellent performance, there are not enough words to compliment what Johnny Musso did the entire night. The

Birmingham All-American was able repeatedly "to take one more step," fighting for additional yardage. The major criticism of Musso's play had been his lack of speed, but perhaps those critics should ask Willie Hall and Kent Carter about Musso's slowness of feet, for he outran both defenders for a touchdown in the first quarter. Musso gained 85 yards on sixteen carries, but on half of those carries he took Trojan defenders for extra yards.

Finally, the Tide was able to play aggressive team defense and make the big play. Repeatedly, when it looked like Southern California had the momentum and was headed for the game-tying touchdown, the defense kicked it up a notch and stopped the Trojans in their tracks. All of the Alabama defenders should be commended, but none more than Robin Parkhouse. He played the game of his life, considering that he was temporarily knocked unconscious early in the third quarter. Very few football players would have stayed in the game, much less made play after play against a larger and stronger opponent. Nobody told that to Parkhouse. Whatever physical skills he lacked he more than made up in the size of his heart and his gritty determination. His leadership on the field spoke volumes of the Crimson Tide victory. In many ways this win replicated the way Paul Bryant had won games at the Capstone in the early and mid-sixties. None of those wins or national championships were more satisfying to him, especially after many commentators had written that his career was in its twilight and his best days were behind him.

The Crimson Tide victory was the front-page headline of every major newspaper in the state of Alabama on Saturday. What the Alabama papers did not mention was that this was the first game in which a black player had participated for the Crimson Tide football team. The national papers, on the other hand, included this detail in every story. The importance of the game coincided with the prior season's 42-21 loss at Legion Field. After the 1970 game, former Bryant player and Kentucky coach Jerry Claiborne noted, "Sam Cunningham did more for integration in sixty minutes than Martin Luther King did in twenty years."[237] It is obvious to most serious observers that Claiborne's comment can not be taken at face value, but it does point to the importance of college football in the South. It speaks volumes that the region's most prominent program achieving a victory over a West Coast team of Southern California's caliber was almost as important as Alabama winning its first Rose Bowl in 1926 over Washington. Both of these wins were loudly heard throughout the South, if not the country at large. In covering the game the national media not only emphasized that this was the first time the Crimson Tide had a team with black players, but some believed Alabama won because of having black players. The Southern perspective was thatAlabama's victory ove the pre-season top-five in the coutnry meant that the team had come back. In terms of race, the South lagged behind the rest of the country and this is emblematic in college football as well, for the SEC was slower to integrate than many of the small schools.

The death of former Soviet premier Nikita Krushchev had to share headlines with the victorious Bama football team. The significance of this victory meant that the Alabama football program was back in business.

WEST COAST COMMENTS

One of the key Bama offensive stars in the victory over USC came from the West Coast. Steve Bisceglia, the junior college transfer from Fresno, had a number of key runs in the win. He ran three times for 27 yards, a 9-yard average. Biscelgia remembered what it felt like to come back to his native region and beat a powerhouse like Southern California. "Growing up in Fresno, all of my family was UCLA fans. I had a number of relatives who went there and some even played football. It was especially gratifying for me to come back here and defeat USC. There was never any love lost for them when I was growing up. I'm sure that it was even better for all my relatives in California."[238]

John McKay was very complimentary of the Crimson Tide and very graceful in defeat. He did not point any fingers and took full responsibility for his team's 17-10 loss: "They took it to us like we did it to them last year and they found us wanting. Alabama out-hit us, out-ran us, and out-coached us. Alabama has a much better team than last year. I knew that, but I thought we would play better than we did, but we sure didn't. They ran the Veer-T at us and, that's tough to stop if you haven't played against it.... We thought that they might use it, but we did not practice against it that much."[239]

Los Angeles Herald Examiner sports editor Bud Furillo called Bryant "the greatest coach who ever lived"[240] after the Alabama victory. Even Jim Murray had a few good things to say about the Alabama head coach. In a column titled "Bear's No Legend," written two days after the game, Murray pointed out that legends were dead, and Bryant had earlier tried to make his career by playing creampuffs for opponents. Finally, perhaps even Jim Murray had to relent: "When Bear's Bama team whipped USC Friday night, 17-10, and the coach, gray-faced and perspiring under his

Tyrolean hat, politely answered questions, the broadcaster Tommy Hawkins came up to me and pointed at Bryant, and avowed, "We're looking at a legend." I thought about it a moment. No, I concluded, legends get run over by trains or lost at sea. We're not looking at a legend, but we're sure as hell looking at a man."[241]

FINAL STATISTICS

TEAM STATISTICS

	Alabama	USC
First Downs	18	16
Rushing plays/Yards	58-302	44-203
Passes Att/Comp/Int	5-6-1	7-13-2
Passing Yardage	58	84
Total Plays/Yards	64-360	57-287
Punts- Average	5-34.8	4-41.8
Punts Ret/Yds	2-54	3-54
Kickoffs Ret/Yds	3-44	4-102
Penalties-Yards	4-39	3-42
Fumbles-Lost	1-1	3-2

SCORE BY QUARTERS

	Alabama	USC
First	10	0
Second	0	10
Third	0	0
Fourth	0	0

INDIVIDUAL STATISTICS

Alabama Rushing	Attempts	Yards	Average	Long	TD
Musso	16	85	5.31	19	2
LaBue	6	59	9.83	24	0
T. Davis	16	59	3.69	19	0
Beck	13	53	4.07	10	0
Biscelgia	3	27	9.00	12	0
Spivey	2	13	6.5	11	0
Knapp	2	6	3.0	3	0
Totals	58	302	5.71	24	2

USC Rushing	Attempts	Yards	Average	Long	TD
Harris	16	116	7.25	20	0
Cunningham	17	76	4.47	15	0
Rae	1	11	11.00	11	0
Hinton	2	2	1.00	1	0
Jones	7	0	0.00	8	0
Young	1	2	-2.00	-2	0
Totals	44	203	4.62	20	0

Alabama Passing	PA	PC	PI	Yards	Long	TD
T. Davis	6	5	1	58	16	0

USC Passing						
Jones	11	7	2	84	18	1
Rae	2	0	0	0	0	0
Totals	13	7	2	84	18	1

Alabama Receiving	Number	Yards	Long	TD
Musso	2	-2	-2	0
Simmons	1	16	16	0
Bailey	1	15	15	0
Beck	1	9	9	0
Totals	5	58	16	0

USC Receiving				
Morgan	3	30	17	0
Swann	1	18	18	0
Hinton	1	17	17	0
Cunningham	1	12	12	0
Young	1	7	7	1
Totals	7	84	18	1

TRIUMPHANT RETURN

The victorious Crimson Tide did not leave for Alabama until late Saturday afternoon. They returned to Birmingham at 10 P.M. A crowd of 10,000 screaming Alabama fans greeted them at the airport. In those days there was much less security, and people could run out onto the tarmac to greet the returning guests. Before the team exited the plane, they had to let Johnny Musso out a different exit because team officials feared for his safety among this large throng of Tide faithful. The players left the plane and were mobbed by the cheering fans. Less than an hour later about 2,000 fans greeted the Crimson Tide squad as they left the bus at Bryant Hall. Needless to say, the team was extremely gratified by this show of support.

Alabama's offensive line surge against the Southern California Trojans. (Jimmy Rosser collection)

Robin Parkhouse (90) trying to catch USC quarterback Jimmy Jones. Parkhouse was knocked unconscious by John Vella just a few seconds after this photo was taken. (Paul W. Bryant Museum)

Quarterback Terry Davis (10) in his first start for the Crimson Tide against Southern California. (Paul W. Bryant Museum)

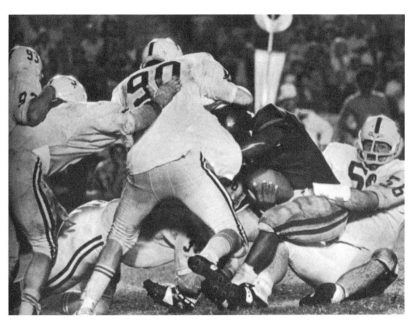

Jeff Rouzie (56), Chuck Strickland (36), and Robin Parkhouse (90) bringing down a running back from USC. (Paul W. Bryant Museum)

Robin Parkhouse, Jeff Beard, Wayne Hall, Steve Williams, and Steve Higginbotham—half of the first-team defense—taking a breather during the big victory over the Trojans. (Jeff Beard collection)

Paul Bryant getting a victory ride after the 17-10 victory over USC. It was his 200th victory of his career. (Paul W. Bryant Museum)

Paul Bryant was all smiles in the locker room as he celebrated his 200th career win. (Jeff Beard collection)

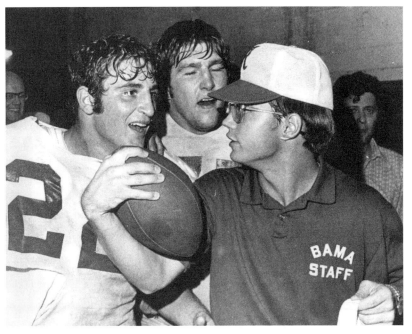

Johnny Musso, Jeff Beard, and Finus Gaston celebrate in the locker room after the Southern California win. (Jeff Beard collection)

Joe Labue, Jimmy Rosser, and Rod Steakley proceed through a gauntlet of happy Alabama students outside Bryant Hall late Saturday night after their arrival on campus after the USC victory. (Jimmy Rosser collection)

MEAT OF THE SCHEDULE

AT ABOUT MIDNIGHT ON SATURDAY NIGHT, PAUL AND MARY
Harmon Bryant returned home from Los Angeles. Awaiting them was a surprise floating in their swimming pool, a 20-foot float congratulating Coach Bryant on his 200th win. The Bryants were somewhat dismayed at the invasion of their private space but the euphoria of the win helped them take it in stride. They were even more astonished when a picture of the "surprise" appeared in Monday's edition of the *Tuscaloosa News*. Kirk McNair remembered the mood around Coleman Coliseum: "The sports information department had been putting something together the past few weeks to honor Coach on his 200th win....Everything was fine until we saw the float in the paper on Monday. We were scared to death that the public would now be coming over to Coach Bryant's house, now that they knew where it was. It had the potential to be a public-relations disaster. As it turned out, nothing really became of it, and we all sighed a breath of relief."[242]

REFLECTION ON THE *BEAR BRYANT SHOW*

During the football season in the state of Alabama, fans and players were glued to their television sets for two hours on Sunday afternoon. The first hour was reserved for the *Bear Bryant Show* which aired at 4 P.M., followed by the *Shug Jordan Show* at 5 P.M. Bryant's show usually received higher ratings in the state than the NFL games shown that day. He used his show to communicate with the people of the state. Bryant was usually very down home and folksy in these appearances, especially if the Tide won the game. If they lost, however, he could be quite testy in this setting. All of the players watched the show to get the first glimpse of what their coach was thinking. It would help them get ready for the next week and know what to expect. They were also listening for their names to be mentioned, hopefully in a positive manner. After the big victory over Southern California, on the first edition of his show in 1971, the Bear was happy and full of compliments for his football team. "Our offensive line did a tremendous job. It has improved more than you can imagine. I've never seen more beautiful offensive drives than the first and third ones that got our touchdowns. Johnny Musso is probably the greatest short-yardage runner I've ever seen. This means that he runs well where it's thick. Robin Parkhouse did a great job on defense. We're getting more leadership than we've been getting in recent years."[243]

LEADERSHIP TAKES PLACE BOTH
ON AND OFF THE FIELD

Observers can easily see that leadership takes place on the football field, but few people get to see those same qualities displayed after the game. Johnny Musso and Robin Parkhouse had clearly been the offensive and defensive leaders on the field that Friday night in California and they, of course, enjoyed the rewards due them. But because football is a team sport, after all, real heroes realize that they have a responsibility to their less-idolized teammates. This game's star players were no exception. Wilbur Jackson described an example of the effort Johnny Musso made to help him after the USC victory:

Johnny would often come by my room during that season. He would always tell me to hang in there and my time would come. When I was a sophomore, I went to Southern Cal and played on a Friday night. I had no idea whether or not I would get to play. As it turned out, I did not get to play. The next day we stayed over and Johnny visited with me and told me not to get down on myself. He told that my day would come and me to keep my head up. That meant a lot to me.[244]

As part of standard procedures the coaches would view the film of the previous week's game and grade the players individually on their performance. They would isolate each player's efforts on every play by rating it a "plus" or "minus." If the player's pluses exceeded 50 percent of his total plays, he was usually rated a "winner." Twenty-four players were graded winners from the USC game; fifteen from the defense and nine from the offense. Bryant rewarded the winning players by allowing them to eat in a separate area of the dining hall. During these occasions they were given the best cuts of meat and enjoyed more exotic fare.

REMEMBER WHAT HAPPENED LAST YEAR

At the beginning of every game, the players received a handout concerning their upcoming opponent. These handouts contained the theme of the week as well as vital information about the opposing team. This information included key players, the foe's offensive and defensive tendencies, keys to beating the opponent, and the like. The theme for the Southern Mississippi game read, "Remember what happened to Ole Miss last year when they were sitting on top of the world at 4 and 0. The score of that game was Southern Miss—30, Ole Miss—14. Now they are on the bottom of the world."[245] That was a game in which Ole Miss entered the contest with an undefeated record and ranked in the top ten in both polls before the Golden Eagles of Southern Mississippi upset their state rival. Paul Bryant was trying to keep his football team grounded. He did not want Southern Mississippi's fate to befall his Crimson Tide, who ranked sixth in the United Press International (UPI) poll and ninth in the AP poll following the first game victory.

On Monday Bryant rewarded the first offensive and defensive teams by having them practice only in their helmets and hip pads. The rest of the players were required to wear full gear. There was some limited scrimmaging between the second and third teams. Perhaps the Bear should have restricted pads to all of his team because there were a few injuries to players who were not starters but certainly were expected to contribute, including Randy Moore, Billy Sexton, and Paul Spivey. Moore, who had been battling Jim Simmons for the starting tight end position just two weeks ago, had hurt his shoulder and as a result had been out of action. He came back full speed to practice on Monday and broke his leg. Moore had been a part-time starter in 1970 at tight end, kicked off, and also was the backup field goal kicker for Bill Davis. Alabama trainer Jim Goosetree announced that Randy would be lost for at least "five or six weeks" as a result of the broken leg, and the Montgomery junior might be red-shirted because of this injury. Billy Sexton, the backup quarterback from Tallahassee, hurt his throwing shoulder at the beginning of the scrimmage. The injury was not thought to be major, but it was unclear whether he would be available for Saturday's game against Southern Mississippi. Spivey pulled the same hamstring he strained the first week of two-a-days back in August. He was listed day-to-day.[246]

OFF-THE-FIELD ACTIVITIES

Meanwhile, on Monday before the first home game, a couple of important activities that occurred off the field impacted the football squad. One was directly related to the Crimson Tide, the other indirectly. In the first occurrence, Robin Parkhouse was named the Associated Press Southeastern Lineman of the Week. Parkhouse was very modest in his acceptance of the honor, thinking of the team first: "It's a big thrill, but not as big a thrill as winning the game, though winning the game was the big thing. I feel great about it. I'm glad I could get it, but I just want to beat Southern Mississippi now."[247] He made seven tackles, six assists, and two sacks of 14 and 4 yards. Parkhouse also contributed heavily toward a pass interception with a heavy rush on one play and forced a fumble on another of Southern California's last offensive possession.

The other activity that got a good deal of press coverage concerned the Bob Hope concert. One may ask what this had to do with the football team, but consider where and when this was. The front page headline in the *Crimson-White* read "Bryant Gets Bob Hope; UA Center Takes Blame." In several previous articles, the student newspaper had criticized the university for scheduling the entertainer; it also voiced disapproval that the Athletic Letterman's Club (A-Club) was sponsoring the event. Charley Thornton, in an interview with Harriet Swift of the paper's staff, went straight to the point:

> Well, Coach Bryant had been telling Hope that we wanted him to come to Alabama, and he said that he would like to come. All the shows in the Coliseum were for the 30-and-under set, rock bands and all that, but they didn't have too much for the community. We thought about Flip

Wilson or somebody like that, but since Coach Bryant and Mr. Hope are good friends, well, Coach asked him and he said he'd come.[248]

The A-Club was the nominal sponsor of the event. Alabama state statutes did not allow any organization outside the university to schedule events or receive profits from an event. Thornton did not address this issue directly and only referred the matter to the comptroller's office. Don Corley, the public relations officer for the University Center, agreed with Thornton's assessment of the situation: "We try to program for everybody, not just the freaks." Bryant was highly instrumental in scheduling entertainers that reflected his generation, like Bob Hope. On the other hand, most of the students were not "freaks" but had different entertainment values and were more receptive to the popular music of the time—like The Who, Three Dog Night, or Grand Funk Railroad. These opposing values sometimes clashed.

SCOUTING REPORT FOR SOUTHERN MISSISSIPPI

Bill "Brother" Oliver was the Alabama assistant coach in charge of preparing the game plan for the Golden Eagles of Southern Mississippi. Oliver was a former Alabama player who had played on the 1961 national championship team. The former defensive back from Livingston, Alabama, had coached football in the high school ranks for three years before joining arch-rival Auburn University in 1966 for the next five seasons. In January 1971, the Bear called him back home and he willingly obliged his former head coach and mentor. Oliver was in charge of the defensive backs. Delbert Reed, sports editor of the *Tuscaloosa News*, would comment some thirty years later, "Bill Oliver was the best assistant coach I ever saw at the University of Alabama."[249] Oliver's assessment of the Golden Eagles was that they were a team not be taken lightly. Southern Miss lost their opening game against Florida State 24-9 and was primed for an upset given what the Tide had done in their first outing. This would be the fifth time in the last six years that the two teams had clashed. "Brother" Oliver was not looking past Southern Miss in his evaluation:

> I think the first thing you have to look at when you evaluate Southern Mississippi is their kicking game, which is probably the best in the country. Ray Guy is the top returning punter in the nation, having aver-

aged 45.3 on 69 kicks last year, and anytime you get inside the 40, they'll be going for a field goal on fourth-down situations. In the spring before his sophomore season, he had a 64-yard field goal, and he kicks off into the end zone virtually every kickoff. Offensively and defensively, Southern has the majority of its starters back.... They'll be a stronger team than they were last year and last year they swamped a fine Ole Miss team.... We certainly can't expect to win on last week's reputation.[250]

PREPARATIONS CONTINUE FOR SOUTHERN MISS

Coach Bryant announced the captains for Saturday's contest with Southern Mississippi: Jimmy Rosser and Robin Parkhouse. Bryant would use different criteria to choose his captains, but all involved merit. Both of these seniors had exceptional games against Southern California. After Wednesday's practice Bryant cautioned his squad against a letdown, and his captains were quite vocal in their remarks to the press concerning this matter. Rosser was adamant when he stated, "We won't be looking past Southern Mississippi. This team will be ready." Parkhouse seconded this: "I don't think that it will be hard for us to get up for Southern Mississippi. We've got something going now and it would be ridiculous for us not to get up for each game and lose it all."[251]

On a rainy Thursday night, a crowd of 1,500 braved the weather to honor Paul Bryant at a pep rally at Foster Auditorium. He was presented a plaque by the Alabama Spirit Committee and the Crimson Girls honoring him for his 200th victory. As always, Bryant was gracious and thanked the student body for their help in the victory against USC. Coach Bryant also introduced Bill Oliver, who gave a brief overview of the Golden Eagles. The captains were also introduced and made a few remarks to the cheering fans. Parkhouse gave a short speech in which he told the students "how grateful the players are for your support."[252] Jimmy Rosser followed up by claiming that "they had not seen nothing yet, and the best was yet to come."[253]

The team went through a light workout on Friday, then had dinner and attended a movie as they always did on the night before a game. Paul Bryant thought it was important to get the players away from the festivities on campus. By doing this, they could stay focused on the task at hand. The team stayed at the *Moon-Wink* in Cottondale, which was 8 miles from campus.

Southern Mississippi won the toss and received the football but did not do anything with it; they ran three plays for 2 yards and punted the ball. The Crimson Tide did much the same thing with their first possession, gaining 9 yards on three plays before Greg Gantt came in to punt. The Alabama defense held Southern Miss again on three plays, and the Eagles were forced to punt. Steve Williams returned the punt for 9 yards, putting the Tide in good field position at the Southern Miss 47-yard line. Terry Davis directed the offense for ten straight running plays as Johnny Musso scored the first touchdown of the game from the 1-yard line. Ellis Beck, Joe Labue, and Musso all carried the ball during this drive. Bill Davis kicked the extra point, and Alabama led 7-0 with 5:42 left in the first quarter. Alabama's one bad spot during this drive occurred when Paul Spivey reinjured his hamstring on a blocking play that allowed Musso to gain 10 yards. Spivey did not play the rest of the day and his injury would be reevaluated on Monday.

On the third offensive series of the game, the Golden Eagles were forced to punt again after gaining only 6 yards on three plays. The front four— Parkhouse, Mitchell, Beard, and Rowell—would not surrender the line of scrimmage. This time Williams returned the punt with another burst of speed for 15 yards, whereupon Alabama took over with good field position on their own 48. Terry Davis kept the ball on the first play as he optioned the left end for 3 yards. Davis then hit David Bailey for 19 yards to the Eagle 31. Musso and Labue exchanged carrying the ball for the next five plays on the first play of the second quarter and Musso ran a counter-play around left end for 16 yards for the second touchdown. The extra point was good, and the Tide led 14-0.

Southern Mississippi managed a first down the next time they got the ball, but they still had to punt the ball away after only five offensive plays. This was against the Alabama second team defense as Paul Bryant was already starting to substitute at the beginning of the second quarter. The Eagle's punt coverage was better this time down the field, as Williams only managed a 3-yard return. Eight plays later, Ellis Beck went over from the 1-yard line to put the Crimson Tide up by three touchdowns. Steve Biscelgia and Beck made several good runs in this series, but the big play was a 43-yard pass completion over the middle from Davis to Bailey. With 8:28 left in the half, Alabama now led 21-0.

Buddy Palazzo was now starting to move the Southern Miss offense after being stymied the first four possessions. With a series of short passes, the Golden Eagles were now in sight of the Alabama end zone at the 13-yard line. John Mitchell rose to the occasion, belting the Southern Miss quarterback on the next play for a 4-yard loss and teaming with Terry Rowell on a 10-yard sack. Ray Guy barely missed a 44-yard field goal as it sailed wide left at the last second.

Alabama made three first downs on its last possession of the half but did not score. The score remained 21-0 in favor of the Crimson Tide. They completely dominated the first half by outgaining the opposition from Hattiesburg in total yards 224-65.

The second half was more of the same as the Tide substituted freely and moved the ball at will. The Alabama first team offense only played parts of the first two possessions in the second half. The first offensive possession yielded nothing and Gantt punted the ball after three plays. Southern Miss made a first down and was starting to show some assemblage of an offense, but another big play by the Alabama defense stopped another drive. David McMakin made a leaping interception of a Palazzo pass at the Tide 18 and ran it back 6 yards to the Alabama 24-yard line.

Terry Davis led the Crimson Tide down the field 76 yards in his last series of the game. He mixed it up a little more on this series and completed passes to Bailey and Dexter Wood. There were a number of outstanding performances on this drive as Joe Labue went 4 yards for a touchdown to put the game almost out of reach. Ellis Beck ran wild in this possession as he gained 44 yards in just four carries, highlighted by a 23-yard burst up the middle of the Southern Miss defense. With 6:38 left in the third quarter, the first team offense took a rest for the remainder of the game.

Benny Rippetoe came in for Davis in the third quarter and looked almost as spectacular when he completed three of four passes for 99 yards. Wayne Wheeler caught his first pass for the Crimson Tide on a 56-yarder from Rippetoe. Rip led the Tide on two touchdown drives. Butch Hobson substituted for Rippetoe for the last couple of offensive series and made a number of good runs with the second- and third-team offense. Wilbur Jackson got to play in his first varsity game on the last two Alabama possessions and remembered, "I did not know if I was going to get to play. I even thought that I might get red-shirted. Against Southern Miss, we had gotten a couple of guys hurt, and Coach Bryant called my name. He told to be as loose as a goose and be reckless as hell. I played four or five plays in that game. That made it better for me the next time that I got in, because I was not as nervous as before."[254]

The Golden Eagles did manage a touchdown in the fourth quarter when Doyle Orange ran 13 yards on an option around the left end. However, they missed the extra point due to a bad snap on the play. The final score was 42-6.

Alabama played sixty-two players in the game. They gained 469 yards with twenty-two first downs. The offense had a lot more balance in this game with Terry Davis and Benny Rippetoe combined for 193 yards passing on a nine-for-ten clip. The defense played an excellent game, pressuring the Southern Miss quarterbacks all day and completely controlling the line of scrimmage. They gave 147 yards all day, much of that by the second and third team defense.

POST-GAME EVENTS

Bob Hope attended the game and got a rousing ovation from the 52,701 fans. Hope had said earlier in the week, "I have got some things to tell everyone in Alabama about my old buddy, Bear Bryant. When I get through with him he'll think he played Southern Cal, Notre Dame, and the Baltimore Colts in the same day." That night he played to a sellout crowd at the Coleman Coliseum. Paul Bryant and many of his players and coaches were in attendance to see the legendary performer. Hope did not disappoint his many fans, throwing out one-liners like "They call Musso 'Top Cat' because he never misses a yard.... Coaching is like show biz. One day you are drinking the wine, the next you are picking the grapes...Alabama is so mean that they keep tackling one hour after practice."[255]

Paul Bryant was highly complimentary of his team on his Sunday afternoon show after the 42-6 shellacking of Southern Mississippi. Being 2-0 and ranked in both of the top-ten polls was all well and good, but now something was changing. Bryant mused to Charley Thornton, "We're getting into the meat of the schedule. We're going to start playing in the conference, where it counts."[256] The first cut of the meat was the University of Florida Gators.

DOUG DICKEY AND THE FIRST SEC GAME

Bryant had a couple of issues concerning the Florida Gators. Since his return to the Capstone in 1958, the Bear had won thirty-seven of thirty-eight games played in Denny Stadium. The single loss occurred in 1963 to Florida by a score of 10-6. That loss probably cost the Crimson Tide a chance for a national title. Historically Florida had not been a regular opponent of the University of Alabama. The Gators had played Alabama only three times since Bryant's reappearance in Tuscaloosa, with Bama leading 2-1. The entire series record was in favor of the Tide at 10-5. Bryant's second issue with Florida concerned its coach, Doug Dickey. Bryant was even with him in head-to-head contests at 3-3-1. Dickey was a former Gator quarterback in his second season as Florida's head coach. Twenty years younger than Bryant, he had been the head coach of the University of Tennessee for the six previous seasons and had been very successful in that position. His five-year record from 1965 to 1969 was 42-10-3, only one game better than Bryant's 42-11-2 for the same period. It was during this span of time that Dickey's Volunteers beat Alabama three straight times, from 1967-1969, and became SEC champions twice. Some who followed the Southeastern Conference thought that seeing the older Bryant being upstaged by the younger Dickey signaled a changing of the guard.

Dickey returned to his alma mater after the 1969 season, but not without controversy. Tennessee was preparing to play Florida in the Gator Bowl that year. While his Vols were getting ready for the late December contest with the Gators, just six days away, Dickey was busy discussing a new coaching job with Florida president Stephen O'Connell. During the season, then-Florida coach Ray Graves had been hinting at retiring from coaching to be strictly athletics director. Graves had made it known publicly that he favored long-time assistant coach Gene Ellenson as his replacement. As it turned out, the Gators defeated Tennessee 14-13. Florida players gave Ellenson a shoulder-ride off of the field and were vocal in their support of him as their next head coach, but it was not to be. Florida hired Dickey on December 30, 1969, just three days after the Gator Bowl. Gene Ellenson was retained as an executive assistant to Graves but would not be on the coaching staff. A number of Florida players were openly critical of the move, and both Tennessee and Florida fans were outraged by the actions.[257] It was not so much that Dickey was leaving one job for another; rather, the timing was the issue. He seemed to have had no good reason not to wait until after the game to discuss his possible move to Florida. Even legendary basketball coach Adolph Rupp of the University of Kentucky could not believe it when he heard the news, questioning, "Why would a man leave the Garden of

Eden? For what possible reason would a coach leave Tennessee?"[258] Doug Dickey claimed it was for personal reasons.

WHO ARE THE FLORIDA GATORS?

Doug Dickey's first season with the University of Florida was a decent 7-4. The Gators won five of their first six games, the only loss having been to the Crimson Tide in Tuscaloosa at 46-15. They finished weakly, going 2-3 the rest of the season with losses to Tennessee, Auburn, and cross-state rival Miami. The Tennessee and Auburn games were blowout losses, but the heartbreaking loss to Miami in the last game of the season knocked Florida out of bowl contention.

Any discussion about the University of Florida football team begins with its offensive threesome of John Reaves, Carlos Alvarez, and Tommy Durrance. As sophomores in 1969, these three offensive stars had put up great numbers and led the Gators to a 9-1-1 record. All three players were now seniors. Reaves had been nothing short of brilliant in his two previous seasons; as a sophomore, he had set SEC records for a single season in attempts (396), completions (222), total yards (2,852), yards gained (2,896), and touchdown passes (25). While his individual numbers were not as high in 1970, Reaves did manage to pass for 2,549 yards and thirteen touchdown passes. His completion percentage dropped 6 points to 50 percent. His favorite target these two seasons was Carlos Alvarez, who had caught eighty-eight passes and twelve touchdowns as a sophomore. As a junior, Alvarez had suffered a serious knee injury and his productiveness had dropped. Yet he still managed to catch forty-four passes and score five touchdowns. Tommy Durrance was a strong running back who had had a stellar sophomore season and a decent junior year. As a sophomore, Durrance had run for 731 yards, caught 26 passes for 331 more, and scored an amazing eighteen touchdowns. His production had dropped off as a junior, but he still gained 583 yards on the ground, caught 20 passes for 172 yards, and scored six touchdowns. They were still the heart of the Gator offense heading into their senior season. In addition, Jim Yancey, a talented tight end who had been on a number of pre-season All-SEC teams, and speedy Willie Jackson, who returned at split end, complimented the Florida offense. In short, the Gators had a number of offensive weapons.[259]

Florida's defense returned six starters from the previous season. Defensive end Jack Youngblood was the biggest loss for the Gators, as the All-American had departed Gainesville to play for the Los Angeles Rams. The Florida defense had performed adequately at times during the previous season but had given 38 points to Tennessee and 63 points to Auburn in back-to-back losses. Bob Harrel and Danny Williams had been two-year starters on the defensive line. Richard Buchanan, a starting linebacker in 1970, replaced Youngblood at defensive end. The top new-comer on the defensive line was David Hitchcock, who was only 5-foot-7 but weighed 210 pounds. He was extremely quick and reminded some Alabama fans of Sammy Gellderstedt, who was an All-America nose gaurd in 1968.. The linebacking corps was a bit thin, as they had lost all three starters from the year before. Harvin Clark and John Clifford were their top defensive backs, both starters from the prior season.[260]

SLUGGISH START FOR GATORS IN '71

Florida lost its first two games 12-6 to Duke and 13-10 to Mississippi State. They had been favored in both contests only to lose in the end. The Gators were able to move the ball between the 20s but could not score. Costly fumbles, interceptions, and penalties had stopped their offense. Reaves had thrown for two touchdowns and 449 yards but had seven passes intercepted in the first two contests. Durrance was hurt and had not played. Mike Rich and Lenny Lucas shared the bulk of the running game in Durrance's absence and performed adequately but did nothing outstanding. After losing its first two games, Florida was primed for a comeback. Coach Dickey said that they had had their best week of practice since he had been there. A new Astroturf surface had been installed at Florida Field, and this was to be the first game played on the new artificial turf.

WOULD THE TIDE BE READY?

Paul Bryant did not sound very happy after Thursday's practice. The Alabama squad worked out in a torrential downpour, and players were slipping and sliding everywhere. If one took everything the wily head coach said literally, there would be reason for real concern. Bryant told the press that he had a lot of injured players who might not be ready to play on Saturday's first SEC game for the Tide. Not only was Parkhouse ill, but Mitchell had a leg injury. Likewise, Paul Spivey definitely would not be available for the game. David Knapp had a hip-pointer and was in questionable condition. Billy Sexton, who had missed last week's game with Southern Miss, had been practicing that week and would probably be ready to play on Saturday.

Earlier in the week Coach Bryant had announced the captains for the game. Johnny Musso and Jimmy Grammer would be the offensive captains, and Robin Parkhouse and Steve Higginbotham would lead the defense. Greg Gantt had been selected to captain the special teams. The team arrived in Gainesville and went through a light workout on Friday afternoon. Parkhouse and Mitchell were much better and were considered likely to start the game. Knapp, who was still sore, was questionable. If Knapp could not go, Wilbur Jackson would be ready for more playing time following his debut against Southern Mississippi the week before.

IT'S 115 DEGREES AND COUNTING

It was 115 degrees Fahrenheit on the field as both teams went through their pre-game conditioning drills. When Alabama came back to the dressing room for the last time before the kickoff, Paul Bryant let his players know what they were there for. As Joe Labue remembered, the coach did not mince words: "He told us 'to go out there and whoop their tails. They're too busy looking at girls' skirts around here.' We all kind of chuckled and went out there."[261]

The Crimson Tide did exactly as their head coach had asked them. They went out there and completely destroyed Florida 38-0 before a standing-room-only crowd of 61,832. This was the first shutout in nearly four years, the last having been 17-0 on November 18, 1967 against South Carolina. The Alabama defense totally befuddled the Gator offense the entire steamy afternoon. The Tide scored the first three times they got the football and led 17-0. They never looked back after that. Johnny Musso played only about half of the game, but gained 97 yards on twenty-one carries and scored four touchdowns. Musso tied two Alabama records and was within one touchdown of a conference mark. The four touchdowns tied the single-game mark of Bobby Marlow, who set the record in 1950 against Georgia Tech. Musso now had thirty career touchdowns, which tied him with Marlow for second place in the SEC behind Georgia Charlie Trippi's record of thirty-one during the mid-

1940s. Musso was his usual modest self in describing what had just taken place, and he was reflective in explaining the team's early success: "We have a oneness. It's something you can't explain. But you can feel it, because all of us are pulling for each other. Take Robin Parkhouse, for example. Last year, he was suspended from the team, and he came back and played great. We all pulled for him. He's a fiery guy. The way he came back after that suspension was a real inspiration. Plus the real responsibility for our improvement lies with our players. And Coach Bryant has that intangible something. If he says something, you just naturally believe him."[262]

Alabama rushed for 363 yards on sixty-six carries at nearly 6 yards a run. Terry Davis scrambled in and out of Gator defenders all afternoon. Davis ran for 64 yards on ten attempts, even though he hurt his shoulder and left the game early in the third quarter. He remembered how his injury continued to bother him the whole season. "The Florida game was one in which I was in a great deal of pain. The Florida player basically knocked the crap out of my shoulder. I told Goose at halftime that I was in a lot of pain, and he got me a shot of novocaine and cortisone. I played the first drive of the second half, and we scored. I came out of the game with a bruised shoulder. It bothered me every time that I was hit there the rest of the season."[263]

Joe Labue gained 52 yards, while fellow backfield member Ellis Beck knocked out 44 yards. Second-teamers Wilbur Jackson and Steve Biscelgia also contributed a great deal in this team effort. Jackson gained 65 yards in his second game, including a 48-yard burst around the right end. Biscelgia picked up 36 yards in a relief effort at fullback. Billy Sexton, the red-shirt sophomore from Tallahassee, played in his first game as an Alabama quarterback and did a stand-up job. He threw a touchdown pass to Dexter Wood late in the fourth quarter. After the game Sexton was reflective about his situation: "I thought it was ironic, that I played my first high school game in Gainesville, and here I am playing my first college game here."[264]

The defense was all over the field and harassed the Florida quarterbacks all afternoon. On the first series the Gators attempted to establish a running game but were not successful. From the second series on, they tried to throw the ball downfield. Again Alabama defenders showed they were up to the task by putting a great deal of pressure on John Reaves and later doing the same to Chan Gailey. Gailey played almost the entire second half with no more success than the record-breaking Reaves.

Reaves was nine out of twenty for 42 yards with three interceptions. Gailey threw two interceptions in his nine passing attempts. Carlos Alvarez caught one pass for 5 yards. Tommy Durrance played in his first game of the season and gained only 21 yards in nine attempts. Steve Higginbotham intercepted two passes while Tom Surlas, Bobby McKinney, and Robby Rowan intercepted one apiece. Steve Wade recovered a fumble to complete the turnover exchange.

The entire defensive line and linebackers played magnificently, but none more than the two Florida natives, Robin Parkhouse and Jeff Rouzie. Parkhouse had recovered from an illness earlier in the week to have his third strong game in a row. Rouzie, who had almost gone to the University of Florida as a number of his relatives had done, led the Tide defense with nine individual tackles and one assist. In recalling how this game made him feel, Rouzie said, "We came down here and beat a supposedly good team like this. It was great for me to do this well in front of the homefolks. I knew Alabama was the right place for me and today added further proof to that."[265]

AFTER-GAME FESTIVITIES

After the game the Alabama football team traveled to the airport on a chartered bus. When they arrived, something was wrong. Their plane was out on the runway but had no flight crew. Bryant was livid and demanded to know where the pilots and the crew were. He marched out to one of the hangars and went inside. Suddenly the crew ran out of the hangar, tucking in their shirttails and putting on their hats. Many of the players got a good laugh out of this, but Coach Bryant was not amused. Jack White recollected what occurred during the trip back:

> Mrs. Bryant asked me on the plane what some of us were doing after the game. She said to the players that they could bring their wives or dates with you over to the house. It was mostly the married players, John Hannah, Kraft, Rosser, myself, Marvin Barron, etc. There were about eight or nine couples who came. We were all hanging out around his swimming pool. I had my shoes off and was really coolint it. I remember Coach Bryant chewed me out up one side and down another. "Where are your shoes? What happens if you get hurt and can't play next week? Get your shoes on!"[266]

Andy Cross was among the players who went to Coach Bryant's house after the game. Being there at this great coach's home in such a relaxed manner equally blew him away. "It was impressive to go his house after the Florida game. He had all these pictures, trophies, mementos, and such. I had only been there one time during recruiting, and I certainly will never forget being there."[267]

ANOTHER BIG CHALLENGE

The Crimson Tide certainly did not have the time to spend ruminating. They had won a big game and had another ahead of them against the Ole Miss Rebels, who were also 3-0 and ranked in the top ten. They knew that in the next week one of the two teams would probably drop out of the top ten. The Tide was determined not to be that team.

In the overall series, the Ole Miss Rebels trailed the University of Alabama 22-4-2 as they prepared to come to Birmingham on Saturday. However, two of their four victories had come in the last three years, and Paul Bryant was anxious to exact some revenge on the Rebels. Bryant had been 5-2 against the University of Mississippi since his return to Alabama. The great Archie Manning, who in 1969 had lost only 33-32 against the Crimson Tide, had engineered those Ole Miss wins. Manning was no longer there, nor was his legendary head coach Johnny Vaught. Vaught had retired after a heart attack felled him during the 1970 season. Although those two were gone, Ole Miss brought an undefeated 3-0 squad that ranked seventh in the weekly UPI poll. Alabama ranked fifth in that poll and seventh in the AP poll.

OLE MISS PREVIEW

The University of Mississippi opened the season with wins over Long Beach State (29-13), Memphis State (49-21), and Kentucky (34-20). Billy Kinard, a former Ole Miss player and Arkansas assistant coach, coached the Rebels. He had won the job over offensive coach Bob Tyler, who had been Johnny Vaught's choice. There was a good deal of resentment from Ole Miss players and fans who had lobbied hard for Tyler to replace the popular Vaught. Tyler was now an assistant coach for the Crimson Tide and was in charge of putting together the game plan. Tyler had a great deal of expertise in evaluating these players since he had been an assistant there for the past three seasons. He offered this assessment:

> Mississippi is impressive in all phases of the game and, of course, they've gained momentum with each of their three games this year. Starting with the kicking game, they've got an outstanding place-kicker in Cloyce Hinton. He'll put the kickoff into the end zone practically every time and he's capable of kicking field goals as long as anyone... Mississippi has some fine kick return men in Bob Knight and Danny Stallings, a sophomore. Both are exceedingly dangerous and they'll both be back on both punts and kickoffs.... Defensively, they are very aggressive and very big... The Ole Miss secondary is relatively young, but they've intercepted a number of passes and by this time will be playing well together.... They have a very consistent offense, one that is potentially one of the most potent and explosive around. Their quarterbacking has probably developed much faster than expected. Brent Chumbler, the backup to Archie Manning the past two years, is now number three. Kenny Lyons, a sophomore, has started the last two games. However, Weese, another sophomore, has played a great deal and started the first game. They have two fine tailbacks in Randy Reed and Greg Ainsworth. A very important part of their attack is the blocking of their young sophomore fullback, Gene Allen. In addition, of course, they have an All-American candidate at tight end in Jim Poole [6-foot-5, 231]. The rest of their offensive is young, but it seems to be coming on fast. It will be a real challenge for us to compete with this fine Mississippi football team.[268]

HANNAH PICKS UP HONORS

On Monday, guard John Hannah received the Southeastern Lineman of the Week award from the Associated Press, determined by a seven-member Southeastern All-American advisory board for football for the news service. Hannah graded an outstanding 83 percent for his actions against Florida. Coach Bryant was happy but not surprised with the Albertville native's play. "John played the way we've always known he's capable of. If he continues to improve as he has so far, he can be a fine football player." On Tuesday the Associated Press presented Hannah with the "National Lineman of the Week." He was charitable in his remarks and refused to take all the credit. "We have a lot of fine linemen. We all know that we'd better block or those backs will be running over us. I'm really just proud to be on this Alabama team."[269]

BRYANT NAMES CAPTAINS FOR OLE MISS CLASH

Monday's practice was spirited as the Tide began their preparation for the University of Mississippi. Paul Bryant named the game captains for the Ole Miss clash: Jim Simmons, Jack White, Terry Rowell, David Bailey, and Steve Williams. All five captains had Mississippi connections. The first four were Mississippi natives, while Williams had a number of relatives who lived there. Ole Miss actively recruited Simmons, White, Rowell, and Bailey, while Williams even tried to recruit himself there.

VAUGHT PICKS THE REBELS

The oddsmakers made Alabama a 10- to 12-point favorite to remain unbeaten and on top of the Southeastern Conference, but Johnny Vaught did not see it that way. He was familiar with both teams, having coached Ole Miss for over twenty years up to the previous season. Vaught had also defeated the Crimson Tide in two out of the last three meetings. He did have some credentials that allowed reasonable judgment:

> I see where the oddsmakers here have made Alabama about a two-touchdown choice over Ole Miss in their Southeastern Conference game Saturday at Birmingham. That's just about two touchdowns too many. The game could decide the winner of the SEC and if the Rebels can detect when Bear Bryant is about to call up some of his mystical trickery, Ole Miss should win it.... Bear is running the Texas Wishbone with a lot of corner offense. I'm glad to see that he finally wised up to the sprint-out moves, it was good to us at Ole Miss for many years. I don't know if the Tide defense has really faced a test so far. It will Saturday...Ole Miss over Alabama.[270]

If the Alabama football squad needed any external motivation for the game, the former Ole Miss coach sure gave it to them by writing this column. It was placed on the Tide bulletin board on Wednesday for all of the players to see. Only time would tell whether the oddsmakers were right.

BATTLE OF THE UNBEATENS

The weather forecast predicted a temperature in the high 80s for Saturday afternoon, indicating only one of the problems the Crimson Tide would face. Another weather-related factor concerned the Alabama training staff; as Sang Lyda recalled, "We knew that it was going to be extremely hot, but we could deal with that. What was more problematical was the smog alert. It was predicted to be at the highest level that had been recorded on the day of the game."[271] As a turned out, the temperature was 88 degrees at game time, with a dangerous smog alert for the Birmingham area. Legion Field was located near the heart of the steel-producing area of the city. Ice and oxygen would be mandatory on the sidelines for both teams, as the temperature on the Astroturf field could be 20 to 25 degrees hotter than elsewhere.

FIRST HALF IS TOUGH

Alabama won the toss and received the kickoff. On their second play from scrimmage, the offense went without a huddle and Terry Davis scampered 25 yards downfield for a first down. The Bama offense went without a huddle the rest of this series, which was a productive one until a fumble by Ellis Beck gave the Rebels possession. This surprised the Mississippi defense, but there were other effects as well. Terry Davis explained, "It was about 120 degrees on the field during this game. The first series of the game was a no-huddle drive that wore me out. You remember those kinds of things because it throws you out of your routine. Every time that I had good run downfield, the fullbacks knew that they were going to get the ball the next play so I could try to catch my breath."[272]

There were several good runs during this series by Johnny Musso, Joe Labue, and Davis. The offense gained 69 yards before the fumble. The defense held Ole Miss to three and out in its first possession. After a fair catch by Bobby McKinney, the Crimson Tide had another good series, driving 48 yards to the Ole Miss 8 before Bill Davis kicked a 25-yard field goal for a 3-0 lead with 5:38 left in the first quarter.

Ole Miss got a first down on their next series but then stalled after only four plays and had to punt the ball again. Again the Rebs had good punt coverage, as McKinney was unable to run it back and called a fair catch on Alabama's own 10-yard line. The offense went to work again moving the ball downfield. Musso's 15- and 30-yard runs were the high-lights of the drive. This drive stalled at the Ole Miss 25, as the Rebel defense stopped the Bama offense two plays in a row for no gain. Davis came in again and kicked a 42-yard field goal less than two minutes into the second quarter to increase the Crimson Tide lead to 6-0.

Greg Gantt boomed his second kickoff in a row into the end-zone as the Rebs took over from their own 20. This series was just like the last. The Mississippi offense managed a first down, with Kenny Lyons sprinting out and completing a short pass but being shut down after that and having to punt again. Three plays by the Alabama offense and Ole Miss took over at their own 21. Two plays later, the Tide forced the first break of the game when Jeff Rouzie recovered a fumble. In great field position at the Rebel 28, Terry Davis fumbled the ball away, giving it back to Ole Miss. It took Kenny Lyons only three plays before he hit Gene Allen for a 48-yard touchdown. A number of Alabama defenders had shots at Allen, but the nifty receiver evaded them all en route to a touchdown. Cloyce Hinton missed the extra point attempt and the game was tied at 6 with 6:11 left to go in the half. It was time for Alabama to go back to work.

This was the first time in the season that Alabama had been tied in a game. The offense really got focused in this possession—and they needed to be focused because they had 85 yards to go. Terry Davis did an excellent job moving the Tide down field in fourteen plays before he hooked with David Bailey on a 12-yard touchdown pass with eight seconds left in the half. Bailey made a good catch right on the sideline before he went out of bounds. He chided the Mississippi defensive back after the play, telling him, "I told you that you should have gone to Alabama, but you just wouldn't listen to me."[273] There were strong runs during the drive by the entire backfield of Davis, Beck, Labue, and Musso. After Bill Davis kicked the extra point, the Crimson Tide led 13-6 at halftime.

As Alabama trotted off the field to their dressing room for halftime, Jimmy Rosser fainted from physical exhaustion. The trainers and doctors hooked him up with fluids for the entire second half.

SECOND HALF TURNS FOR THE TIDE

Ole Miss took the opening kickoff from their own 20-yard line and started their comeback against Alabama. Kenny Lyons looked a lot like his predecessor Archie Manning as he marched his Rebel teammates down the field. Lyons passed for 28 yards then ran for 17 more in this 69-

yard drive. The Crimson Tide defense finally stopped the drive at the 11-yard line. Jim Poole missed a chip-shot field goal from 28 yards. The Rebels seemed to melt in the heat after that.

Terry Davis took over for the Crimson Tide and moved them down the field literally by running down the throats of the opposition. Jack White replaced Jimmy Rosser at guard and Bama was off to the races. Seven plays and 80 yards later, Joe Labue scored on an option play around left end for a 29-yard touchdown. Davis carried the ball for the first 8 yards and pitched to the trailing Labue, who outran the Ole Miss defense to the end zone. After Bill Davis kicked the extra point to make it 20-6, Alabama dominated both sides of the line of scrimmage and never looked back.

The next time they got the ball the Ole Miss offense made a couple of first downs but fumbled this opportunity. Steve Williams hit Greg Ainsworth with a crushing lick and the Ole Miss tailback lost the ball to the Alabama defense when Wayne Hall recovered the fumble. The very next play, Ellis Beck blasted up the middle for 27 yards. Ten more running plays later, Musso scored his thirty-first career touchdown on a 7-yard jaunt to tie Charlie Trippi, completing the most career touchdowns in the SEC. With the successful extra point, the score went to 27-6 with only five seconds left in the third quarter. On the extra point attempt Terry Davis was the victim of a cheap shot by Elmer Allen and reinjured his shoulder. The hit resulted in the expulsion of the Rebel tackle for unsportsmanlike conduct.

Butch Hobson replaced Davis for the remainder of the game. Hobson, who was listed as the fourth-team quarterback for much of the fall drills, was now the number-two quarterback behind Davis. Benny Rippetoe and Billy Sexton shared the number-two spot for most of the season, but it seemed that Hobson had moved ahead of them. He did not have the arm strength of the other two quarterbacks but was a much better runner. Hobson showed off his running skills as he led the Alabama offense to two more scores on drives of 53 and 59 yards. He gained fifty-one yards in six carries in the 40-6 romp over the previously unbeaten Ole Miss Rebels.

WHY SUCH A LARGE MARGIN?

There were several reasons for Alabama's dominance over Ole Miss. First, the Crimson Tide was unquestionably a much better football team. Second, Alabama was in better shape physically, as evidenced by their strength in the fourth quarter. Third, the Tide offensive and defensive lines of the football accounted for the second consecutive blowout of an Alabama opponent. Last, by running a new offense, Alabama created a learning curve as the defenses struggled to respond appropriately.

Coming into this game, Ole Miss had the highest scoring offense at 37.3 points a game. The Rebels had done this against the likes of Long Beach State, Memphis State, and Kentucky. The Crimson Tide was much stronger than their first three opponents. Ole Miss was held to only 27 yards rushing and 164 yards passing. Alabama gained 531 yards on 73 attempts for a 7.3 average. In over 100 years of football history, the Ole Miss defense had never been that porous. Johnny Musso led the Tide runners with 193 yards on twenty-two carries. He had a lot of support, with Ellis Beck gaining 88, Terry Davis 74, Joe Labue 72, Butch Hobson 51, and Steve Bisceglia 38 more.

Alabama was a much better conditioned football team than their opponent. Paul Bryant always used to say that his teams were in better shape and "would wear down their opponents in the fourth quarter."[274] Certainly the Rebels from Ole Miss would attest to that. Jim Simmons, the giant tight end for the Tide, recalled this some thirty years later:

> I got a big kick out of beating Ole Miss. Coach Bryant was such a genius when it came to being creative and catching the opposition off-guard. We lined up in a no-huddle against them that whole first series. I was talking to Reggie Dill, who was one of the starting linebackers for Ole Miss at the time... Reggie told me, "Man, have you ever in your life been as hot in a football game." I told him, "No, not on God's green earth have I ever been as hot as that." We both agreed. Reggie said that he and Johnny Chandler were alternating at linebacker all throughout the game. He told me that by the end of the third quarter, neither one of them wanted to go back in the game. They had had enough.[275]

One other surprise characterized the game. Most observers did not notice it at the time but it became more obvious years later. Ellis Beck observed some defensive tendencies that served him well during this period, but later the team had to make some adjustments:

By the time that we played Ole Miss, the fourth game of the season in 1971, the defensive secondary was trying to take us on when we blocked downfield, instead of trying to get around us or brushing us off. They would learn this later in this season and certainly the next two. Toward the end of that season, defensive backs were using their hands more and trying to keep on their feet instead of manhandling us. We eventually had to change our technique in response to that, but it was not the case in the Ole Miss game. It took a while before defenses could do anything with a good wishbone offense.[276]

WAS BAMA REALLY THAT GOOD?

Paul Bryant would sleep well on Saturday night after this big victory over Ole Miss. His next opponent would be the Vanderbilt Commodores. Vanderbilt had not been that strong in recent years, but they tended to play their best football against his Crimson Tide. The last time Alabama journeyed to Nashville, they lost to Vanderbilt 14-10 in a huge upset. Bryant would certainly be reminding his team of that score in the next week. He was determined that this would not happen again.

After the first elation of the win, Bryant had a chance to view the game films. By the time he appeared on his Sunday afternoon television show, he no longer sounded quite so happy. While he had a good track record, having had three national championships during the 1960s, he pointed out that his current team had done things that great football teams just don't do. Bryant explained this to Charley Thornton and the television audience. "It's very simple, great teams don't fumble the football or get penalties at the wrong time. Great teams don't allow a long run or long pass like we did Saturday. Those are the main things."[277] The Crimson Tide did have four fumbles against Ole Miss, but luckily they did not do much damage. One, however, did harm the Tide. After recovering a Rebel fumble at the Ole Miss 26, Bama fumbled it away all the way to midfield. Two plays later, Gene Allen ran in and out of Alabama defenders 48 yards for a touchdown. This tied the score at 6-6. These were the kinds of mistakes Alabama was going to have to cut out if they were to be a great team. Coach Bryant thought this team had the capacity to be great, but it was up to him and his coaching staff to minimize such shortcomings.

MORE HONORS FOR THE CRIMSON TIDE

On Monday the Alabama football team found out that they ranked fourth in the UPI poll and sixth in the AP ratings. Tom Surlas and Johnny Musso won the weekly honors as the most valuable lineman and back, respectively, from the Associated Press panel of Southeastern writers. Surlas, the senior linebacker from Mt. Pleasant, Pennsylvania, had played his best game of the best season, grading 93 percent on defense, recovering a fumble, and making tackles all over the field. Musso received the award for his 193-yard performance on twenty-two carries. He had tied the SEC record for career touchdowns with thirty-one on his 7-yard run at the end of the third quarter. Musso had also led the SEC in rushing with 440 yards on seventy-one carries for a 6.2-yard average through four games. Both of these stars knew the headlines would mean little when they journeyed to Nashville to face the Vanderbilt Commodores.

UPDATES FOR BAMA

Paul Spivey would not play this week against Vanderbilt. After passing out during the Old Miss game, Jimmy Rosser also had to stay in the infirmary and missed Monday's practice. However, he did practice during the remainder of the week and regained full strength. Offensive line coach Jimmy Sharpe could not say enough good things about the two-year starter from Birmingham and what he meant to the Crimson Tide:

> He gave it his all. We had played him too much during the first half. When he came to the sideline after we had lost the ball on a fumble, he was dizzy and weak. But he knew that we had to get the score, and he wanted to go back out there. He just got off the field before he passed out. He was lying there unconscious from heat prostration while the doctors tried to cool him off. The players came in and saw him there. In the second half, they all went out and took up where he had left off.... In his senior year he has really developed in the shadow of John Hannah into one of the real outstanding lineman in the league. He has been very consistent in his play so far. Being a senior and having the most experience of anybody on the line, he's sort of the patriarch of the flock. He seems to hold the guys together.[278]

Paul Bryant announced the captains for Saturday's game with Vanderbilt: Johnny Musso, Steve Higganbotham, and Greg Gantt.

VANDERBILT WILL BE A TOUGH TEST

On Monday afternoon Paul Bryant made his case that Vanderbilt might be the toughest opponent of the season so far. The theme of the week was "Man can climb over the highest mountain, but he can stumble over an ant hill."[279] Bryant wanted to make sure that his top-ten-ranked squad did not stumble against the Commodores. His team was listening, and they remembered what had happened two years ago. The Tide was fresh off a thrilling, nationally televised 33-32 victory over Ole Miss and came into Nashville 3-0 with visions of grandeur. Bryant pointed to the reasons this game would be a tough one: "They beat us two years ago, and they've got a lot more ability than they had then—twice as much, in fact. Coach Pace did a great job of getting his team ready to play. They beat us with inferior material. We expect them to be toughest game we've played so far on Saturday."[280]

Less sophisticated sports fans at the time might have thought Bryant was merely talking up his next opponent. On one level that was the case, but one has to consider that this was the SEC, and it was still relatively early in the season. Less talented teams like Vandy tend to play better earlier in the season before injuries and eagerness to finish the season take over. What occurred just two years earlier should have given the Tide more reason to listen to their well-seasoned skipper.

Mike Denson was the only Nashville native on the Crimson Tide squad. He was a reserve tackle who remembered what it had been like in his hometown when Vanderbilt had upset Alabama. "I was only a freshman at the time, and we were not allowed to play, but every time that I went home for the next few years were difficult. All these Vandy fans were giving me hell for that loss. I knew exactly what Coach Bryant was talking about concerning that loss."[281]

WHO ARE THE COMMODORES?

Alabama led in the series with Vanderbilt 27-17-4. However, the Crimson Tide was only 13-10-2 when the game was played in Nashville. Alabama was reminded all week what occurred the last time they went to the Music City. Vanderbilt was coming into this game with a 2-1-1 record. They had defeated Chattanooga 20-19 in their opener, tied Louisville the next week 0-0, blown out Mississippi State 49-19 in their third game, and lost a heartbreaker to Virginia 27-23 in last week's contest. Bill Pace was in his fifth season as head coach, and his overall record was 17-25-3 at Vandy. The Commodores ran a wishbone offense like Bama. Quarterback Steve Burger, tailback Jamie O'Rourke, and split end Gary Chesley would lead their offense. Burger had rushed for 102 yards on forty-five carries and passed for 309 more on twenty-seven completions. O'Rourke had tallied 181 on fifty-three carries for the Vanderbilt rushing attack. Chesley, Burger's best receiver, had caught eight passes for 94 yards for an 11.8-yard catch average.

The Commodores had a good kicking game. John Shaffler had punted the ball thirty-one times for a 41.5-yard average. Kicker Taylor Stokes had kicked all 10 extra points and missed his only field goal attempt. Alabama coaches rated their special teams as being excellent when describing their punt and kickoff coverage. Cornerback Doug Nettles had returned six kickoffs for 178 yards for nearly a 30-yard average and had run back one kickoff against Virginia 95 yards for a touchdown. Walter Overton, a wide receiver, had hauled in eleven punts for a 10.1-yard average and had also broken one for a touchdown.

Physically, this was the largest Vanderbilt team in history. Their offensive line of John Drake, Sandy Haury, Jim Avery, Charles Parrish, L. T. Southall, and Robert O'Neal averaged 6-foot-1.5 and 229 pounds. Drake and Haury were their best offensive linemen, and they both were two-year starters. Their defensive front five of John Carney, Mike Kirk, David Haun, Mark Ilgenfritz, and George Abernathy averaged 6-foot-2.5 and 225 pounds. Ilgenfritz and Abernathy were strong candidates for post-season honors, as was their senior captain John Carney.

The rest of the Vanderbilt defense had better-than-average speed, and it had been very good on occasion this season. The linebackers were adequate with Joe Wood and Joe Cook. Ken Stone and Doug Nettles led a strong secondary.

VAUGHT PICKS THE TIDE

Former Ole Miss Coach John Vaught wrote a weekly column that appeared in a number of Southeastern newspapers. In his column he admitted his shortcomings, particularly as they applied to the previous week's game with his Rebels. Vaught had nothing but praise for the Crimson Tide after their victory and predicted even greater success this week:

> I have often said that a successful coach is one agreeable to changing his mind. This philosophy most certainly includes the business of evaluating football teams. Alabama has made a believer out of me.... I was unaware of the potential of such an offense because of the national attention attracted by Texas and Oklahoma. Yet, as the afternoon wore on in Birmingham, it became even clearer that this particular Alabama attack creates tremendous problems defensively.... I pick Alabama over Vanderbilt and they will keep going strong.[282]

The oddsmakers agreed with Vaught and made Alabama a 28-point pick over Vanderbilt.

WAS VANDERBILT TOUGHER THAN EXPECTED?

Steve Williams received the opening kickoff at the 6-yard line and flew up the right sideline for 41 yards. Starting their first series near midfield, the Alabama offense struggled and had to punt after three plays. Vanderbilt did the same thing on offense, with the Tide getting the ball again on its 47-yard line. Again they could not move the football. The Vandy defense was cutting off the outside by overloading the ends and cornerbacks to stop the option from going wide. However, the Commodores could not do much better as they punted the ball away again to the Crimson Tide.

The third offensive series for Alabama was much better. They started running the ball more up the middle and were quite successful. It took Terry Davis and crew eleven plays to move 79 yards for the game's first score. They did not throw a pass during this drive. Johnny Musso broke the SEC career touchdown record with a 17-yard belly play up the middle for his thirty-second touchdown. After Bill Davis made the extra point, the Crimson Tide led 7-0 with 3:44 left in the half.

The Alabama defense was strong again on their third series, as they shut Vandy down after three plays. Again the Commodores were forced to punt. The Tide defense was extremely stingy, and it did not yield a first down during the first quarter. The Vanderbilt defense stiffened and forced the Tide to punt. Greg Gantt came in to punt for the third time and kicked the ball into the end zone for a touchback.

The Vandy offense was much more effective in its next series. Steve Burger led the Commodores to three first downs, one by running 18 yards on an option and passing another to Gary Chesley for 16 yards. The Alabama defense was penalized 15 yards for a facemask after Jamie O'Rourke had already run for another first down on a 13-yard gain. Vanderbilt had its first real threat going on Alabama's 29-yard line. The Bama defense dug down and stopped the Commodores on three consecutive plays. Taylor Stokes came in for Vanderbilt and attempted a 49-yard field goal only to see it fall short of the crossbars.

Alabama was stopped on its next offensive possession after making three first downs but bogged down and had to punt again. Gantt put Vanderbilt deep in their territory with a 50-yard punt on their own 12. After a 5-yard run up the middle, Steve Williams recovered an O'Rourke fumble on the Vandy 17. This time the Commodore stiffened and did allow a first down. Bill Davis kicked a 34-yard field goal to give the Crimson Tide a 10-0 lead with 4:35 left in the half. Davis added another field goal right before the half to make it 13-0 at the intermission.

SECOND-HALF BREAKOUT

Vanderbilt received the second-half kickoff and made one first down before they had to punt it away to Alabama. The Tide offense broke out of its first half "funk" and marched down the field 58 yards for its second touchdown. Terry Davis threw only one pass during this drive, a 14-yarder to David Bailey. Twelve plays later, Ellis Beck blasted over from the 1-yard line for the score. Johnny Musso took a pitch around the right side for the 2-point conversion to make it 21-0 with 4:17 left in the third quarter.

The next time the Commodore offense received the ball they were not able to do much, but they were aided when the Alabama defense roughed the punter on fourth down. They continued their drive only to have Robin Parkhouse, John Mitchell, and company stop them cold in their tracks. Jeff Beard made two strong plays in a row on Burger and forced a fumble on the Vanderbilt quarterback. Mitchell recovered it on the Alabama 32. The Vanderbilt offense was completely stymied by the Tide defense for the remainder of the game.

On the other hand, the Alabama offense was now starting to really pick up the tempo. Jim Simmons caught a 9-yard touchdown pass from Terry Davis toward the end of the third quarter, making the score 28-0 after three quarters of play. Davis made the kick. Butch Hobson and Johnny Sharpless relieved Davis for the rest of the game. Both did a good job of running and throwing the football. Sharpless scored a touchdown on an 11-yard run with less than a minute to go in the game. Sandwiched between these two touchdowns, Bobby McKinney ran 55 yards for another score on a punt return. Alabama substituted freely the rest of the game. They played sixty-two players in the 42-0 drubbing of Vanderbilt.

LOOK WHO'S NEXT

Paul Bryant was relieved to leave Nashville with a victory. His team had learned two years earlier that you could never take anything for granted. They had not "stumbled over an ant hill." Bryant hoped they were up for the team coming next, the Tennessee Volunteers. They were the Crimson Tide's second biggest rivals, having defeated Alabama four times in a row. Bryant had never before suffered such defeat and he was resolved to break this streak. Would his team be as resolute as its head coach?

Johnny Musso (22) laughs it up on the bench with John Mitchell (97) as Glenn Woodruff (7) tries to catch his breath. (Paul W. Bryant Museum)

Bryant directing his troops as Bobby McKinney (26) and Tommy Lusk (81) look on. (Paul W. Bryant Museum)

FOUR IN A ROW IS ENOUGH

THE SCORES OF THE LAST FOUR GAMES THE ALABAMA CRIMSON
Tide had played against the Tennessee Volunteers were 24-13, 10-9,
41-14, and 24-0, with all four in favor of the Volunteers. In Alabama's
seventy-seven years of collegiate football, only one other team had
defeated them four times in a row. One has to go back to the first decade
of the twentieth century, when Sewanee defeated them six times in a row.
In Bryant's twenty-five-year career, no team of his had been beaten by the
same opponent four times in a row until the Vols accomplished this feat
from 1967 to 1970. After the 1967 loss, Tom Siler of the *Knoxville News
Sentinel* thought he had just witnessed the beginning of the end for the
famous head coach: "Bryant lost more than a football game Saturday
afternoon on Legion Field. No more is he the Big Daddy of Dixie football. Throw away the jokes about walking on water. Sweep away the good
luck charms. Junk that old blue sweater which he always said brings good
fortune. That's all passé, cleaned out and no more… Bryant and
Alabama are stripped of the cloak of invincibility… And he isn't likely to
get another streak going, not at his age." [283] The total series with the Big
Orange and the Crimson Tide was tied at 23-23-7. Maybe Siler was right
when he asserted that Bryant had ceded the crown of Southern football
supremacy to the Tennessee Volunteers.

ALABAMA'S SERIES WITH TENNESSEE

The University of Alabama certainly had a football history with the University of Tennessee that was older than the rivalry with Auburn. They played eleven times between 1901 and 1913, the series resumed in 1928, and the two teams have been playing every year, usually on "The Third Saturday in October" as the well-known series is called. The series resurrected itself after Tennessee head coach Robert Neyland wanted to put Alabama back on the schedule so that his team could get some national recognition. Alabama had won national championships in 1925 and 1926. However, Bert Bank, long-time producer of the Alabama Radio Network and a former University of Alabama classmate of Bryant, remembered a time when the series was almost broken up:

> I can remember being at an SEC meeting in Birmingham right after it was announced that Paul Bryant was leaving Texas A&M to come to the University of Alabama. Bowden Wyatt was the football coach at Tennessee at the time, and Robert Neyland was the athletics director. I was sitting at a table across from them before the meeting started. Neyland told Wyatt that he ought to give some consideration about taking Alabama off their football schedule because of Bryant. Neyland told his head coach that when Bryant comes back to Alabama that he was going to be beating up on everybody in this league. Luckily for both schools, this did not happen.[284]

BRYANT'S HISTORY WITH THE VOLUNTEERS

Paul Bryant had played with a broken leg against Tennessee in the 1935 game. When he was a player at the University of Alabama, Bryant's teams won three games in a row from 1933 to 1935. Tennessee had also been a thorn in Bryant's side in his eight years at the University of Kentucky. During that period his record against the Vols and its famous coach, Robert Neyland, was 0-5-2. Arguably Tennessee cost Bryant's 1950 Kentucky team the national championship by defeating them 7-0 in a snowstorm in Knoxville during the last game of the season. Since Bryant returned to the Capstone, Tennessee had had more success than anybody else. His record was 5-6-2 against the Volunteers. His only vicotry against Tennessee was in 1953, the year after Neyland's resignation as coachIt was time to even things up and maybe even start a streak of his own. The Bear thought that his 1971 squad was up to the task.

NOTHING COUNTS NOW BUT THE VOLS

Paul Bryant would always say that nothing matters more than the next game, and this next game was upon him. On his Sunday afternoon show, the head coach complimented his squad for their 42-0 win against Vanderbilt, but he was really concerned about the Tennessee Volunteers. Bryant was looking forward when he said of his next opponent, "Tennessee is a physical team. They're big, strong, and quick. They're not fancy, but they could be. They're just doing what they have to do to win. It's a big challenge for us. I'm just glad we've got another chance at them. This is always one of the great games of the year and, if we do our part, this year's game should certainly continue that pattern."[285]

Tennessee ranked thirteenth in the UPI poll and fourteenth in the AP ratings. They were 3-1 with wins over the University of California at Santa Barbara (48-6), Florida (20-13), and Georgia Tech (10-6). Their lone loss was a 10-9 decision against Auburn. Bill Battle, a former Alabama-player who played for Bryant from 1960 to 1962, was coaching the Vols. He was a three-year starter at end and a member of the 1961 national championship team that replaced Doug Dickey after the 1969 season. His Volunteers went 11-1 in his first season and ranked fourth in both the AP and UPI polls in the final ratings of the season.

Richard Williamson was the Alabama assistant coach designated by Coach Bryant to come up with a game plan to defeat the Tennessee Volunteers. Williamson believed that the Tide would have to play their best if they intended to win Saturday's game at Legion Field. He knew how much beating Tennessee meant to his head coach, being another of the coaches who had been a member of the '61 championship squad. This was his second time around as an assistant for the Crimson Tide. He had been an offensive coach from 1963 to 1967 before coaching at Arkansas from 1968 to 1969. This time he came back as a defensive coach who worked primarily with the defensive ends. Bryant convinced his former wide receiver that he would be more likely to get a head-coaching job if he coached both sides of the football.[286] Williamson would later become a head coach at both the college and professional levels. He was highly complimentary of the Tennessee Volunteers when he filed the scouting report:

> Whenever you talk about fine football teams, you are usually talking about teams that have, first of all, a strong defense and secondly, sound kicking. Tennessee has both of these traits... And although the

Tennessee offense has not been awesome, it has been putting enough points on the board to win and it has been putting them where it counted.... Tennessee people think that they have the best three linebackers on one team in college football, and they can make a pretty good case of it. Jackie Walker, their captain, is outstanding. He's strong, tough, quick, and smart and will turn in big play after big play. Moreover, Ray Nettles and Jamie Rotella, like Walker, are returning starters. Safety Bobby Majors can beat you in a lot of ways.... George Hunt is the Tennessee place-kicker, and he can really boot them. He's extremely accurate and can hit them from a long way out. As always, Tennessee is well coached.[287]

TENNESSEE AND THE CRIMSON TIDE CONNECTION

Mike Denson, Mike Eckenrod, Benny Rippetoe, Chuck Strickland, and Tommy Lusk were the five Alabama football players from the state of Tennessee who would dress for the game. Most likely only two players from the Volunteer state would see action in the contest. Strickland was the only starter from Tennessee. Lusk would probably see quite a bit of action at either defensive end or weakside linebacker, being listed on the second team. The other three players were unlikely to get into the game.

Two days before the game a noteworthy story of the Tennessee connection appeared in the *Knoxville News Sentinel*, bearing the headline "Tide's Strickland Is Primed for Vols." This certainly was no big shocker of a headline given that Strickland was a starting linebacker for the Crimson Tide and a native of Chattanooga. However, Marvin West's story contained a few inaccuracies. It indicated that the Tennessee coaches had told Strickland's high school coach [Ray James] that he would never play football in the Southeastern Conference because they thought he was too slow to play in the SEC.[288] That part of the article was accurate. Furthermore, his coach was quoted as saying that Strickland wanted badly to be a "Volunteer" and only went to Alabama because they offered him a scholarship and Tennessee did not. Strickland claimed that this was never the case. The two schools he seriously considered outside of Alabama were Auburn and Georgia. He said, "Tennessee was never a serious option for me. I don't where they got that information. It certainly did not come from me."[289] One might feel that it would be shocking for anyone in Tennessee to think that any football player from the state would ever consider any school besides the

University of Tennessee. Yet this was an added incentive for the big line-backer to excel on the third Saturday in October.

Alabama had always recruited well from its bordering states. There were at least two reasons for this. First there was the lure to play for Paul Bryant, who was generally considered to be the best coach in the country at the time and arguably already a "legend" in the South. Second, and perhaps less important, Jim Goosetree and Ken Donahue were the two Tennessee links to the area. Both of these coaches were linked to the Neyland era of Tennessee football and grew up in Tennessee. Goosetree, from Clarksville, had been a trainer under Neyland. "Goose" was the only member of the Whitworth staff Bryant retained when he returned to his alma mater. "Keno," who hailed from Knoxville, had played for the legendary coach. Donahue also coached for the Vols for the five seasons from 1956 to 1960. He came to Alabama in 1964 from Mississippi State. Donahue believed that "his connection to General Neyland was the main reason that he wanted me. Coach Bryant wanted to know everything he could about Neyland. In addition, it did not hurt that I had known Jim Goosetree since my days at UT."[290] While Bryant did not have an official defensive coordinator in 1971, the de facto position belonged to Donahue. Goosetree was the primary Tennessee recruiter, but Donahue had done some recruiting there, too.

BRYANT NOT SHOWING TOO MUCH

Paul Bryant was not telling the press much during the week leading up to the Tennessee game. He did say on Monday that John Hannah missed practice because of a leg bruise, but he indicated that the big offensive lineman would play. On Friday he would not give any information concerning who was not going to be available to play. Bryant remarked to the media that he was not going to telegraph anything to the Volunteers. In regard to the injury situation, the Bear said to the gathered reporters at Thomas Field, "Let them find out Saturday who's hurt."[291] He was definitely keeping things close to the vest. The stress of losing four in a row to the Vols was showing on Bryant. However, he did announce the game captains: Johnny Musso, David Bailey, Jeff Beard, Steve Wade, and Steve Williams. Alabama was a 14-point favorite to defeat its old rival.

THE FIRST HALF IS DEFENSE AND TURNOVERS

The first half of the Tennessee-Alabama game was one in which the defenses out-performed the offenses. There were no first downs in the first eight minutes of the game. In addition, there were eight turnovers in the first half, five by Tennessee and three by Alabama. The Vols had three fumbles and two interceptions yielded by their offense. Bama had two fumbles and an interception. All of the points scored in this half were after turnovers. Alabama led 15-7 at the intermission. Bama gained 166 yards total offense, while the Volunteers had 99 total yards. Each team had eight offensive series during the first thirty minutes of the game. Neither offense was terribly effective. Tennessee had the ball for three plays or less on six of its eight offensive drives. Alabama had it for three plays or less on five of its eight offensive series.

Alabama scored first on its fourth series of the game after Curt Watson fumbled when hit hard by Jeff Beard. Terry Rowell recovered the ball at the Tennessee 22. Three plays later, Terry Davis hit David Bailey on a crossing pattern over the middle for a 20-yard touchdown pass. Bailey beat Vol linebacker Jackie Walker on the play. Bill Davis missed the extra point but Alabama led 6-0.

Tennessee scored on its sixth offensive possession by going 44 yards on six plays. Curt Watson scored the touchdown on a 2-yard plunge. George Hunt made the extra point to give the Volunteers a 1-point lead. The two key plays during the touchdown drive were on passes by Dennis Chadwick, one for 8 yards to George Silvey and another to Gary Theiler for 24 yards. Tennessee led 7-6 at the end of the first quarter. This was the first time all season that the Crimson Tide had trailed in a game.

Alabama finally started to get off track offensively in its last three possessions. In the first quarter, the Tennessee defense shut down the Tide offense. They were bunching up at the corners and completely shutting down the outside running game. Terry Davis remembered that the Volunteer defense was one of the factors involved, the other factor was the Crimson Tide sideline:

> The first half was a close game and normally Coach Bryant did not send in many plays. He had always told me if I don't like it, don't run it. Sometime in the first half, they starting running in a bunch of plays, and it was option-left and option-right. I was calling the plays that he sent in. Normally he did not do this, so I thought that he wanted to run these plays and we did. We kept one series after another with no suc-

cess. It was because their linebackers were cheating to the outside. I went to the sideline and Coach Crow met me coming off the field and he was furious. He said, "Davis, what in the hell is going on out there?" I told him that if he would let me call the damn plays, we would be all right. I then stopped and realized what I had said to him. I thought he was going to hit me right there on the sideline, but he didn't. I told him that I was sorry for what I was said. He said that it was okay, and that I was exactly right about calling the plays. After that, I called the plays for the rest of the half and the game.[292]

Following this exchange Alabama began to do much better in the last three series of the half. The first five series netted only 43 yards, while the next three series nearly tripled, gaining 123 yards. The Crimson Tide scored on two of these possessions. A poor pitch on an option play, which resulted in a fumble, stopped an Alabama drive on the Tennessee 10-yard line on the sixth possession, but there was a lot of consistency to the offense as they moved 65 yards in nine plays before the fumble.

The next series by the Alabama offense saw more consistency that led to a 27-yard field goal by Bill Davis to retake the lead at 9-7. The Alabama defense continued to make big plays, as Steve Higginbotham intercepted a Chadwick pass deep in Tennessee territory and gave the offense great field position at the Vol 17, with less than three minutes to go in the half. Terry Davis ran the ball three straight plays, while the Tennessee defense was concentrating on the halfbacks on the option. Terry scored on a 6-yard run just before the half. Again there was a problem on the exchange, and the extra point was no good. Bama led 15-7. The defense held Tennessee for three more plays as the half ended.

BRYANT'S ADMONITIONS

Bryant always told his team that there are a number of things that are important in a football game, and one of them is that there are usually four or five plays that decide a game. He said you need to be ready for every play because you do not know when it will occur. He also said that the last five minutes of a half and the first five minutes of the next half are very important to setting the tone for the winner of the game. Alabama would receive the kickoff to begin the second half.

COULD THE STREAK BE BROKEN?

Steve Williams took the second-half kickoff 55 yards to the Tennessee 42, and the senior sprinter just missed breaking away for a touchdown. Alabama was in good field position for their first offensive possession. Terry Davis and the Alabama offense took good advantage of the field position and scored eight plays later. Davis hit David Bailey in the right flat for 16 yards and a touchdown. This time Bama made the extra point and led 22-7.

The Tide defense took over for the rest of the quarter as they limited the Volunteers to just one first down in the third quarter. The first time Tennessee got the ball in the second half, the Vols netted 11 yards on three plays. This did, indeed, set the tone for the rest of the game. The entire defense was magnificent. A breakdown on a 57-yard pass midway through enabled the Vols to get inside the Bama 10. Curt Watson went 8 yards the next play to cut into the Alabama lead. Dennis Chadwick ran around left end on the extra point to make the score 22-15 with 7:28 left to play.

When the Bama offense surrendered the ball to the Volunteers after six plays, the Tide defense went right back to work. Tennessee got the ball back with three-and-a-half minutes to play and 80 yards ahead of them. Again they rose to the occasion. Chuck Strickland and Terry Rowell stopped Vol runners on the first two plays for two yards. This set up a third and 8 from the 22. Chadwick avoided a heavy Alabama rush, sprinted around the right end, and appeared headed for an apparent first down. Lanny Norris made a great open field tackle that left him 1 yard short. On fourth down, Haskel Stanback was stopped just a few inches short of a first down by John Mitchell and a host of Alabama defenders. This ended Tennessee's hopes with only a couple of minutes to play.

Alabama ran the ball three times for 8 yards. Bill Davis came in to seal the victory with a 39-yard field goal with only fifty-seven seconds left in the game. Tennessee would get the football one more time, but to no avail. They fumbled on the first snap, and the Crimson Tide recovered the football at the 5-yard line. Johnny Musso scored on the next play to extend the margin to 16 points. Davis made the extra point, making the final score 32-15.

OFFENSIVE AND DEFENSIVE STARS

The Alabama offense had come into the game averaging 432 yards per game but fell short of that number by getting 325 yards total offense. However, they did control the game by keeping the ball for eighty-one offensive plays to forty-nine for Tennessee. Two hundred eighty-three yards of that offense came on rushing plays. They also tallied seventeen first downs. Musso again led the rushing attack with 115 yards on twenty-two carries. He had a lot of help from Ellis Beck, who ran for 62 yards, and Joe Labue, who ran for 61 before a shoulder injury forced him out of the game in the third quarter. Wilbur Jackson replaced Labue and gained 25 yards against a stingy Volunteer defense. Terry Davis was only three for five passing for 42 yards, but two of them went to David Bailey for touchdowns. Bailey reflected on the difference between this Tennessee game and the previous two contests: "The ironic aspect of this change from a pro-style passing offense to a wishbone running offense was reflected in the Tennessee games. I caught twelve passes in each of the 1969 and 1970 games, and they whipped our ass. I catch two passes against them in my senior year and score two touchdowns. This time, we kicked their ass. All that mattered to me was winning. I did not care about individual statistics."[293]

The offensive line did a great job against the best three linebackers in the country. A couple of the unsung heroes in this Tennessee win were the "two Jimmys"—Grammer and Rosser. Both linemen were tired of losing to the Vols. What they both remember were their entanglements with All-American linebacker Jackie Walker. Grammer graded the highest of any of the offensive linemen in the game, and his main responsibility was Walker. He recalled, "The Tennessee game was a lot of hype, especially about me trying to block Jackie Walker. I'm not tooting my horn, but I graded 88 percent that game. Walker was the primary guy that I had to block."[294] Grammer also separated his shoulder. Rosser recalled a play in which the primary target was Walker. "Coach Sharpe had put in the Jackie Walker play. Of course, there was a nose guard on Jimmy Grammer, but his primary blocking assignment was on Walker. It was Jimmy's responsibility to stand him up on this play. After that I would hit him on the right side. Either Kraft or Hannah would come right after that and hit him from the other side. It was like a sandwich. We did this on other people that year, but it was called the "Jackie Walker play" after that."[295]

John Hannah was another Tide lineman who performed at a high level against Tennessee. Hannah had a Tennessee connection, having attended Baylor High School in Chattanooga. The Volunteers had made strenuous efforts to recruit him. What Hannah remembered about this game was actually not the game itself, but what happened afterwards: "It was about 120 degrees on the field that day. I remember talking to Jim Krapf, who was the player in the locker beside me in the locker room after the game. It was right after the prayer. I told him that I was feeling kind of dizzy. He told me to go see Goose, and that was all that I remember about that. The next thing that I remembered was I was packed in ice and I saw my brother David looking down at me. I had a 108-degree temperature. I was very fortunate to pull through this one."[296] Assistant trainer Sang Lyda remembered, "We packed him in ice and got some IVs going in him. It was a really scary situation. His temperature went extremely high."[297] Fortunately for Hannah and the Crimson Tide, John's temperature came down and he would play the next week. This was the second Alabama player this season that had overheated and had to be packed in ice.

The entire Alabama defense played a great game. They held Tennessee to just eight first downs and Bama yielded just 161 yards total offense, 62 in the second half. All-Southeastern Conference tailback Curt Watson was held to 24 yards on sixteen carries, his worst individual performance in his three years at Tennessee. Three Bama defenders—Jeff Beard, John Mitchell, and Steve Higginbotham—stood out in this 32-15 victory. Beard played his best game of the year, making one big play after another: "Tennessee was a big win for us. I had a great game and was wild-eyed for that one. I can still remember one of those slants and chasing their quarterback."[298]

John Mitchell had what was possibly his greatest game as a member of the Crimson Tide. He played on all the defensive snaps during the game. Mitchell and teammate Terry Rowell were involved on the big fourth-down play that sealed Alabama's victory in the last three minutes of the game. Mitchell remembered seeing the movie *Shaft* during the week of the game and how the Bama defense shafted the Volunteers by holding them to forty-nine offensive plays. "This victory was just great. We've got a team that's good enough to go undefeated. This was our big test. It's great playing with these guys. We have a heck of a defense and a lot of the credit has to go to the coaches."[299]

Higginbotham, a teammate of Beard's at Hueytown, also had a fabulous game, with two interceptions. He also graded 90 percent on his defensive performance. Higginbotham rated the significance of the Alabama victory: "The defense overall played well. It was as well as any game this year. That front four really did a job. It just has to be our best game of the year. Beating Southern Cal was great, but this one was better. This one was Tennessee."[300]

COACHES' CORNER

In the victorious Alabama locker room, Paul Bryant had to wait to talk to reporters following the 32-15 Tide victory that broke Tennessee's four-year winning streak. Before Bryant could address the media, trainer Jim Goosetree passed out cigars to the winning Alabama players. This had become a tradition for Goose after victories over the Vols. He also performed a little dance for the players celebrating a win over his alma mater. Coach Bryant made a few comments to his team before talking with reporters, and he was liberal in his praise: "Needless to say, I'm tremendously proud of our team, in spite of the fact that we made quite a few mistakes. I think Tennessee came well-prepared. Coach Battle and his staff did a good job making us run our strength against their strength, which made us do a lot of things that we didn't want to do... And I think, in spite of the fact that they scored two touchdowns against us, that our defense did a terrific job. They played a tremendous game."[301]

SILER'S MUSINGS

Knoxville sportswriter Tom Siler had been complimentary of Alabama throughout the season, especially after the victory over Southern California. Going into the Tennessee game he had ranked the Crimson Tide second in the nation in his own personal poll, but he was not ready to concede that Bryant and Alabama were headed for further greatness: "Alabama's undefeated Crimson Tide was ready to be taken, but Tennessee wasn't ready to take them. Alabama did not play like the national championship contender. Tennessee's moment of glory beckoned time and time again, but each time a horrible mistake cut them down. Tennessee had eight turnovers, four on fumbles and four on pass interceptions. Alabama had four turnovers and maybe it isn't a coincidence that the Tide doubled the score and got two points for good measure, 32-15."[302]

BRYANT BREATHES A SIGH OF RELIEF

After four straight losses to the Vols, Bryant was glad to get the Tennessee monkey off his back. He knew he would have only about twenty-four hours to savor this victory before he would have to start getting ready for the next game. There would also be no letup on the pressure, as it was not going to get any easier for the Crimson Tide. The Houston Cougars were coming up next and were looking for revenge for the previous season's 30-21 upset in the Astrodome. This vengeance-seeking team was not exactly the one Bryant wanted to face after the demanding Tennessee contest. As always, he carried the heaviest burden of responsibility for seeing that his team was prepared for the Cougars.

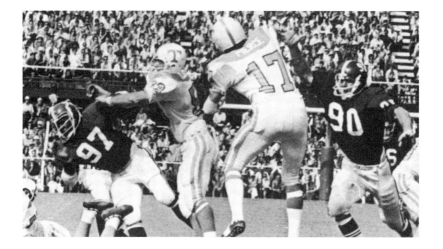

John Mitchell (97) and Robin Parkhouse (90) pressure Tennessee quarterback Phil Pierce on the "Third Saturday in October." (Paul W. Bryant Museum)

Ellis Beck (35) runs for daylight against the Volunteers of the University of Tennessee. Buddy Brown (65), John Hannah (73), and Jimmy Rosser (72) are helping the Alabama fullback. (Jimmy Rosser collection)

John Mitchell (97) and Lanny Norris (40) help the referee decide that the Crimson Tide recovered a fumble from a Tennessee ball carrier. (Paul W. Bryant Museum)

YOU HAD BETTER BE READY TO PLAY

THIS TEAM HAD GIVEN BRYANT A WIN OVER THE TENNESSEE
Volunteers, one for which he had waited four years. He knew that this
was going to be a very special team, but how special was still an unan-
swered question. When reporters began asking him how this team ranked
with his national championship teams, he still was not quite ready to put
this squad in that category. With injuries beginning to take their toll
going into the game against Houston, the Bear commented: "It's a little
early to compare them. Anyway, we won't be a national champion or any
other type of champions if I don't do a better job of teaching them.
Evidently, I've done a poor job so far because we made a lot of turnovers
and got penalized a lot. National champions don't get penalized and
fumble like that."[303]

The Bear often downplayed wins, even a big one against Tennessee.
He did not want his squad to become overconfident. Bryant had grown
up extremely poor and never forgot where he came from. He felt it was
his job to bring his players down to earth. In formulating these plans,
Bryant implored his players to "expect the unexpected." In this way the
veteran head coach made sure that his squad always had a plan to deal
with any situation. He did not want this team to take Houston for
granted.

Even though Paul Bryant was all smiles and confidence on his show on Sunday, he had a big worry on his mind—the upcoming contest at Denny Stadium with the Houston Cougars. Houston was one of those teams that would sneak up on you before you knew it. An extremely talented team, one-third of its starting players was black. Houston had integrated its athletics program in 1964 when they signed Warren McVea, about five years before the rest of the Southwestern Conference integrated.[304] Even though they were not a member of the conference until 1971, the players they recruited were from the same region. Houston got a jump on recruiting black players from the rest of the big Texas schools. It would take a great effort on the part of the Crimson Tide to defeat them, especially after the big win against Tennessee.

Bill Yeoman was coaching Houston, which had been 8-3 the previous season. This was Houston's first season in the Southwestern Conference (SWC). Before this they had been an independent. Alabama was Houston's biggest game of the year. The Cougars came into this game with a 4-1 record, their only loss having been to Arizona State 18-17 on a last-minute field goal. They had wins over Rice, Cincinnati, San Jose State, and Villanova. In their 42-9 win over Villanova, they gained 632 yards in total offense. This explosive team was not even ranked in the top twenty, but not because it was not worthy. Bryant knew this better than the pollsters. Alabama was considered to be a two-touchdown favorite.

In the handout the players received on Sunday about their upcoming opponent, Coach Bryant let them know that this was going to be a difficult game. The players would have to be mentally prepared to play a tough, physical game against a Houston team that was ready to beat them. After outlining their kicking game, which he called "outstanding," Bryant also evaluated the offense:

> Offensively they are explosive and can score anywhere on the field. Number 46 Robert Newhouse will be as good as any running back we play against. They have great ability at tight end in Riley Odum #86, split end Willie Roberts #2, flanker Pat Orchin #7, and Robert Ford #4. Gary Mullins #11 is their starting quarterback who is a great competitor, although he is still having trouble running with the ball. D. C. Nobles #3 is the second quarterback and looked good running the option and throwing against Villanova. He is extremely quick and he could play a lot against us.[305]

Pat Dye was the Alabama assistant coach in charge of scouting Houston. He echoed much of what Bryant had earlier said concerning the offense. Even though the defense had lost five starters to graduation, he believed they were strong and underrated. Dye reminded the players to think back to the prior year's contest in the Astrodome when the Crimson Tide upset the then-fifteenth-ranked Cougars. The linebacker coach reminded the players that Houston would love to do the same to the fourth-ranked Alabama squad this year:

> Defensively, Houston is big, strong, and physical. They all are football players and at least three of them are outstanding: defensive end Butch Brezina, who has a brother playing for the Atlanta Falcons; linebacker Frank Ditta, who made several All-American teams last year; and Nick Holm, who has five interceptions in Houston's first five games. At the first of the year it looked like they would have an inexperienced defense, but you can't tell it by the way they've been playing.... We can expect a real physical game from a highly motivated team because we are the biggest game on their schedule. We know from last year that they will hit you, and you can bet they haven't forgotten our upset win over them in the Astrodome.[306]

WILL THE CRIMSON TIDE BE READY?

On the eve of Saturday's afternoon game with Houston, Paul Bryant was singing the blues, worrying whether his team would be prepared. He told the reporters that yesterday's headlines had nothing to do with the current game, and that the Tide had better wake up if they intended to remain unbeaten.[307] Jimmy Grammer would not play because of his injured shoulder. Pat Raines would replace him in the starting lineup at center. Don Cokely would likely start in place of the ailing Jim Krapf if needed, but Krapf would probably be able to play. Bryant did name the captains for the game. Johnny Musso and Jack White would be the offensive captains, while Robin Parkhouse and Tom Surlas would captain the defense.

The captains were not nearly as pessimistic as their head coach. Musso said that Alabama would be ready to play by the time the game started at 1:30 on Saturday afternoon. "I don't think a team works hard and prepares for a game, then lets down on Saturday. A letdown comes when a team or player doesn't study films or prepare, and we're not letting down."[308]

White had been playing with the first team in practice during the last two weeks because of injuries to John Hannah. He also had gotten more playing time in the games. The extra snaps in practice had helped his preparation and timing. White liked his team's chances especially since they switched to the wishbone: "Pass protection just wasn't my bag. I wasn't cut out for that. But I like to go after a man and block, and the running game is just right for me."[309]

Robin Parkhouse knew it was up to him on the defensive side of the football to get the players ready to play. Going into the seventh game of the season he had no illusions what it meant to be undefeated and rank number four in the country. Parkhouse fully understood the importance of this game. He had come to the University of Alabama to have the opportunity to play for a champion. The senior defensive end knew that Houston would be a tough game, but he also believed that the Crimson Tide would be prepared. As he put it, "the games get bigger every week. Everyone is out to knock you off. That is the way it's going to be from here on out."[310]

Tom Surlas believed that the team's disappointing 6-5-1 record a season earlier would motivate them during the current campaign. Surlas was philosophical as he talked to reporters after practice: "This team is a lot closer than the one last year. We've got the right attitude to play, and you've got to have that to win. It's going to be hard for us to get beat now that we've gone this far."[311]

IS THE BEAR QUITTING?

In the middle of the week leading up to the Houston game, a rumor was floating around the Southeast that the Bear might retire after the 1971 season. An article titled "No Bear Facts" appeared in the *Knoxville New Sentinel*, and there was no byline on the story. The writer was merely referencing a comment that had appeared on an Atlanta television show. The station had stated that Bryant would retire after the 1971 campaign and that Bill Battle would replace him at the Capstone. Battle vehemently denied the rumors: "I don't know anybody who'd want to succeed Coach Bryant. Besides, no one has ever talked with me about going to Alabama. I like it fine at Tennessee."[312] There was no press coverage in the Alabama newspapers concerning this rumor. Subsequently there were no quotes attributed to Paul Bryant. One can only speculate as to the origin of this unverified story.

A REAL STRUGGLE

This game was much different from the one a week before. In the Tennessee game the offense had made four turnovers, and they had not executed as well as they had done in previous contests. The defense saved Bama in the Tennessee game by allowing only eight first downs and 162 yards. The reverse was true against the Houston Cougars. The offense performed almost mistake-free with no turnovers, and they had only one penalty called against them. They scored on their second and third possessions on drives of 50 and 62 yards. David Bailey caught a 25-yard pass for the third Alabama score of the first half. The Crimson Tide led 20-7 at the half.

Again Johnny Musso led the way for the Tide, as he picked up 123 yards on twenty-two carries and two touchdowns in the winning effort. He had good support from the offensive backfield with Beck gaining 66 yards, Labue 45, Bisceglia 44, and Terry Davis 27. Davis also completed five passes for 59 yards, two of them for touchdowns. David Bailey caught both touchdown passes in the Crimson Tide's winning effort.

The defense had to fight for their lives as the Cougars gained 418 yards, 300 of them on the ground. Robert Newhouse picked up 182 yards on twenty-two carries, while his running mate Tom Mozisek gained 105 yards in eighteen rushing attempts. Newhouse was listed at 5-foot-11 and 190 pounds but played much bigger than that. He was built very low to the ground and had enormous leg strength. Newhouse would later have a stellar career with the Dallas Cowboys as their starting fullback. Larry Norris remembered how difficult the player was to bring down. "Newhouse was like trying to tackle a conference table. You could never quite get a hold of him. He was the toughest running back that we faced that entire season."[313] Gary Mullins was fourteen of thirty for 118 yards passing and two touchdowns in the loss. Yet there were some bright spots for the Bama defense. Steve Higginbotham, Jeff Beard, Jeff Rouzie, and Tom Surlas all had strong games.

Higginbotham was the top defensive player of the game, graded 95 percent by the Alabama coaches. Higgs had ten individual tackles, four assists, and one interception. Two of those tackles came on 6-foot-4, 238-pound tight end Riley Odom. After his career with Houston, Odom was an All-Pro tight end with the Denver Broncos for a number of seasons. Tackling Odom was a remarkable feat for a 6-foot-1, 166-pound player who only gave up 3 inches and more than 70 pounds in this exchange. A comparable analogy was the Parkhouse-Vella match-up in the Southern California game. Higginbotham played much bigger than his physical attributes.

Jeff Beard graded 65 percent for his effort against Houston. He remembered that they had great talent but were inconsistent. Yet what Beard remembered most was his verbal banter with Gary Mullins. "The quarterback [Gary Mullins] had given me a hard time, because I came close to him several times when he kept saying, "You can't get me 77 because you are too slow," and these types of comments. Finally, I sacked him for a loss and asked him how he felt now being that I had just knocked him on his butt. He didn't have much to say about that."[314]

Alabama linebackers Rouzie and Surlas had good games against Houston, too. Rouzie was involved in twelve (8-4) total tackles, one for a four-yard loss, and he graded at a 66 percent level. Surlas was credited with ten (5-5) stops and deflected one pass in the victory. Surlas graded just below Rouzie at 65 percent, but both of these linebackers hit hard all day in helping the Tide defense to victory.

Houston out-gained Alabama in total yards 418-327, but when one considers kickoff and punt returns the numbers were much closer. The Tide gained 145 in return yards versus 84 for the Cougars. For the second week in a row, the kicking game played a prominent role in the victory. Bobby McKinney had a great day returning two punts for 81 yards and two kickoffs for 50 yards. A 64-yard punt return late in the third quarter to the Houston 9-yard line put Bama in great field position. It only took Musso one play to run it in from there. As it turned out, that was the winning score and it gave Alabama the lead at 26-7.

The Cougars did not roll over and quit. They drove 97 yards in ten plays to cut the lead to 26-14. Alabama returned the favor by going 69 yards in eleven plays for their final touchdown, and they extended the lead to 34-14. All of the eleven plays during this possession were running plays. Houston got the ball again, starting their next drive at the Bama 20. They drove 80 yards in eleven plays to score for the second straight series. Five of these plays were passes during this offensive possession. However, the Cougars stilled trailed 34-20. The score did not change again as the Crimson Tide defense bucked up and stopped Houston on their next two possessions. The final outcome moved Alabama to 7-0 for the season, while Houston dropped to 4-2.

Alabama defeated Houston 34-20 for their seventh straight victory of the season. This marked the Tide's thirty-seventh win in thirty-eight attempts at Denny Stadium during the Bryant regime. The game had been a real struggle for the Crimson Tide, as it had been as physical as the Southern California and Tennessee contests.

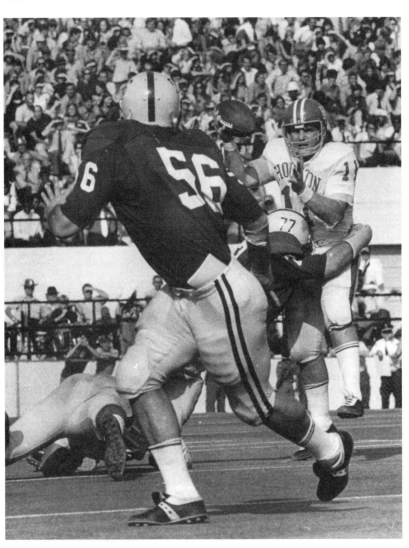

Jeff Beard (77) lowers the boom on Gary Mullins (11), the Houston quarterback. Mullins had earlier taunted Beard saying that he was too fat and slow to ever touch him. Beard had the last laugh in this exchange. Jeff Rouzie (56) is in the foreground defending for the Crimson Tide. (Jeff Beard collection)

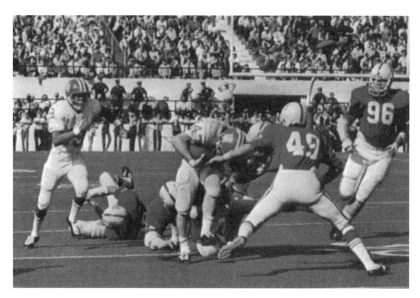

Steve Higginbotham (49) coming up to tackle a Houston running back. Jim Patterson (96) is running up from behind to assist him. (Paul W. Bryant Museum)

AND YEOMAN REMARKS

Many of Paul Bryant's post-game comments were negative, even though he was happy with the win. The negative remarks had to do with his defense. In fairness, Bryant knew that part of the problem with his defense was the great offensive performance by Houston. His offense was another story. In the locker room after the game, the Bear explained himself to the media:

> Our defense did not make any big plays. Houston carried it to us. They've got some offense. I'll tell you...I think that our offense did pretty well except for the time at the beginning of the second half when they should have taken it in for a score (clipping penalty). I don't know who blocked well. I know Johnny ran well as he always does. He had to get it inside where it's thick today. Beck and Biscelgia ran well, too. Terry operated the attack pretty well. I don't recall any bad pitches or bad mistakes that he made. He threw a couple of perfect long passes that our receivers just couldn't get to, so I guess I'd have to say that Terry did well. He would have done better, I'm sure if I'd left him alone.[315]

Bill Yeoman was not quite as demonstrative as the Alabama head coach. It was not his nature to explain things in the long, drawn-out manner that Bryant often did. A graduate of West Point, Yeoman usually conversed much more succinctly. He was extremely proud of his own players in spite of the loss. Many of the questions from reporters were about his preparation for the Crimson Tide and how they compared with Arizona State, another highly ranked opponent of the Cougars. Yeoman was straight on with his comments:

> They're a really good football team, very strong, and their offense was very effective. They did pretty much what we expected them to do. They're far better than they were last year. I don't think there's any comparison. I don't mean that in a negative way, but their defense is much better... Alabama is not as fast as State, but they've got more good people. They did what we expected them to do, but when you have good coaches, good personnel and execute well, you do what is expected of you.[316]

THE SAME AS LAST WEEK?

The circumstances were different, but Paul Bryant thought that perhaps his squad had "dodged a bullet" for the second week in a row. His Crimson Tide was now unbeaten in seven straight games. The last two games had taken their physical toll on his squad but the team would keep moving forward, traveling next to Jackson, Mississippi, to play the Bulldogs of Mississippi State. The Bulldogs were certainly no pushover, no matter what their record was.

Starkville, Mississippi, home of the Mississippi State Bulldogs, was only an hour-and-a-half's drive from Tuscaloosa. "State" (as people at the University of Alabama called the team) had been a member of the Southeastern Conference since its inception. Mississippi State had played Alabama every year since 1931 except for a one-year break in 1943 during World War II. The overall series was 42-10-3 in favor of the Crimson Tide. In football terms, it could be said that the Bulldogs were much farther away from the University of Alabama. When one looks below the surface during the Bryant era, however, another picture arises. While Bryant had won thirteen games in a row over the Bulldogs, many of these games were hard-hitting contests in which the better team just squeaked by with the victory. Six of the thirteen victories had been accomplished by seven points or less. Bryant believed that Mississippi State would be ready to play on Saturday night.

Alabama would be playing at 7:30 on Saturday night in Jackson, Mississippi. This was the second game of a doubleheader being played that day. Ole Miss would host LSU in the afternoon contest. The last three games played in the state of Mississippi between Alabama and Mississippi State had been played in the state's capital city, as Jackson Memorial Stadium had a larger seating capacity than Scott Field in Starkville. A near-capacity crowd of 43,000 was expected for the game. The game was played on natural grass, only the second time that season the Tide played on grass. The Crimson Tide was a three-touchdown favorite.

MISSISSIPPI STATE BREAKDOWN

Charlie Shira coached the Mississippi State Bulldogs, who were 2-5 coming into the game with Alabama. The Bulldogs wins had been over Florida and Lamar Tech. State had losses to Oklahoma State, Vanderbilt, Georgia, Florida State, and Tennessee. Tennessee was the best team they had played to date, and they had only lost 10-7 in that game.

Coming into this season it was thought that the defense would be the strong point for the Bulldogs. They had been 6-5 in 1970, and all of the defensive starters were returning in 1971. However, that was not been the case this season. In four of the five losses, the opponents averaged 34 points a game. On the other hand, they had yielded only 17 points in the last two weeks. Maybe the Bulldog defense was starting to play to their potential.

Defensively, Mississippi State ran a 4-4 formation. Jerry Conrad was their best defensive lineman at tackle. Chuck Dees and Billy Southward were the two best linebackers. Their cornerbacks were the strongest defensive positions. Frank Dowsing and Ken Phares were great cover cornerbacks and both had great speed. Dowsing had run a 9.5 in the 100-yard dash, and he was perhaps the fastest player in the SEC. Phares was not as fast as Dowsing but played the run better than his counterpart. Phares was fast enough to have returned a punt 90 yards in the Bulldog victory over Lamar Tech.

Offensively, State was primarily a running team. They had run the ball about twice as much as they had passed the football. Lewis Grubbs was their best running back. The quarterback position had been a revolving one. The Bulldogs had used four quarterbacks that season, and none had performed consistently enough to keep the offense moving down the field. Hal Chealander was most likely to be the starter in Saturday's night game. Chealander was a 6-foot-5, 225-pound junior college transfer from California. Should Chealander falter against the Crimson Tide, Bill Baker, Ronnie Everett, and Jerry Spraus could all see action in relief at quarterback. All had seen action that season and had played well on occasion. Tommy Strahan was their top wide receiver. He was only 5-foot-11, 170 pounds but had good speed. Strahan also had the best hands on the team.

Glenn Ellis and Lanny Sheffield led their kicking game. Ellis had scored 20 points as a kicker. He had hit four of six field goals and had only missed one of nine extra point attempts. Sheffield, the Bulldog punter, averaged 40 yards per kick in the first seven games of 1971.

BRYANT QUIET DURING THE WEEK

Paul Bryant was quieter than normal during the week of the Mississippi State game. He had stated earlier in the week that Alabama expected a tough game with the Bulldogs, but he said little else. On Wednesday Bryant announced the captains. Four of the five captains—Jack White, David Bailey, Terry Rowell, and Jim Simmons—were from the Magnolia State. Steve Higginbotham was the fifth captain. All four of the players who came from Mississippi had been game captains earlier in the season against Ole Miss. They talked to reporters after Wednesday's practice and echoed what the veteran head coach had said concerning their upcoming opponent. In addition, all of the players were now beginning to feel some pressure.

PRESSURE COMES WITH BEING A CHAMPION

White acknowledged that "there's pressure, that's for sure, and that's something that we haven't had in a couple of years." Bailey echoed White's concerns. "We're a good team and there is a lot of pressure and tension now that we've got a good chance for an undefeated season." Rowell was not as caught up in the moment as White and Bailey, explaining that "they're all big games now, and we've come this far. We can't afford to look ahead now. This team started out playing each game as if it were the only one, and that's the way it has been all the way." Simmons thought that playing at night was as much a concern as the pressure. He said that "waiting for a night game sometimes causes a little letdown because we all sit around and get bored watching television or something." Higginbotham, the only non-Mississippi captain, was not concerned with the pressure, considering the alternative of having no pressure. Higgs stated that "sure there is pressure, but everybody is working harder, too, now that we have a chance at a championship." Alabama had not been playing for championships this late in a season since 1966. All of these senior captains came to the University of Alabama to play for championships, something they had not experienced in their collegiate careers. The players knew what they were up against, and they welcomed the challenge.[317]

GAME CLOSER THAN THE SCORE

This time the defense saved the day for the Tide. They only allowed 39 rushing yards in thirty-four carries. The stubborn Alabama defense recovered four fumbles and intercepted three passes in the victory. Steve Higginbotham returned an interception 29 yards for a touchdown. The only Mississippi State touchdown came on an 80-yard punt return by Frank Dowsing. Glenn Ellis kicked a 41-yard field goal after recovering an Alabama fumble deep in Tide territory. The Alabama defense rebounded after last week's 400-plus yardage performance against Houston. Bryant was thrilled with this offering by the Crimson Tide defenders: "Mississippi State deserved better than they got. Their defense whipped our offense. I think that the defense won the football game for us. State got all of their points off of our offense, the punt return by Dowsing and the field goal after recovering a fumble. They did a great job on the punt return, but our coverage was terrible. We just fell right in the trap they set for us. I don't know who made the plays on defense, but I think everyone on defense played well."[318]

The offense played just good enough to win. It may have been their worst performance all season. One of the reasons for this was that State had proved to have a tenacious defense, which pretty much cut off the corner game for the Bama wishbone. The majority of yards were gained up the middle. Birmingham All-American Johnny Musso was limited by an elbow injury that had been bothering him for the past couple of weeks and gained only 69 yards on seventeen carries. Musso unfortunately suffered the additional injury of a bruised shoulder in the hard-hitting contest. Ellis Beck was the leading ground gainer for the Tide, with 78 yards on twelve carries. The second cause for the lackluster playing was injuries suffered by a number of players. The past three weeks had seen several offensive players absent from or limited in practice. Bryant reflected on this when he said, "We've gone back since the Tennessee game. We've been so crippled with injuries. We can't have any contact work. It's a lot different when you're out there learning on dummies all week and then have to go out and play against men. We had a lot of people hurt simple during the game because they were out-hitting us."[319]

A few bright spots on offense are worth noting. Greg Gantt punted the ball five times for a 52-yard average. Wayne Wheeler caught a 31-yard pass from Terry Davis. David Knapp and Glenn Woodruff scored their first career touchdowns for the Crimson Tide in the victory over the Bulldogs.

Alabama defeated Mississippi State 41-10 for their eighth consecutive victory. Even though in a number of statistical categories the Crimson Tide clearly defeated the Bulldogs, on further inspection the game was much closer than the score indicated. Bama doubled the number of first downs (18-9) and total yardage (362-170) on State, but it took 24 fourth-quarter points to provide the winning margin. The score was 17-10 after three quarters of play.

Charlie Shira did not have much to say to reporters following his team's 41-10 loss. He was short and to the point. "I thought we played well defensively, but we were on the field too much. I think when we did break down it was just a case of running out of gas. We gave the ball too much to a real good football team who took advantage of it."[320] Shira's reservation had less to do with the game itself than with an unrelated loss. The Mississippi head coach found out right after the game that his longtime friend and coaching associate Jim Pittman had died during the TCU-Baylor game. Pittman was the head coach at TCU and the father of former Alabama player Alec Pittman. Shira and Pittman had both been assistants for a number of years under Darrell Royal at the University of Texas.

BRYANT LOOKS FORWARD

Paul Bryant won the 207th game of his career on Saturday night. He tied Jess Neely for fourth place on the all-time victory list in college football. Bryant knew that it would take a much greater effort on the part of his troops to succeed in the next week's game. They would have to travel to Baton Rouge, Louisiana, to play the LSU Tigers in a nationally televised Saturday night contest. The Tigers were the defending SEC champions. This could be the toughest opponent the Crimson Tide would face all year. The pressure was tremendous.

THE WAR-AND-A-HALF AND MORE

PAUL BRYANT WAS LOOKING TO THE FUTURE WHEN HE APPEARED on his Sunday show. He just hoped his players realized that the next few weeks were going to be crucial to their futures. Bryant wanted to impress upon the players that their actions have consequences and that these consequences would follow them for the rest of their lives. Even though the players were young and had many years to pursue their future goals, what lay ahead of them in just the next month was critical. Bryant was philosophical when he claimed, "I don't know if they realize how much of a chance they have to do something big. I think that if they realized what they could do, they wouldn't sleep at night and would be waiting to practice four times a day. They have a long life ahead of them, but they have only four weeks to do the job."[321]

Bryant was mindful of what had just occurred as well as what was in front of his Crimson Tide. He apologized to the television audience for the 41-10 victory Alabama "won in spite of me."[322] The team was able to accomplish the win despite injuries to three frontline players, Steve Wade, Jimmy Rosser, and Johnny Musso. Wade injured his hand on the second play of the game and did not return. Rosser bruised his ribs but remained for half of the offensive snaps during the Tide victory. Musso injured his shoulder but played for the majority of the game. The status of all three players was uncertain.

One of the more complimentary parts of the Sunday show was Bryant's comments concerning a great block by Bubba Sawyer, which he got Charley Thornton to replay. While viewing this, Sawyer told an interesting story that coincided with the show: "All the players would always watch his show to see if he would say anything about them. I, along with Musso, had dates who watched it with us at the A-Club room in the Coliseum. When Coach Bryant singled me out with that great block, I about fell out of the chair that I was sitting in. I couldn't believe it. It made me feel like the best player in the world when he said that. What made it even better was that my girlfriend was there to hear it."[323]

LSU IS THE STRONGEST TEAM IN THE SEC

The Bayou Bengals from Louisiana State University were the defending SEC Champions. They had come within 5 points of the eventual national champion Nebraska in last year's Orange Bowl. The Tigers came into this Saturday-night clash with the Crimson Tide with a 5-2 record and ranked fifteenth in the nation. Their only losses were in their opener with Colorado 31-21 and the previous week's 24-22 loss to Ole Miss. In between those losses, LSU had won five in a row over Texas A&M, Wisconsin, Rice, Florida, and Kentucky. A former Bryant player at Kentucky, Charlie McClendon ("Cholly Mac" or "Charlie Mac" depending on who you talk to), coached LSU. He had won nearly 75 percent of his games in his nine years as head coach of the Bayou Bengals.

Mal Moore was the Tide assistant coach in charge of formulating the game plan against the Tigers, and he believed that this was the biggest test Alabama had faced all season. LSU also had the distinct advantage of playing this game on their home field. Tiger Stadium has a capacity of 67,510—certainly not the largest arena Alabama had ever played in but most likely the loudest, as the oval-shaped stadium sits right on top of the playing field. Opposing quarterbacks have trouble calling signals because of the noise of the always-raucous crowd, which gave the Tigers an edge.

In addition to the stadium advantage, this LSU squad had twelve starters returning from last year's 9-3 season. Eight of the players were on offense and four on defense. Assessing their offense, one must begin with their two fine quarterbacks, Paul Lyons and Bert Jones. Lyons, the starter, was the best runner of the two and could run the option well. He also had done an excellent job of executing play-action passes. Jones was his backup and would see plenty of action, as he was the better passer and had a very strong arm. Sometimes the two quarterbacks would alternate every other offensive series. Which one was in the game did not really matter. They had combined for 1,143 yards passing on 78 completions out of 159 attempts. LSU led the SEC in total offense, averaging 419.3 yards per game.

LSU had a number of good running backs and wide receivers. The Tigers had 1,792 yards on the ground during the first eight games of the season. They averaged 224 yards rushing per game. Art Cantrelle, their best running back, was a great inside runner and possessed great speed (9.8 seconds in the 100-yard dash) to get outside. Their best receiver was Andy Hamilton, who had broken many career-receiving records for the Bayou Bengals. Jimmy LeDoux backed up Hamilton at wingback and also would see a lot of action. LeDoux had 9.5 speed in the 100-yard dash. Both Cantrelle and Hamilton had been picked as pre-season All-SEC selections. Their veteran offensive line consisted of four seniors. Mike Demarie and Charles Stuart were three-year starters at guard and tackle. The Alabama defense would have their hands full.

The LSU defense during the McClendon era had always been the strong point of his teams. The defense had been known for its sound fundamentals, excellent pursuit, and gang tackling, and the 1971 team was no different.

The defense is just what you expect from LSU. They have a very well coached unit. The LSU lineman and linebackers have as good of techniques as you'll ever see on movement and gang tackling. Ron Estay is the best individual defensive lineman we'll play against this year. We expect Tommy Casanova [All-American safety who has been slowed by a back injury] to start against us. He's been out for several games, but he's a truly great football player when he is healthy.[324]

Casanova and linebacker Richard Picou returned to practice that week for the Tigers. Both were expected to start for LSU on Saturday night. The Crimson Tide offense would have to be at its best against this defense if they were to remain in contention for the national championship. This was the most powerful defense they had faced all year. LSU was likely to have seven or more players on their defensive front, daring Alabama to try to throw the ball.

TERRY DAVIS COMES HOME

Terry Davis was the leader of the Alabama offense who would attempt to better the LSU defense on Saturday night. He had grown up in Bogalusa, right in the middle of Tiger country. Bogalusa is on the Louisiana-Mississippi border, about an hour-and-a half's drive from Baton Rouge. Davis had followed LSU growing up and always figured that he would go there to play football. However, when Alabama came calling, the slender quarterback knew that he really wanted to play for the Crimson Tide. In his freshman class were five other quarterbacks who had signed with the Tide. Davis showed a great deal of perseverance during the three years he was forced to wait for an opportunity to really showcase his talents. With the switch to the wishbone, he had made the most of his chance for advancement. The Crimson Tide was 8-0, with Davis leading the offense. His feelings were high on the eve of his biggest game as a starter: "It's pretty important to me, of course. Being from Louisiana and knowing some of the guys on the other team, it'll be an exciting experience. And it's good to get back home anyway. I think we've been able to run against everybody that we played, so I think we can do it. We've been running all year and winning and there is no sense in changing now."[325]

OFFENSIVE CHANGES?

Even though the Alabama players and coaches had not talked to the press about any offensive changes for the LSU game, they certainly were preparing for some. Coach Bryant knew that the Tiger defense was the best they had faced all season, including Tennessee. He wanted to put a few wrinkles in the offense for the game in Baton Rouge. Bryant had Musso (who was pretty banged up physically) running at quarterback behind Davis throughout the week. He was fearful of the way LSU bunched their defense on the corners and how that might affect the Tide's running attack. They ran a 5-2 set and brought their safeties up on the inside to hit the quarterback. Coach Bryant feared this might take a physical toll on Davis, who only weighed 170 pounds. He wanted to be ready for this if it occurred. Bryant had scheduled to run Musso as quarterback in several series during the second quarter. By doing this, Bryant hoped to get the safeties to back off somewhat. This would give Alabama more offensive options.

TIDE READIES ITSELF FOR THE BENGALS

Paul Bryant continued the work for Saturday's clash with LSU. On Wednesday he named the captains for the game: Robin Parkhouse, Steve Higginbotham, Bubba Sawyer, Don Cokely, and Lanny Norris. He was very aware of his opponent's strengths and weaknesses.

Alabama was a touchdown favorite to remain undefeated against LSU. This was the first time since 1966 that the Tigers had been underdogs at home. ABC television would broadcast the game to a national television audience at 8:35 local time in central Alabama. Chris Shenkel and Bud Wilkinson would be the announcers for the prime-time football clash. In those days, still a decade away before ESPN, a team was usually not on television more than twice during a season, and ABC had the exclusive rights to college football during the 1970s. The rules that governed this arrangement stipulated a team could not appear on television more than five times during a two-year period. This would be the Crimson Tide's first showcase during the 1971 season.[326]

DESTINATION: BATON ROUGE, LOUISIANA

On Friday the Alabama football team flew to Baton Rouge. After checking in to the hotel, they got ready for their last practice at Tiger Stadium that night. The players loaded up as usual and rode the chartered buses to the stadium. When the team arrived, students surrounded the buses, yelling and screaming obscenities at the Crimson Tide players. Before the team exited the buses, Bryant went to talk with the students. Soon thereafter the students dispersed and the team was allowed to go on to their practice at the stadium. Jimmy Grammer remembered that the players felt this was "a real scary situation. The whole student body surrounded the bus when we got to the stadium. Coach Bryant came out and parted the waters. We knew that we were in for a tough time."[327] This was another instance in which Bryant's charisma and demeanor spoke volumes. This was coupled with the way that fans/students in the South viewed college football differently from the rest of the country. If this had happened in one of the large urban areas outside the South, the result might have been different. It could have very well turned violent, but luckily it did not.

Coach Bryant was mum on the Tide injury update. The three starters Steve Wade, Johnny Musso, and Jeff Rouzie were still ailing, and they were the ones the media wanted to know about.

On Friday night after practice the team watched, ironically enough, *The Undefeated* starring John Wayne, for the Crimson Tide was undefeated and clearly intended to stay that way. The team's hotel was water-ballooned by LSU students, a number of the balloons containing liquid other than water. John Hannah said, "A bunch of balloons with piss were thrown around me. It was not a pretty sight." These were just some of things that visiting teams had to put up with when they played in Baton Rouge. Many of the players on the 1971 squad understood what this experience was all about. The others would soon find out.

On Saturday morning Bryant, as a favor to McClendon, took part in a charity football game for muscular dystrophy that was staged by the Delta Tau Delta fraternity. Both coaches, along with former Oklahoma coach Bud Wilkinson, participated in the event. The final fifteen minutes of the competition took place in the stadium two hours before the game. The event raised several thousand dollars to help find a cure for the degenerative muscle disease.

GAME TIME

After warming up on the field, it was customary for the Alabama football team to go back to the locker room to hear a few comments by Coach Bryant. They would then run back onto the field approximately ten minutes before the start of the game. As the players began to leave the locker room and run onto the playing field, a most unexpected thing happened, one they would never forget. Wayne Adkinson and John Hannah were among the first players to come out the door. Adkinson recalled, "I was really fired up for this game. I was the first person out of the locker room getting ready to run into Tiger Stadium. As soon as the door opened, I saw this huge tiger [Mike II] right in front of me in a cage. He opened his mouth and growled loudly. It scared me to death. I almost peed in my pants. I was not expecting this."[328] Hannah was right behind Adkinson. After such a spectacular fright, Hannah was very reluctant to come out of the locker room. He remembered exactly what was going through his mind at the time: "I remember before the game standing besides the door. I was one of the first ones to run and did not know that they had that tiger up there. He jumped up in that cage right outside the door. I jumped back into the locker room. I told the other players that they could go out there, but not me. I thought the tiger was going to eat me up. It was unbelievable. It was the most scared in my life I had ever been."[329]

LSU won the coin toss and received the football. The Alabama defense was to set the tone for the first series of the game. Robin Parkhouse tackled Andy Hamilton, who had bobbled the ball on the first play for a 10-yard loss. In the two subsequent plays, the Tigers did not get back to the original line of scrimmage and they were forced to punt. The Crimson Tide received the ball with good field position at the LSU 46-yard line but could not do anything with it. The patterns continued, as the Tigers went three and out again on their next possession.

Alabama started their second offensive series on their own 37-yard line. Johnny Musso went outside the left end on his first carry of the game for a 19-yard gain. After 9 more yards by Terry Davis and Ellis Beck, Musso took the ball 18 more yards before Tommy Casanova knocked him out of bounds at the LSU 17. It was a vicious lick that temporarily knocked out the star tailback. He tried to get up but fell back to the ground. Musso finally got up and would only play one more offensive series before being sent to the locker room for the remainder of the first half. Jim Simmons recalled what actually happened on the play and his father's reaction after Musso was hit:

Johnny went out of bounds. When he did, Casanova grabbed him by the back of the jersey by the shoulder pads and slung him down. Johnny hit his head on a drain grate. After this happened, my daddy and uncle were in the stands, and got into a little altercation... My mother was also sitting with them. When Johnny got slammed down, all those Cajuns, who were pretty rough anyway, starting hollering, yelling, and the like. There was a lot of drinking and carrying on among those fans in the stands. Like I said, you would have to know my daddy. He jumped up and yelled back at them and told them that "it would take a dirty bunch of sons of bitches to cheer when one of these kids out there gets hurt." One of the LSU fans got up and told him that he "cheered when he got hurt." Daddy said back to him, "Well, you're a dirty son of a bitch." That guy did not say anything else. Everyone around there knew that daddy meant business. He was an old bulled-up guy who was not going to put up with that around him.[330]

Three plays later, Bill Davis kicked a 29-yard field goal to give Alabama a 3-0 lead with 7:21 remaining in the first quarter.

The third time the Tigers got the football, they made a mistake and the Bama defense tried to take advantage. Wayne Adkinson intercepted a Paul Lyon pass and returned it 10 yards to the Tiger 42. This put the Tide in good position again. With Musso sidelined, the quarterback experiment for the Crimson Tide was shelved. They were held to 6 yards in three plays and had to give up the ball. Greg Gantt punted the ball into the end zone for a touchback. This time LSU started to move the ball down field again. They went eight plays for 49 yards before being stopped at the Alabama 31. Jeff Beard caused Lyons to fumble the ball as Chuck Strickland recovered it. Bama gained only one first down before punting it away to the 6-yard line.

LSU was on the move again in their next offensive possession. They gained 28 yards on the first four plays to move to their own 34. After that the Alabama defense took over. Three consecutive losses that totaled 19 yards by Beard, Mitchell, and Parkhouse backed up the Tigers to their 15-yard line. Ronnie Estay punted for LSU for the third time in the game.

Alabama started their fifth series with the football at the Tiger 49-yard line. It took the Tide six plays to move 27 yards before Bill Davis came back onto the field to kick a 39-yard field goal to extend the lead to 6-0. The big play on this drive was a 16-yard run by Joe Labue around right end. What people remembered most about that play was not Labue's run but Paul Spivey's punishing block on Casanova that set up the run. Spivey said about the block, "What I recall about the LSU game was my block on their All-American safety. ABC Sports ran my block a number of times on their college football game advertising for the next several years. I still have people come up to me and tell me that they remember that block that I put on Casanova."[331]

The Tigers got the ball one more time before the half. Chris Dantin took the Alabama kickoff and ran it back 41 yards to the LSU 42-yard line. Only a shoestring tackle by Steve Williams kept the run from being a touchdown. Paul Lyons and company went to work. They drove the ball to the Tide 27 before a fourth-down stand by Parkhouse and Beard stopped the final drive before halftime. Alabama led at halftime by 6-0.

Terry Rowell (57) sacks LSU quarterback, Paul Lyons (16), in the fierce battle in Baton Rouge.
(Paul W. Bryant Museum)

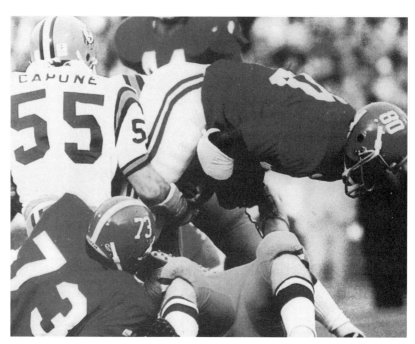

Wilbur Jackson (80) runs the ball against the LSU defense. John Hannah (73) helps lead the way for the talented Alabama running back. (Paul W. Bryant Museum)

Chuck Strickland (36), Robin Parkhouse (90), and Terry Rowell (57) bring down Art Cantrelle (24) of the LSU Tigers. (Paul W. Bryant Museum)

THE SECOND HALF

The final half was much like the first, with the defenses dominating the action between the two teams. The second time Alabama got the ball in this half, they went 52 yards in four plays to extend their lead. Just before the Crimson Tide scored, something strange occurred; as Jimmy Rosser recalled, "We had been driving down there for our second touchdown. Cholly Mac was running all the way down the sideline on each play. We're in our huddle and we glance over at their sideline and he is on his knees exhorting his defense to 'beat this guy one more time. Do it for me.' It didn't work because we scored on the next play. I just remember how weird it was seeing their head coach on his knees yelling at his defense this way."[332] Terry Davis went 16 yards on the right side to put the Tide up 12-0. Musso, now back in the game, took the ball into the end zone for the 2-point conversion to extend Bama's lead to 14-0.

LSU took the kickoff and drove 69 yards in sixteen plays to cut the lead in half. Paul Lyons led the Tigers on this drive. They made two critical third-down plays and another fourth-down conversion before Lyons hit Andy Hamilton in the end zone for a 7-yard touchdown pass. Jay Michaelson made the extra point to make the score 14-7. Alabama was pretty much held in check for the rest of the game, as they gained only 34 yards in the four offensive series after the touchdown. However, LSU kept coming at them.

The Tigers got the ball with 5:06 left in the game and hoped to tie the score. Bert Jones was now quarterbacking for LSU, who started this drive at their own 19-yard line. Jones moved LSU down the field with short passes to Hamilton and Allen Shorey. A pass interference call against the Tide put LSU on the Bama 38. On the next play, Steve Williams made a game-saving deflection at the 10-yard line on a halfback pass. Jones went back to pass on the next play only to have John Mitchell strip him of the ball at the 43. Wayne Hall recovered the fumble for Alabama with three minutes to go. Glenn Woodruff recalled that before that last series, Coach Bryant had had a heart-to-heart conversation with defensive tackle Jeff Beard: "Beard came over to Coach Bryant, who told him that he needed him one more time. Coach looked him right in the eye and asked Jeff if he could count on him. With a tear streaming down his face, Jeff told him that he could. I remember that Jeff went into the game and pressured Bert Jones a number of times during that series before John Mitchell cracked him on that last play."[333]LSU got the ball one more time with fifty-seven seconds left in the game. Parkhouse sacked Jones for an 8-yard loss on the first play from the LSU 20. The next pass was incomplete. On third down, Terry Rowell nailed the Tiger quarterback for a 2-yard loss to put in on the LSU 10-yard line. Jones hit Art Cantrelle for a pass over the middle for a 9-yard gain as time expired. Alabama had just won its ninth consecutive game by the score of 14-7 over the Bayou Bengals.

KEYS TO THE VICTORY

No mistakes, defense, and the kicking game were the keys to Alabama's ninth win of the season. While LSU nearly doubled the first downs (17-9) on the Tide, out-gained them 232-214 in total yards, and led in offensive plays, by 76-52, they still were not able to win the football game. All of Alabama's yards were gained on the ground, as they had thrown only three passes all night, none to completion. Johnny Musso's quarterback debut never took place because the Birmingham star missed the second quarter due to a concussion. He was also suffering from other injuries. However, Musso did lead the Tide in rushing with 61 yards on only five carries. Joe Labue and the rest of the Alabama backfield took up the slack in Musso's absence. Labue remembered what a tough game this was:

> It was a war and a half. Johnny got knocked out and they took him to the dressing room. Here he comes in the second half and he does not know what to do. In the wishbone, we were the high backs and would line up in the three-point stance. Terry would call the play and we'd break the huddle. Johnny would look at me and say "Joe, what do I do, what do I do?" I would tell him like, go to the right and take the pitch or whatever the play was. This went on the entire second half. I was talking to him and telling him what to do on every play.[334]

The Tigers had a much more balanced offense, gaining 157 yards on the ground and 75 passing. LSU committed five turnovers on three interceptions and two fumbles, while Bama made none.

The Crimson Tide defense made big play after big play. They had their best pass rush of the season. They sacked LSU quarterbacks eight times for 48 yards. Robin Parkhouse had three sacks, Jeff Beard and Terry Rowell two, and John Mitchell one. Jeff Rouzie and Tom Surlas had great games from the linebacker position. Rouzie, who played with a severely bruised shoulder, was in on sixteen tackles (10-6), while Surlas took part in fourteen stops (10-4). Wayne Adkinson, substituting for the injured Steve Wade, had his best game of the year. Cornerbacks Steve Higginbotham and Steve Williams all had stellar games against LSU.

Bill Davis, Greg Gantt, and the kicking team all had excellent games. Bill Davis kicked two field goals and added an extra point that gave Alabama their margin of victory. Greg Gantt punted the ball eight times for a 41.8-yard average. The Crimson Tide's kicking game was largely responsible for keeping LSU in bad field position all night. The Tiger's offensive possessions were at their 20-, 25-, 20-, 6-, and 42-yard lines in the first half. The second half was more of the same, as LSU took over at their 24-, 31-, 19-, 4-, 15-, and 20-yard lines. On Gantt's last punt of the night, he was instructed by the Tide coaches to try to pooch it inside the 10-yard line. When he went into the huddle, he knew that he was going to do something a little different. "When I came running out onto the field and looked at our offensive lineman, I knew that they had had enough. We decided between ourselves that I would kick it in the end zone because they were exhausted. It turned out all right in the end."[335]

ONE OF THE UNSUNG HEROES

A number of players contributed to this hard-fought win for the Alabama Crimson Tide. Needless to say, they are too numerous to mention. One player's contributions were hardly recognized in this game or any other in the 1971 season, even though he played in every game. Freddy Marshall was the designated snapper on extra points and field goals. The LSU game was the most memorable to him because of his children's memories of LSU games:

When I was a little boy growing up in Montgomery, I can remember my parents listening to the LSU-Alabama game on radio when I was eight or nine years old. My bedroom was upstairs, and I had to go to bed. I can remember putting my head to the floor and listening to them talk to each other as they were listening to the radio telecast. The next morning as we were eating breakfast, I told my mother that I heard part of that game that they were listening to and that I was going to the University of Alabama and play football for Bear Bryant and get to play against LSU. She just smiled and said, "I'm sure you are, Freddy." After we beat them 14-7 on national television, I called her from right outside our dressing room. I told her that I was reminding her what I had said many years ago about playing for Alabama and against LSU. As I was telling her, I almost broke down and cried because it meant so much to me.[336]

COACHES' EXPLANATIONS FOR THE BAMA WIN

Paul Bryant moved into fourth place all-time in victories with his 208th win. The Tide was now 9-0 for the season. Bryant was almost as tired as his exhausted team when he commented on why he thought they had won the game:

> I think it was a typical LSU game. Coach McClendon and his staff had them ready to play. They had the ball an awful lot. I think we made some big plays on defense and that was what won it for us.... I know that Wayne Adkinson came from a mile away to cover on that halfback pass they threw. Rowell and Parkhouse made some key plays, too. We played too many of our players too much, but you have to go with the best you have. Some of our people got tired in the fourth quarter.... We've got to get patched up and get our offense straightened out. Our defense gave us the ball enough that we should have scored, but LSU was just too tough for us.[337]

Charlie McClendon had just seen his own two-game winning streak over Bryant broken with the 14-7 Alabama victory. McClendon did not make any excuses for his team's loss:

> We played good enough to win, but I said before the game Alabama didn't make many mistakes, and we had to keep our mistakes to a minimum. Unfortunately, we had three important turnovers, and that's enough to beat you when you're playing a team like Alabama. Our defense was just sensational. They were right after them and contained them. After all, they held them to one touchdown. It's been a long time since anybody has held Alabama to only one touchdown. Our boys were ready and they did themselves proud. They never quit, even though we had a lot of bad breaks. Our field position was terrible virtually the entire game, but we stayed right in there...I'm proud of the Tigers, and they showed a national television audience what kind of stuff they're made of.[338]

WHAT NEXT?

Paul Bryant thought that the LSU game was the most physical game of the season. In this game he had played the fewest number of players in this game since the opener with Southern California. Only the 62-degree temperature saved the weary Alabama players. In preparation for Alabama's homecoming game, Bryant wanted to rest a few of his players during the next game with the Miami Hurricanes. Whether or not the wily head coach would be able to do so had a lot to do with the competition. Miami surely was not of LSU's caliber, but when a team is undefeated after nine games and ranked fourth in the country, all of their opponents are gunning for them. Bryant did not believe that the Hurricanes would back down from the Crimson Tide.

When he appeared on his Sunday afternoon show, the Bear was complimentary of his defense's efforts in the victory over LSU. The entire defense had played an excellent game. They had consistently made the big plays and cut the Tiger offense production to nearly half its normal output (232 yards compared to a 419.3-yard average). Bryant felt that the offense had gone backward in the past few games. Johnny Musso's injuries had certainly taken their toll on him as well as the offense. Without Musso this was still a good offense, but with him it was outstanding. Due to the concussion early in the game, Musso had carried the ball only five times for 61 yards. Coach Bryant called that "ridiculous."[339]

MONDAY'S GOOD AND BAD

On Monday sportswriters across the country agreed with Bryant's assessment of his team's defensive performance against LSU. Five of these players received weekly honors for the nationally televised Tide victory: Jeff Beard, John Mitchell, Robin Parkhouse, Terry Rowell, and Tom Surlas. The Associated Press honored Beard, who had played over the game with a broken hand, as the Southeastern outstanding defensive player of the week. United Press International noted Mitchell and Parkhouse for the same citation. The defensive ends had cut off the outside running game and harassed Tiger quarterbacks all night. Rowell received the same honor from the *Atlanta Journal-Constitution*, for he had been all over the field in perhaps his best game of the season. Finally, Surlas won the National Defensive Player of the Week award from *Sports Illustrated*. He had been in on fourteen tackles and graded 70 percent at his linebacking position. This was the highest grade of any of the Alabama linebackers, who all had outstanding games.

The bad news that came out of Monday's practice was the injury list. Bryant was forlorn as he discussed the long list of injured players, explaining, "We came out of the LSU game badly crippled. David Bailey, David McMakin, Johnny Musso, Jeff Beard, and Terry Rowell were all injured and unable to practice. Musso is the most seriously injured. The doctors don't think that Musso will be able to play before the Auburn game. Beard had surgery after the game. He is not likely to play this week."[340]

HOMECOMING WITH THE HURRICANES

Bryant immediately had to get on with the job of preparing his squad for the homecoming game against the Miami Hurricanes. He believed that this Miami team was as good as any he had faced during his career at the University of Alabama. He insisted however that his team would be ready to play on Saturday afternoon: "Miami is in a fine position as far as an upset goes. It's going to be difficult for us to get ourselves to play. On the other hand, if we realize how much we have at stake, we'll be all right."[341]

Miami had a 4-3 record coming into the homecoming clash with Alabama. They had wins over Wake Forest (29-10), Baylor (41-15), Navy (31-16), and Army (24-13). The losses were to Florida State 20-17 in the opener, 17-0 to Notre Dame, and 13-7 to North Carolina State the previous week. Fran Curci was in his first season as head coach of the Hurricanes.

John David Crow, the assistant coach who scouted the Hurricanes, prepared the game plan for Coach Bryant. Crow adamantly warned about the Tide being complacent just because this game fell between the LSU and Auburn games. He said that this Miami team was vastly improved over the prior year's 3-8 season, when Alabama had defeated them 32-8: "A lot of people seem to have the idea that Miami is some kind of an off-week for us because it comes between two real big games. Well our players had better believe that this is a big game, too, or everything that we've worked for this year will be down the drain. Miami is a sound football team fundamentally…Coach Fran Curci has instilled a lot of pride and made them a 60 minute football team."[342]

GAME CAPTAINS ASSURED OF NO BREAKDOWN

On Wednesday Paul Bryant announced the captains for the home-coming game with Miami: Johnny Musso, Robin Parkhouse, Jimmy Rosser, Steve Higginbotham, and Steve Williams. This was the last game the five seniors would ever be a part of in Tuscaloosa. Even though Musso would not play, Bryant felt that the star running back should still be a captain for his leadership contributions. Wilbur Jackson was going to make his first start for the University of Alabama in Musso's place.

Parkhouse, the top defensive end in the SEC, was certain that Bama would not look past Miami, telling the media assembled after Wednesday's practice, "We've got to get up for all of them now. They just keep getting bigger and bigger. We've got to realize we could be playing for a national championship. We'd better realize what it means. We're not looking ahead. We've got two weeks to get ready for Auburn. This game right now is just as big as the Auburn game."[343]

Rosser believed that Miami would be a tough challenge for the Crimson Tide. In addition, the offensive lineman thought Musso's absence could have a positive effect on the rest of the players because they knew how much Musso meant to this team. "Miami is a team that gets after their opponents. They've got a good ball club. I think the players will put more into it because of his absence."[344]

Higginbotham and Williams echoed what the other captains had said. Higgs added that "it's hard not to look to Auburn, but when you've got a national championship at stake, you concentrate more on each team."[345] The other senior cornerback had done a little bit of everything on defense and special teams. Whether it was making a big play in the open field on a tackle or a pass deflection, you could count on Steve Williams. The Moline, Illinois, native had been outstanding on the special teams, whether running the ball back or trying to block the kick, and this week would be no exception. Williams said that the Tide "would be ready for anything."[346]

PRE-GAME UPDATES

Bryant was circumspect as he talked to reporters after practice on the eve of the homecoming contest with Miami. He was tired of talking about how beat his team was. Yet the head coach did report on those players who would not play, and he named those who were questionable.

Of course, Bryant mentioned at the beginning of his comments that Musso would not play. Later he said that Jeff Beard would only play in an emergency. Joe Labue and Paul Spivey would be game-time decisions. Finally Bryant stated that Steve Wade would be returning that week after a foot injury had kept him off the field for nearly two weeks.

FIRST-HALF HIGHLIGHTS

After spotting the Hurricanes a field goal after a fumble on the first offensive play of the game by Biscelgia, the Tide roared back to take the lead on a nine-play 63-yard drive. Terry Davis went 22 yards around the end for the first touchdown of the day. Bill Davis kicked the extra point to put Alabama ahead by a score of 7-3 halfway through the first period. The Tide defense held Miami to three plays and out before Steve Williams blocked a punt. The offense took over in great field position at the Hurricane 27 but was unable to capitalize on the turnover. The Bama defense again held Miami, this time for six plays. It took the Tide offense only three plays to go 72 yards, which increased the lead to 13-3 with twelve seconds left in the first quarter. Jackson's 67-yard touchdown run made the difference. Bill Davis missed the extra point.

The second period was a defensive battle with Alabama coming out on top. Miami had the ball for four offensive possessions but the players were unable to make any headway against an aggressive Tide defense. The Hurricanes gained only three first downs during the quarter, all on their last possession. Jeff Rouzie and Terry Rowell led the Crimson Tide defense throughout the first half, allowing only 3 points. The Alabama offense was slowed during the second quarter, as they only had one meaningful drive that resulted in 3 points. Bill Davis kicked a 34-yard field goal with 3:02 left in the half to extend the lead to 16-3. The highlight of this scoring possession was Bisceglia's 39-yard run. At halftime the score remained at 16-3 in favor of the Crimson Tide.

SECOND HALF SIMILAR TO THE FIRST

The second half of the football game was very much like the first. Bobby McKinney returned a Miami punt 39 yards to put Alabama in excellent field position for their first offensive series. It took the Tide offense only four plays to go 22 yards for their third touchdown of the

Johnny Musso watches from the sideline in street clothes against the University of Miami. The All-American running back was resting his hurt foot before the Auburn game. (Paul W. Bryant Museum)

day. Terry Davis scooted 6 yards on an option around left end for the score. He also ran 3 yards as Bama went for 2 points after the touchdown. This widened the Alabama lead to 24-3 with 11:14 left in the third period.

The only serious Miami offensive threat was midway through the fourth quarter. John Croyle stripped Hurricane quarterback John Hornilbrook of the ball at the 15-yard line and Terry Rowell pounced on it before the Tide offense took over. Butch Hobson ran 10 yards for a touchdown, having replaced Davis late in the third quarter. After the extra-point kick was good, Alabama led 31-3 with 7:10 left in the game. Neither team scored after that, as the reserves finished up for both sides.

The Alabama defense picked up where they left off in the first half and shut out the Miami offense in the second half. It was another fine defensive effort by the Crimson Tide. Miami gained just 180 yards total offense during the entire game. Chuck Foreman, who would later be a star running back for the Minnesota Vikings, was the leading offensive performer for the Hurricanes, as he gained 61 tough yards on sixteen carries. Hornilbrook was only nine for nineteen passing for 71 yards. The Tide defense even amazed injured All-American tailback Johnny Musso. He was delighted with the defense's performance, even though his action was limited to cheerleader status on the sideline: "I thought our defense looked pretty good. I enjoyed watching them play. It was really the first time I've been able to watch the defense play."[347]

SECOND-TEAMERS LEAD THE WAY

Alabama cruised to its tenth straight victory 31-3 as the second-team running backs led the way. Wilbur Jackson, David Knapp, and Steve Bisceglia combined for 247 yards on thirty-three carries in leading the Crimson Tide to a homecoming win. The average-per-carry on these rushes was more than 7 yards. Jackson, subbing for Musso, gained 90 yards on thirteen carries, one a 67-yard touchdown jaunt at the end of the first quarter. Knapp, starting in place of Labue, rushed for 81 yards on twelve carries in his first start of the year. Bisceglia, playing in front of Ellis Beck, collected 76 yards in only eight attempts, one of which was a 39-yard burst up the middle late in the second quarter. As a team, Alabama gained 345 rushing yards to set a new conference single-season rushing record of 3,293 yards. This eclipsed the previous record of 3,068 set by the Tennessee Volunteers in 1961.

CURCI IMPRESSED WITH THE TIDE

Fran Curci made no excuses for his team's defeat. His Hurricanes evened their season's record at 4-4 after the Alabama loss. Curci did not mince words when describing how his Hurricanes had lost 31-3: "They were just too big and too tough for us. It was a mismatch all the way. We're trying to build a team, and we are just not a match for a team like Alabama yet. We've had a lot of people hurt, we don't have any depth, and we got more of our people hurt today. Alabama punishes you like Notre Dame. They come at you hard, and they just beat you down."[348]

DID BAMA DODGE A BULLET AGAIN?

With all the injuries surrounding the Crimson Tide, Paul Bryant was feeling less anxious in the winner's locker room after the homecoming win over Miami. It was his thirty-eighth win in thirty-nine tries at Denny Stadium. Much of the questioning from reporters concerned Auburn, not Miami, but Bryant was much more interested in talking about the Miami game. He had two weeks to think about Auburn, and the winning head coach illustrated this to the members of the fourth estate: "Fran had his team well prepared and before the game, I would have been happy to win by one point. I think our defense played real well.... Our offense sputtered around or maybe I should say that Miami was making us sputter around. We were getting people open on pass plays, but our quarterbacks would start scrambling around and running out of the pocket, and we didn't get anything done. I don't think that this was one of our better games."[349]

THE SEASON FINALE

Paul Bryant knew exactly what was next. It was the last game of the season with his biggest rival, the Auburn Tigers. Both teams were undefeated and ranked in the top five in the country. Bryant and Alabama had two weeks to get ready for this one, and they would need every bit of it given the number of injured players who needed to heal before the season finale at Legion Field in Birmingham. This was the Crimson Tide's first week off in the season. The team had lost the last two games against this vaunted rival, and they sure did not want to make it three. Bryant was going to make every effort for this one.

THIS IS THE BIGGEST GAME OF YOUR LIFE

THE ALABAMA HEAD COACH CALLED HIS NEXT OPPONENT, the Auburn Tigers, a "great team."[350] This game was for the championship of the SEC, and it would be the first time in history that two undefeated teams met on the last game of the season to determine the championship. Alabama was 10-0, Auburn 9-0. Bama had just defeated Miami 31-3 on Saturday. Auburn, then ranked number six, had just come off a 35-20 win over previously undefeated Georgia, then ranked number seven. With this loss Georgia dropped out of the race for the SEC championship. Both Alabama and Auburn would have an open week before the big game on November 27. The Crimson Tide ranked third in both polls; their cross-state rival ranked fourth in the UPI and fifth in the AP in the new ratings.

A WELL-DESERVED REST

There was not a formal team meeting on Sunday, and the players were told to continue their conditioning on their own. There were two reasons for this: first, there was an Elvis Presley concert at the Coleman Coliseum that afternoon, and second, the team had been given a reward for being 10-0. Coach Bryant felt that his team deserved a short break from the practice schedule before coming back on Tuesday for meetings with their position coaches. These were the players' first breaks from practice since the middle of August. During this recess the seniors also voted to play Nebraska in the Orange Bowl, but their decision would not be made public until Saturday, one week before the Auburn game. On Wednesday practices would resume for the biggest game of the season for the Alabama players. They would have a little more than a week and a half to prepare for the Auburn Tigers.

While some of the players enjoyed the free time, Bryant was fast at work in anticipation of the final regular-season game of the year. If the Crimson Tide were to prevail over its archrival, it would be because of "dedicated preparation and little things," claimed Bryant as he spoke to the Tuscaloosa Quarterback Club on Monday night.[351] He knew that over the season Auburn had shown great improvement and would be the biggest test to date that the Tide would face. The eyes of the college football world would be focused on Birmingham in twelve days, and it was up to Bryant and his coaching staff to see that the Tide was ready for the task. The Tigers would certainly be prepared for the upcoming clash, as the crafty head coach explained to the crowd assembled on Monday night: "Auburn can do all the big things. They have probably the greatest passing attack that's ever been. Pat Sullivan can beat you in more ways than any other quarterback I've ever seen. Auburn is a terrific team."[352]

BACK TO PRACTICE

On Wednesday the team returned to practice for the first time since their win over Miami. The workout was a spirited one, done in sweats. Eight injured players did not practice, but Bryant told the media that he was not going to talk about who was or was not going to play. However, he did say that Bama "needs to get some of the cripples back and needs to get quick" before the big game with Auburn. Coach Bryant played down rumors that his team had already decided to play in the Orange Bowl opposite top-ranked Nebraska. Bryant's focus was the game at hand: "We need to improve on the things we've done poorly and work on quickness. We're going to try to get ready for Auburn and let the administration handle the bowl, like always. I'd a lot rather beat Auburn, but it would be nice to do both."[353]

On Thursday and Friday practices continued for the Crimson Tide, who were readying themselves for the "Iron Bowl" that was now a week away. This name was given to the Alabama-Auburn football game because it was played annually in Birmingham, known for its steel mills. For at least part of the day on Saturday, the game had to take backstage to the freshmen game at Auburn. The Alabama freshmen defeated their counterparts on the "plains" 13-6 before a crowd of 15,000 at Cliff Hare Stadium. This was the one time during football season when the Bear gave the freshmen some well-deserved recognition. The players usually practiced by themselves or on the scout team. However, it was different when they played Auburn. Paul Spivey remembered that the prior season, when he was a freshman, Coach Bryant had talked to them only about the importance of their next opponent: "He came to the dorm and met with us separately from the varsity. We were all excited about this. Coach Bryant let us know in no uncertain terms that this was not just another game. This was Auburn. If we were going to play football for the University of Alabama, it was explained to us about this rivalry. We certainly knew it after this meeting. He had made it clear to us."[354]

The freshmen could now go back to helping the varsity get ready for Auburn. Their season was over, but the task of helping the upperclassmen prepare was not. When the freshman returned to campus after the game, university president David Mathews announced that Alabama had accepted an invitation to play the Nebraska Cornhuskers in the Orange Bowl at Miami, Florida, on January 1, 1972. If both teams won their final games, this game would be for the national championship. Nebraska had to beat the Oklahoma Sooners on Thanksgiving Day if they were to retain the top ranking in the country. The Sooners were also 10-0 and ranked number two in both polls. The college football season had come down to its final weekend, with the top-four-ranked teams playing each other. Meanwhile Auburn had accepted a bid to play Oklahoma in the Sugar Bowl in New Orleans.

THE SENIORS KNEW WHAT WAS AT STAKE

Only a quarter of the 1968 University of Alabama football freshman class was still there in 1971, and they were well aware of the magnitude of the upcoming game with the Auburn Tigers. Alabama had a history with this team. The seniors on the squad had not been able to defeat their cross-state rival in their last three tries. In two of the three games, Alabama had raced out in front, only to fade in the end. As freshmen, the Baby Tide had led 27-0 before Auburn stormed back to win 36-27 at

Denny Stadium. As sophomores, the Tigers had simply had too many weapons and outgunned Bama 49-26 at Legion Field. The last season had been another missed opportunity, as the Crimson Tide jumped out to a 17-0 lead midway through the second quarter. They were inside the Auburn 10-yard line before Tiger linebacker Ronnie Ross intercepted Scott Hunter's pass in the end zone to thwart the drive. After that interception, Pat Sullivan and Terry Beasley came roaring back to lead Auburn to a 33-28 win.

The seniors did not want to be remembered as the ones who never beat Auburn. They were determined to see a win this time. There were more than enough incentives at hand for the Tide seniors because they were playing for the state championship, the SEC championship, and a chance at the national championship on New Year's Day. Perhaps more than all of these reasons, they were playing for their own pride. A number of the seniors talked to the press over the weekend about what this game meant. Jimmy Rosser stated, "I imagine that not having beaten them really does mean something, especially living in this state. It means even more to me that I am a senior, and we have never beaten them."[355] Bubba Sawyer echoed what Rosser had said and more: "It means a great deal. I think we should have beaten them before, but we helped beat ourselves. I feel like we owe them something."[356] Steve Williams, the senior cornerback, was right on target in his slightly different assessment: "The biggest thing to me is that we've got a chance for a perfect record this year. There's much more at stake than just to say we've beaten them one time."[357] In addition, Alabama now had someone on their coaching staff who knew the Auburn personnel intimately, because he had been coaching there for the past five seasons. He also knew what was at stake in this game, having played for the Crimson Tide and the Bear. Assistant coach Bill "Brother" Oliver, who was in charge, knew these things.

BILL OLIVER AND AUBURN

Bill Oliver returned to the Capstone after an eight-year hiatus that included stops in Marietta, Georgia, and Guntersville, Alabama, where he had coached at the high-school level. He spent his next five years as an assistant coach for Ralph "Shug" Jordan at Auburn University. Oliver coached the defensive backs during his five seasons on the plains. In February he returned to his alma mater to do the same thing he had done for Auburn. His impact on the defensive backs was nothing less than spectacular, as they had all performed at an above-average to excellent level all year long. All of the defensive backs had nothing but praise for their position coach. Steve Wade illustrated why this was the case:

> Coach Oliver has made a whole lot of difference. Before he came, we were all tentative and afraid that we were going to make a mistake. When Bill Oliver came over from Auburn, he made it fun for us in the secondary. He would do little things that made the difference.... He helped us enjoy practice. He wouldn't demean you, and he respected you as a person. Coach Oliver was more like a father to us than anything else; when we made a mistake, you felt like you were letting you him down.[358]

"Brother" was trying to tone down any talk that he would be able to make any difference in the Auburn-Alabama game. He correctly pointed out that he was just one of the coaches, that the players played the game, not the coaches. Publicly Oliver was very respectful in his comments concerning his former employers. Any meaningful discussion of the Auburn football team must begin with its offense. The All-American tandem of Pat Sullivan and Terry Beasley led this offense. In the scouting report to the media, Oliver made this observation perfectly clear:

> When I was at Auburn, I said during his sophomore year that I wouldn't mind playing against him. I never said that when he was a junior. By then, it was obvious that he could do more things than any quarterback I've ever seen could. And what I'm building up to is the improvement that he has made from his junior year to now. As of today, he is the most poised quarterback in the United States. Of course, he's got Terry Beasley to throw to and having Terry on your team is the equivalent of playing with a 13 or 14 man squad on offense. He has so much ability— particularly great acceleration—that he will lure two or three extra people, leaving the defense vulnerable and allowing other Auburn players to perform well. He has strong speed [9.6 seconds in the 100-yard dash], quick speed, and great strength. He is a complete football player and it is easy to understand why he leads the conference in receiving. Their other receiver, Dick Schmaltz, is the most underrated receiver in the SEC. Beasley makes Schmaltz, Schmaltz makes Beasley, and Beasley and Smaltz make Pat Sullivan.... Auburn stretches a football field about as wide and long as you can. They present many problems to the defense.[359]

The Auburn defense was highly underrated. On the defensive line, Bob Brown and Tommy Yearout were their best lineman. Both were starters from a year ago, and the two were extremely quick. Yearout was an All-SEC player at defensive tackle. He was only 6-foot-0, 210 pounds but promised to cause problems for the Alabama offense. All four of the Auburn starters at linebackers were returning. Rick Chastain, Mike Flynn, Mike Neel, and John Hayworth were of average size and speed, but all were good hitters and unafraid of contact. Their secondary was strong with Johnny Simmons, Dave Beck, David Langner, and Phillip Gilchrist. Simmons and Beck were first-teamers in 1970.

David Beverly was one of the top punters in the SEC, averaging over 40 yards a punt. Gardner Jett handled the extra points and short field goals, while Roger Pruitt kicked off and took care of the long field goals. The kicking game was one of the strong points of any Shug Jordan team. Finally, it was no surprise to the Alabama coaches that Auburn was now undefeated.

Bill Oliver believed there would be a couple of keys to Alabama's winning the game. One would be to slow down the Auburn offense. In order to do this, the Tide defense would have to give up the short passes but not allow the big play from Sullivan, Beasley, and company. Secondly, Alabama would need to control the ball and keep it away from Auburn. The offense needed to do what they had done all season—run the football. If Bama could do that, they had a good chance of winning the game. They had done so ten times already that season, so why not once more?

REASONS FOR SUCCESS IN '71

Kirk McNair wrote a story that ran in the *Huntsville Times* the Sunday before the Auburn game. He related the story to the general public based on an interview he had done with Coach Bryant during the off week. The article offered a glimpse into Bryant's reasoning as to why this team had done so well:

1) We have more good football players than we have had in a long time,
2) New coach, Bob Tyler, who lives in the dorm and who is given much credit for the morale and leadership on the new team,
3) Coach Oliver,
4) A tough defense that was made tough because it had to practice against the wishbone offense,
5) Luck in personnel.[360]

On Monday, Paul Bryant had his first-team offense and defense practicing in sweats. There were just so many injuries to front-line players that the veteran head coach did not want to risk any more during the week of the biggest game in Southeastern Conference history. However, the rest of the squad practiced in full pads and even did some scrimmaging. A great deal of the press's injury discussion centered on Johnny Musso. He had tried to come back to practice too soon during the off week, and this was a mistake. Musso ended up on crutches for the rest of the week. While Bryant still evaded the media's questions regarding team injuries, on Monday he did give them some hints concerning his star running back: "Musso walked through about twenty minutes of plays. We don't know how it will affect him, but the doctor and Jim [Goosetree] will see how he does between today and tomorrow. If it doesn't delay his recovery, we'll let him do some more. Otherwise, we'll wait until Saturday to see whether he can get around or not."[361]

During the buildup to the game many of the stories that circulated through the Alabama press had to with the connections players on both teams had with each other. The connections were numerous since the majority of players on each roster were from the state of Alabama. No story got as much attention as the relationship between Johnny Musso and Pat Sullivan. Representative of this was the article "Musso Has Special Fan in AU's No. 7," written by Roy Riley of the *Birmingham Post-Herald*:

> Johnny Musso will have many fans Saturday when Auburn plays Musso's Alabama team in Legion Field. The great Bama runner deserves his cheers, and he'll get them. And one of his fans will be wearing Auburn blue. The number on the blue jersey is "7." It's worn by Pat Sullivan, Auburn's quarterback and long-time friend of Musso. "Gosh, I really hope Johnny plays a great game," Super Sully said earlier this week. "I hope he plays real good, just like he did against us last year. Johnny is real fine player and I have a lot of respect for him as a person, too. I am looking forward to the game. I hope Johnny is able to play and I hope he has a great game." Sullivan and Musso, from John Carroll and Banks respectively, have been friends since their boyhood days and they'll be playing their last regular season game in that wild one on Saturday.[362]

Tuesday's practice was just as Bryant had indicated it would be. The first team continued to dress in sweats while the rest of the squad wore full pads. Bryant still would not comment on the Alabama injury situation. Tuesday's big news was the announcement by the Associated Press of the 1971 All-Southeastern Conference football team. Seven Alabama players made the first team. On offense, they included Johnny Musso, John Hannah, Jim Krapf, and David Bailey. Robin Parkhouse, Steve Higginbotham, and Tom Surlas were listed on the first-team defensive squad. Jimmy Grammer and Jeff Rouzie were on the second team.

On Wednesday and Thursday the Tide continued with their preparations for Auburn. The team ate a big Thanksgiving lunch at Bryant Hall on Thursday. After practice they huddled around the dormitory's color television to watch the Nebraska-Oklahoma game, which Nebraska won 35-31 in the match-up between the first- and second-ranked teams and in the country. At the conclusion of the game, the Downtown Athletic Club of New York announced the winner of the Heisman Trophy, Pat Sullivan of the Auburn Tigers. Johnny Musso finished fourth in the balloting for the prestigious award. Cornell's Ed Marinaro and Oklahoma's Greg Pruitt were sandwiched between the Birmingham natives in the voting by the college football media. Former winners of the Heisman had also participated in the voting. John David Crow had indicated a couple weeks earlier that he had voted for the top running back of the Crimson Tide.

Much of the media's speculation continued to center on whether or not Johnny Musso would be ready to play on Saturday. Bryant still was not talking publicly, but privately something else was going on. Jim Goosetree and the training staff had been treating Musso's injuries several times daily with the hope of readying the All-American for his last regular-season contest. Sang Lyda explained what the training regimen involved:

> Coach Goosetree had built a brace to go around Johnny's toe. The problem with the brace was with his shoe going over it. We had to put a shoe two sizes bigger than his regular size to fit with the brace. In addition, we were treating him in a number of different ways. They included ultrasound, heat, and icing treatments. We were not allowing him to practice but did let him ride a stationary bike to help keep his wind up. On Friday we let him run with the team in their last workout before the game. Musso seemed to do fine. We were confident that he would ready to play on Saturday.[363]

On Friday both teams went through light workouts at Legion Field in Birmingham. Forecasters from all over the country were focusing on the "Steel City," making their predictions. The national writers, among them the Associated Press and *Sports Illustrated*, tended to side with Alabama while the regional writers slightly favored the Tigers.[364] The sportswriters from both the *Birmingham Post-Herald* (4-3)[365] and the *Birmingham News* (9-7)[366] predicted that Auburn would win their third straight over Alabama. The national oddsmakers made Alabama 3 1/2-point favorites despite what those closest to the scene prognosticated. Johnny Vaught picked the Tide to roll, explaining, "Bear Bryant will have his full complement of players in there, and my decision is based on Alabama's defense and personnel."[367]

On Saturday morning after the team breakfast, the players got their ankles taped before they went to the stadium. This time was a little different. Jeff Beard was very apprehensive when he realized that he had left his lucky white belt back in his room at Bryant Hall. Jack White, his roommate, explained: "Jeff was very superstitious. He always had this white belt that he wore. On the Auburn trip, Beard had left his white belt back at the dorm in Tuscaloosa. He was panicking and didn't know what to do. The police radioed down to the campus police in Tuscaloosa; they went to his room, got his white belt, and brought it to him in Birmingham. Jeff was quite relieved."[368]

HOW THE TEAMS/SCHOOLS MATCH UP

Popular folklore in the state of Alabama led many to believe that the University of Alabama was home to the vast majority of lawyers, doctors, politicians, prominent business people, and the wealthy, while Auburn University was home to the state's farmers, agricultural types, and working-class people. While historically speaking there was some truth to the myth, by the early 1970s both schools had had their share of successful graduates in all fields. The class and political divisions that had separated the two schools were fading as were the differences between the football teams.

Auburn led the SEC in total offense with an average of 393.7 yards and 34 points per game. Alabama was third in total offense with an average of 361 yards and 33.1 points per game. Alabama ranked first in the conference in total defense, allowing 223.8 yards and only 7.7 points per contest. Historically speaking, the series was almost dead even. The two teams had played thirty-five times each since 1893 and only .3 of a point separated the schools in this series. The series has been played every year since 1948. Alabama has averaged 16.1 points per game while Auburn has been right behind at 15.8 points per game. The Crimson Tide had an 18-16-1 record over the Tigers in this famous rivalry. The Bear had been 9-4 since returning to his alma mater in 1958, and Shug had an 8-12 record against Alabama during his twenty years as head coach of the Tigers.

ROLL TIDE OR WAR EAGLE?

Auburn won the toss and received the football. Greg Gantt kicked it deep into the end zone. The Tigers' first offensive possession started from their 20-yard line after the touchback. The Alabama defense held them to 9 yards and David Beverly went back to punt for Auburn. The snap from center was bounced back to Beverly, who fumbled for the first turnover of the game.

Alabama took over at the Tiger 20, and it only took five plays to score the first touchdown. Johnny Musso was fine and carried the ball once during the drive for 4 yards. Terry Davis ran for 16 of the 20 yards. He scored a touchdown around left end on an option play. Bill Davis made the extra point and Alabama led 7-0 with 10:43 left in the first quarter.

The second series for Auburn was similar to the first, except this time they did make one first down on a 16-yard pass play over the middle to Terry Beasley. The Tide defense stiffened and stopped the drive on their 41-yard line. Again Beverly went back to punt and did much better this time by punting it into the end zone. However, the punt was almost blocked by a couple of Bama defenders who came blowing in from Auburn's right side.

Alabama went to work again, this time 80 yards from the opponent's goal line. They marched down the field in businesslike fashion, running the ball twelve of the next thirteen plays before Davis scored his second touchdown of the game. The one pass play was a 17-yard hitch to Joe Labue. This was just one example of the number of new offensive plays Mal Moore had developed for this game. Labue lined wide-left directly behind the pass receiver on that side of the field. In addition, Musso ran the ball five times for 32 yards during the drive and showed no sign of the painful toe injury that had slowed him for the past several weeks. The

Crimson Tide held the ball for nearly seven minutes and led 14-0 with fifty-eight seconds left in the first quarter.

Auburn began their third offensive series at their 30-yard line. This time, however, they started to click. Sullivan completed a couple of short passes for 5 yards or less before he hooked up with Beasley on the first play of the second quarter with a 40-yard strike. The Tigers were now on Alabama's 29-yard line. The Tide defense rose to the occasion and held Auburn to just 4 yards on the next four plays. Terry Rowell recovered a fumble by Harry Unger on the 26. However, Ellis Beck fumbled on the next play and Auburn got the ball back. The Tigers got on the scoreboard on an option pass from Unger to Terry Beasley in just one play that covered 31 yards. Gardner Jett kicked the extra point and cut the Alabama lead in half to 14-7 with 13:08 left in the half.

The Crimson Tide started their fourth possession at their own 32-yard line after a 24-yard kickoff return by Bobby McKinney. The offense strung together three first downs before surrendering the ball on a fumbled pitch by Davis in Auburn territory at the 37. Before the fumble, Davis and Musso had combined for 36 yards on the drive. All the yards were on the ground except for one 10-yard pass on a quick slant to David Bailey.

A ferocious Alabama defense halted the next two offensive drives by Auburn. They went three plays and out in two consecutive series. Steve Higginbotham broke up two passes, making up for the defensive lapse on the touchdown pass earlier in the quarter. The defensive line had great surges on these possessions and forced Sullivan to hurry his passes.

The Bama offense failed to convert after three plays and punted on their fifth possession as the Tigers had done. They got the ball again with 4:40 to play in the half. This time they did much better, though they did not score. The Alabama offense held the ball for twelve plays before their drive was halted at the Auburn 14-yard line. Bill Davis missed a 31-yard field goal as the buzzer sounded, ending the first half of play.

The score was somewhat misleading at halftime, with Alabama leading 14-7. The Crimson Tide had completely dominated the statistics during the first half. They had led thirteen to four in first downs and 224-111 in total yards. Auburn had gained 71 yards on two plays. Both teams had had two turnovers. Sullivan and Beasley had been held in check for the first thirty minutes. It would be up to the Alabama defense to see that trend continued if the Tide were to break the losing streak.

WOULD AUBURN COMEBACK
FOR THE THIRD TIME IN FOUR YEARS?

Alabama led statistically and certainly kept the ball away from Sullivan and Beasley. They had controlled the line of scrimmage and doubled the output of their opponents but only led by a touchdown. From the Auburn perspective, one could say that this had been their worst offensive performance of the season, even though they were only behind by 7 points. Of course, the Tigers knew from previous experience that once their offense got in sync, anything was possible. They had fallen behind Alabama before, only to roar back and win the game. Would 1971 be any different?

Alabama started the second half at their own 16-yard line. Their first series was similar to the last one of the first half. They had the ball for a long time but did not score. The Crimson Tide held the ball for the first six minutes and forty seconds of the third quarter. They ran thirteen plays and gained four first downs before surrendering the ball to Auburn. Greg Gantt's punt went 47 yards before landing at the 1-yard line surrounded by five Crimson Tide players.

Auburn got out of a big hole by making two first downs before having to punt the ball away from their own 32-yard line. Sullivan completed four passes during the possession, but none was over 8 yards. Steve Williams and Steve Higginbotham were covering the Tiger receivers as if they owned them. As soon as an Auburn receiver caught the ball, he was immediately tackled. Robin Parkhouse and Jeff Beard made a couple of big plays during this drive, each batting down a Sullivan pass in this series.

The Crimson Tide began their next possession on their own 22-yard line after a Bobby McKinney fair catch. Again they played keep-away from the powerful Auburn offense. They held the ball for over 6 minutes before Bill Davis kicked a 41-yard field goal with 13:03 left to play in the game. This drive was just a repeat of the last one. Alabama had run the ball eleven out of twelve plays before the Davis field goal. Musso was spectacular on this drive, carrying the ball six times for 44 yards. As the game entered the final quarter, the much smaller Auburn defense was starting to wear down while the Alabama defense was just hitting its stride.

The Tigers got the ball for the second time in the half with thirteen minutes left in the fourth quarter. They only had the football for one play before Chuck Strickland intercepted a pass from a hurried Pat Sullivan and ran it back to the 7-yard line. After a 5-yard penalty for illegal procedure, Musso took the pitch from Terry Davis around right end for 12 yards to extend the Bama lead. Bill Davis kicked the extra point to make the score 24-7.

The vaunted Auburn offense had a little over twelve-and-a-half minutes to come back on their bitter rival. They had done it before against the Crimson Tide and only time would tell if they could do it again. On the first play, Auburn gained 3 yards on a rushing play-off tackle. Sullivan missed on the next two passes under a strong rush by the Alabama defense. The Tigers were forced to punt it.

The Bama offense picked up right where they left off. It was Musso right and left with a little Labue and Biscelgia mixed in between. Terry Davis also completed three passes for 34 yards during this possession. However, the drive stalled as the "Italian Stallion" fumbled at the goal line, and Auburn recovered the ball in the end zone. This was only Musso's second fumble of the season.

The clock now showed now just over four minutes to play as Auburn went back to work offensively. Sullivan completed two passes in a row, one for 9 yards and the other for 7. Jeff Rouzie intercepted Sullivan's third pass of the drive and ran it down to the Auburn 5-yard line. It took Musso only one play to run 5 yards for a touchdown, erasing the memory of his last carry. The Crimson Tide was in complete control, leading 31-7 with 3:33 left in the regular season.

The Bama defense held Auburn to four plays and one first down before giving the ball back to the offense one last time. It took the Tide offense only four plays to run out the clock. The final score was Alabama 31, Auburn 7, and the Tide players carried their victorious head coach off the field on their shoulders. In the midst of all this celebrating someone even stole Coach Bryant's houndstooth hat in the hubris after the game, but a valiant recovery effort by one of the assistant coaches saved the day. Jack Rutledge ran down the offender and retrieved the hat before the winning team went to the locker room.

THE NUMBERS TELL THE STORY

Both the offense and defense were responsible for the Crimson Tide's 31-7 victory. The offense controlled the ball for nearly 42 minutes (41:49) compared to a little over 18 minutes (18:11) for Sullivan and Beasley. Bama was able to keep the ball away from the high-powered

Auburn offense, which had averaged over 34 points and almost 400 yards total offense. This was the lowest offensive output of Pat Sullivan's career at Auburn. The Bama defense held their archrival to three plays and out in five of eleven possessions. The Tigers were able to gain a mere 68 yards and three first downs in the second half. Alabama had twenty-four first downs compared to seven for the Tigers. The Tide gained 400 yards total offense to Auburn's 179. Both teams had three turnovers. The game was nearly penalty-free, as the Tide was penalized for 30 yards and the Tigers only 10. Any way one looks at this game, Alabama completely dominated both lines of scrimmage.

Offensively, the big stars for the Crimson Tide were the same ones who had been in the forefront all year long. Johnny Musso was brilliant, especially considering how little he had practiced in the three weeks leading up to this game. He gained 167 yards on thirty-three carries and completed a pass for 17 yards. Musso also scored two touchdowns. Terry Davis had perhaps his best game of the season for he completed nine of eleven passes for 105 yards, ran for 36 more on eighteen carries, and scored two touchdowns. Davis remembered how great it was to beat Auburn:

> We made some adjustments to the wishbone and stacked Labue out behind the wide receiver. Auburn could not do anything with it. It was very similar to what Steve Spurrier did at Florida during the 90s, with the stacking of the three receivers on the same side of the football. This was the first time we had beaten them in three years, counting the freshman game. All of these games were ones where we had the lead and could not hold it. Sullivan and Beasley always found a way to come back and beat us. We had a history with this team. Johnny had a hurt toe in that game and had a great game. The defense just smothered Pat Sullivan the entire game. In all fairness, their offense was one-dimensional; drop back and where is Beasley? He was always outrunning everybody down the field. Trying to run down that one guy was difficult, but we did in that game.[369]

Once again the offensive line did an excellent job. The entire interior lineman graded 73 percent or better. Jimmy Grammer had the best day, grading 88 percent in his last regular-season game. The two guards, Jimmy Rosser and John Hannah, had perhaps their best individual games ever. Rosser had a very clear memory of what this game meant to him:

There was a little inside story about the Auburn game. Auburn was going to move Tommy Yearout to the left side over John Hannah. Hannah didn't want to block him. He [Yearout] was not a very big guy, but he was very quick. Hannah did not want to block him because of his quickness. So finally Hannah said that "we could flip-flop the line and put Rosser over there." Of course that pleased John being blocking on Yearout. The rumor was that we were going to make all those changes, so I went along with it. I said, "Okay Hannah can block him just as well as I can." He wasn't sure if he could or not. I told him that he could, and he did...I know that we had the ball for over forty-five minutes of the game, but I felt like we did not have it all. I had so much adrenaline going through my body during this game. I wanted to beat them so much.[370]

As it turned out, Rosser was lined up on Yearout the entire game and did a great job. Meanwhile Hannah was having an excellent game from the other guard. The Auburn game indicated that he was fast becoming the most dominating offensive lineman in the SEC, and he was just a junior. Hannah recalled how the team came together and literally willed itself to win over their most hated rival: "I remember a lot about this game. Beasley and Sullivan were the cat's meow, and rightly so. Sullivan had just won the Heisman a couple days before the game. A lot of people did not give us much of a chance to win against them. It was us and Auburn and Nebraska versus Oklahoma playing each other over the Thanksgiving weekend. All of us were undefeated at the time. We made a pact among ourselves to beat them, and we did."[371]

The entire defensive starting team played flawlessly. Only a handful of substitutions were made during the game. None of the subs played more than seven plays. Terry Rowell participated in all fifty-one plays while Steve Higginbotham and Steve Williams missed only two defensive plays. The entire defense graded out as "winners" during the 31-7 win. The four defensive linemen scored 67 percent or higher while Robin Parkhouse and John Mitchell led with a grade of 75. The three starting linebackers scored 85 percent or better, with Chuck Strickland earning a phenomenal 91. All four of the defensive backs graded 83 percent or better. Steve Wade scored an unbelievable 100 percent at the free safety position.[372]

EXPLANATIONS FOR THE WIN

Different players and coaches have varying memories and interpretations of this game, but almost everyone mentioned one factor above all others: Bill Oliver's game plan was the key to the victory. While not taking credit for the win, Oliver explained what he had wanted from the defense:

> Auburn had only one protection for the passer. The biggest thing in that game was very unusual, but it was designed that way. We did a couple of blitzes with the strong and weak safeties. We blew them away with this. We could come right back and run the same thing with the other safety and knock them for a loss or no gain. The biggest thing was the pass protection part of it. Alabama was not overly deep in the defensive line that year. We told those guys to watch Pat's eyes and jump when he threw the ball. If we did that, we could bat down some of those passes. We did knock some of them down.[373]

The defensive backs had a much better sense of Bill Oliver's impact because they dealt with him on a daily basis. It was no surprise to them that the Auburn game plan was excellent, but they also knew that it was the players who had to execute the plan. It was up to them to do what they were told. In this game they had done so and they were all extremely complimentary of their position coach. Steve Williams talked about how the "tendency sheet for the Auburn offense that we had to memorize was right on target. We knew exactly what they were going to do in every situation."[374] Steve Higginbotham echoed Williams: "Everything Auburn did, we knew what it was. It was my responsibility to take everything short and not worry about getting beat deep. There was help back there."[375] That deep help to which Higgs referred came from Steve Wade and Lanny Norris. Wade credited Oliver with his 100 percent grade for the game. Wade thought he "was more prepared for this game than any other one this season. Coach Oliver knew their personnel."[376] Norris remembered how the previous year's game had left him more focused than ever: "We had several injuries in the defensive backfield last year against Auburn. I thought we had better personnel than they did, but we just did not show it on the field. Brother Oliver had us ready for anything."[377]

Four of the other biggest stars from the Auburn game were Robin Parkhouse, Jeff Beard, Tom Surlas, and Jeff Rouzie. All except Rouzie were seniors. They remembered how they had known exactly what Auburn was going to do. In addition, Parkhouse, who had been the leader of the Alabama defense during the 1971 season, recalled what this game meant:

> Auburn was our third defining game of the 1971 season. The first two were USC and Tennessee. We were both undefeated and playing for the SEC championship. Brother Oliver had the best game plan that I can ever remember us having while I played at Alabama. We were able to shoot them down. We knew what their tendencies were and how we needed to watch Sullivan's eyes. His eyes would tell us that he was getting ready to throw the ball. When we saw this, we always had our hands up and would try to block his pass. We did knock down a few passes at the line of scrimmage. This win was extremely gratifying to the seniors on this team, myself included.[378]

Jeff Beard was another of those senior players who had never beaten the cross-state rival. Beard almost went to Auburn, but after this win he was glad he had not. He felt everything had fallen into place for him, but only after his anxiety attack over the lost belt subsided. Beard described his feelings after the big win that thrust the Crimson Tide into the national championship game against Nebraska: "Everything I ever went through playing football was worth it for this. This is what I've been waiting for since I was in high school and heard all that talk about national champions. Now I know what it was all about. There ain't nothing like this feeling."

Tom Surlas was another of those seniors who wanted to put the past behind him. Yet Surlas was somewhat different from the other seniors on the 1971 squad. Surlas had not grown up in the state of Alabama. He had played junior college ball in the Midwest for his first two collegiate seasons, and it had not taken him long to learn the tradition of Alabama football and what playing Auburn meant. Surlas commented to the press after the big win, "I knew that we had the makings of a great football team. We had size and speed equal to anybody in the country. We could do whatever we wanted to do. I think the entire team knew we could beat Auburn. The offense knew that they could move the ball, and we [the defense] felt we could shut off Auburn's running game. We put it all together."[379]

Bill Oliver thought that Jeff Rouzie was "as good as any linebacker in the country during this season."[380] Rouzie's big interception in the fourth quarter was one of the turning points in the game. He graded 87 percent during the Auburn contest and just missed scoring a touchdown. He remembered how badly the players wanted to beat Auburn: "I'll tell you one of the great experiences of that year was beating Auburn's ass. We hadn't beaten them in a few years. The defense was incredible that game. I think they had only forty-something offensive snaps that day. We absolutely kicked their butts, 31-7. It was a great feeling beating those guys."[381]

BRYANT AND JORDAN AGREE ON THE BETTER TEAM

Maybe with the exception of the USC win earlier in the season, Paul Bryant was as happy as he had been in several years. The win over Auburn left him smiling from ear to ear. President Richard Nixon had even tried to call to congratulate the winning head coach, but he could not get through. The Bear was highly complimentary to all the players and coaches who had contributed to the Auburn win, but especially to Bill Oliver. Bryant was visibly moved by the resounding Alabama victory as he talked to reporters afterward in the locker room. The coach had just come out of the showers, having been tossed in there fully clothed by his overjoyed players. He explained to them the reasons for the win:

> Actually, my limited vocabulary doesn't permit me to express how proud I am for the players for winning. I'm proud of everyone who played and the ones who didn't, because they all contributed something to the preparation. The assistant coaches did a great job, but Bill Oliver was responsible for the game and did an excellent job... Our kicking game was excellent. The defense took away those things Auburn had been getting on everybody, including us last year. And the offense did put some points on the board and keep the football....I'm more proud for the players more than anything else.[382]

The Auburn locker room was quiet as players and coaches cleaned up in order to return home. Coach Shug Jordan was very gracious as he absorbed the reality of what had just happened to his football team. Reflecting on his first loss of the season, Jordan showed class in describing to reporters why Auburn had lost the football game: "It simmered down to possession football. They could move it and keep possession. And we couldn't move it and keep possession. Alabama had a much better team than we had, anyway you look at it, offensively, defensively, even passing. We take our hat off to Alabama. They came to play."[383]

TIME FOR CELEBRATION AND REFLECTION

Paul Bryant would have a few days to celebrate his first SEC championship since 1966, and he sure was glad to be back among the powerhouses of college football. Coach Bryant had come close to leaving this game less than two years earlier to go to the professional ranks. More than ever, Bryant knew that he had made the right decision. Alabama football was back where it belonged, and he had certainly helped put it there. Now the Crimson Tide head coach had a little over a month before his team played in the Orange Bowl—but first things first. Bryant would reflect on what this team had come through to be where they were now. The Orange Bowl preparations could wait a couple of days.

Paul Bryant chats with ABC sportscaster Jim McKay before the Auburn game. (Paul W. Bryant Museum)

Terry Davis (10) runs upfield in the thrilling 31-7 victory over archrival Auburn. Jack White (66) and John Hannah (73) are assisting their quarterback.(Paul W. Bryant Museum)

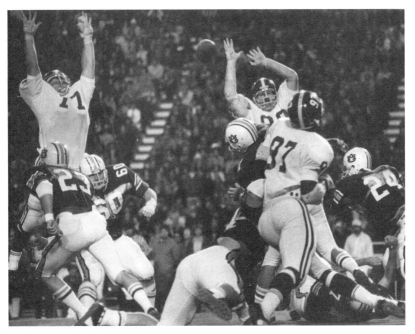

Jeff Beard (77) and Robin Parkhouse (90) leap high into the air to try to bat down an errant pass by Heisman Trophy winner Pat Sullivan (7) during the game with the Tigers. John Mitchell (97) is also in position to hit the famous Auburn quarterback. (Jeff Beard collection)

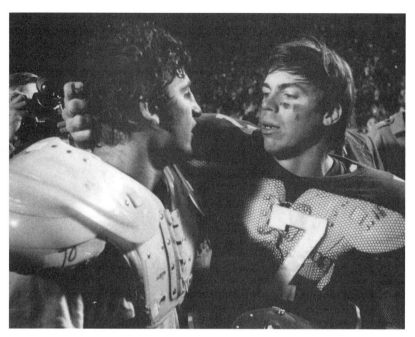

Two Birmingham All-Americans from Auburn and Alabama meet on the field after the game. Pat Sullivan won the Heisman Trophy two days before the game. Johnny Musso finished fourth in the balloting. (Jeff Beard collection)

The Bear celebrates the Auburn victory in the locker room with Johnny Musso (22) and Jack White (66). (Jack White collection)

Assistant Coach Richard Williamson is shown in the victorious Alabama locker room after winning the SEC title against Auburn. You can see the sign in the background the sign that says "Break Beasley," referring to the talented All-American wide receiver for the Auburn Tigers. (Jack White collection)

IT DOESN'T GET ANY BIGGER THAN THIS

PAUL BRYANT WAS ALL SMILES ON HIS WEEKLY TELEVISION
show following the Auburn victory. He announced to the viewers of the
popular program that he thought his Crimson Tide could play with
anyone in the country. Bryant proclaimed to the Alabama nation: "If we
can get everyone well—and I think, there's time for that—, I think we
can entertain anybody."[384] Coach Bryant also introduced the seniors to
the viewing audience and explained how proud he was for their contributions during their 11-0 season.

BRYANT AND PLAYER SCHEDULES

On Monday the veteran head coach announced that he would be in
and out of his office for the next two weeks. He had at least three appearances out of town, not counting recruiting trips. On Tuesday and
Wednesday of that week, Bryant and Curt Gowdy went quail hunting
outside of Selma, Alabama. The two filmed for the popular ABC television show *American Sportsman*, which would air across the United States
later in the winter season on Sunday afternoons. Bryant accompanied
Johnny Musso to New York the following week for the Football Hall
of Fame dinner, where Musso was honored with a graduate academic

scholarship. Finally, Bryant went to Palm Springs, California, to meet with Bob Hope and John McKay. If this were not enough, between stops he visited would-be recruits for the December 11 national signing date.[385]

For the next two weeks the players were running and working out on their own. During this period they also prepared for their final exams. On Tuesday, December 14, formal practice would resume for a week until the players began their Christmas break on December 21. Afterward the team would report back to Tuscaloosa the day after Christmas and fly to Miami to continue preparations for the New Year's clash with Nebraska. The players and the press found out about the specific timetables for the Florida trip after the December 21 practice.

SUPERLATIVES ABOUND FOR THE CRIMSON TIDE

Johnny Musso and John Hannah were honored by the Associated Press for their accomplishments in the 31-7 win over Auburn, which propelled the Crimson Tide to their tenth SEC title. Musso was named top back in the South and Hannah the top lineman in the South. Musso was as modest as ever when questioned by reporters: "Certainly, I'm honored, but the award really needs to be spread around. I had the easiest job on the team because our blocking was fantastic, and Terry Davis did a great job of running the option. Every time I saw one of those blue jerseys, I'd see Hannah or someone knocking them down."[386]

John Hannah led an offensive line that had experienced one of its best performances of the season in the Auburn victory. All of the line starters graded 73 percent or better, with the Albertville junior grading a whopping 83 percent in Alabama's eleventh win of the season. Hannah was extremely gratified with the personal honor but refused to take all the credit. "They say the most unnoticed man on a football team is an offensive lineman, so of course it's pleasing to be recognized. But I think it's probably hard to pick one outstanding individual in our line."[387]

On Tuesday, A. H. "Tonto" Coleman, the Commissioner of the Southeastern Conference, announced its 1971 Academic All-SEC team. In order to make the team, each player had to average at least a "B" or better in the classroom. Three members from the Alabama Crimson Tide were included on this squad—Johnny Musso, Jim Krapf, and Jimmy Rosser. All three players were majors in the College of Business.

Meanwhile, on the same day that the SEC announced its All-Academic team, the *Nashville Banner* proclaimed that Pat Sullivan and

Johnny Musso had tied for the annual SEC Player of the Year award. This was only the second time in the thirty-eight-year history of the honor that it would be shared by two players. The voting was completed on Monday after Alabama's convincing victory over Auburn. This differed from the Heisman Trophy voting that had occurred three weeks before the end of the regular football season. In addition, the paper announced that their Coach of the Year award went to Paul Bryant. Shug Jordan and Billy Kinard were runners-up for the prestigious honor. This was the third time in Bryant's career at Alabama that he had won the award, having also won in 1961 and 1964. The three winners were to receive their awards on December 15 at the Banner Banquet of Champions ceremony and dinner.

LARGEST ALUMNI GROUP HONORS THE TIDE

The Jefferson County (Birmingham) Alumni Association hosted its annual awards dinner on December 10 for the 1971 Alabama football team. The event, at which the University's largest alumni association honors its gridiron stars, had become an annual occurrence since 1923. More than 1,000 people attended the banquet at the Municipal Auditorium to honor the SEC Champions. The specific honorees of the team were the seniors and the coaches. The seniors received watches while the coaches were given silver bowls for their service to the Crimson Tide. Alabama radio broadcasters John Forney and Doug Layton presented the coaches and players with gifts from the alumni association. In addition, the master of ceremonies, R. P. McDavid, III, read the poem "A Season to Remember," written by an unknown Tide fan. The final stanzas can be found below:

> A week of rest...and then the big day
> The biggest day ever, for two teams to play
> The first time in history our state schools had vied
> For the privilege of staying unbeaten, untied.
>
> The tension, it mounted...the whistle, it blew
> And the Tigers were served with so much wishbone stew
> And the defense from Bama stood so strong and tall,
> That the Eagles from Auburn still ain't seen the ball!

Coach Jordan was asked if he would like to name
What he thought was the turning point of the game,
"Well, you're so right, Carl," he said in his manner.
"It was when they played the 'Star Spangled Banner.'"

So, pride in the red jersey, that's the main reason
That we have enjoyed this remarkable season.
God bless you, red jerseys, in Miami, you run
To prove to the world that you are number one![388]

John McKay, head coach of the University of Southern California and long-time friend of Coach Bryant, was the guest speaker for the annual event. Much of McKay's dinner speech was laced with satire and humor. However, the Trojans head coach was dead serious when he spoke to the Alabama players dressed in red travel blazers and ties "You won 11 games because you wanted to win more than the teams you played. You're going to be playing a team in Miami [Nebraska] which is going to be wanting to win, too. The team that wins down there (for the national championship) will be the team, which wants to win the most.... Paul Bryant is the best coach who ever lived."[389]

Alf Van Hoose, sports editor of the *Birmingham News*, interviewed McKay as he left from the alumni awards dinner. McKay talked about Alabama's season, particularly the game against his Southern California squad, and the Tide's chances in the upcoming Orange Bowl:

Alabama just beat us. Paul just had a better team. We played well. Defense, Alabama played defense. They brought it to us. Paul's wishbone stuff wasn't the difference—though Alabama ran it well, extremely well.... The two best teams in the country are playing for the national championship in Miami. The reasons they're the best are because they're the two best defensive teams I've seen. I saw Paul's team on television against LSU and Auburn. Defense won both of those games. The Auburn game was 14 to 7 going into the fourth quarter. That was defense. Nebraska can play defense, too. It ought to be a classic match. Both teams are going to move the ball, but that's to be expected. But the team that plays the best defense is going to win it.[390]

WHO ARE THE NEBRASKA CORNHUSKERS?

Mal Moore was in charge of the scouting report for the Nebraska game. Moore knew that this would be the biggest challenge Alabama would face for the entire season, as the Cornhuskers were the defending national champions. All Nebraska had done during the 1971 season was go 12-0 en route to their current number-one ranking. Moore was under no illusions concerning the Tide's chances against this opponent. He described this in his summary of the Nebraska Cornhuskers:

> They're as strong, offensively and defensively, as any team that we've faced all year. As far as size and ability go, they've got more than anybody has. The offensive line is big and tall and come off the ball well. The thing that concerns us is their ability to keep the ball on offense with the strength and size that they have. If we give them the ball in four-down zone, they'll walk it in on us. Defensively, they have All-Americas at end, tackle and nose guard, have plenty of speed and are aggressive. They don't present a lot of different looks, but they play one or two well, and do it with cool, perfected execution. Rich Glover [nose guard] is probably the best we've run into in several years.... Quarterback Jerry Tagge doesn't make any mistakes and he is an excellent faker. Jeff Kinney is a big and tough inside runner. He breaks more tackles than anybody I've seen this year. He simply runs through men. Johnny Rodgers (wingback) does everything well and I don't know what we'll do in regard to punting because of him. The coverage doesn't matter to him; he's great. He's the best I've ever seen at running back kicks, and he could beat us alone if we are not careful on our kicks.[391]

Coach Bryant always gave his team a written evaluation of their next opponent at least a week before the upcoming game. In the case of the Orange Bowl, the team received their Nebraska evaluations three weeks before the game. In these reports were various comments and indications of formations the opponents were likely to run in particular situations. The packet also included the starting lineups with specifics about each of the players. Listed below are the particulars Bryant gave about the Nebraska starting lineups.

Offense

Position No.	Name	Ht	Wt	Comments
SE#32	Woody Cox	5-9	180	Sr. Second-leading receiver; fine speed
T #72	Daryl White	6-4	238	Soph.
G #77	Dick Rupert	6-1	221	Sr. Quickness & Agility; fine blocker
C #54	Doug Dumler	6-3	237	Jr.

G #65	Keith Wortman	6-3	238	Sr.
T #71	Carl Johnson	6-4	252	Sr. Strong, overpowering blocker
TE #85	Jerry List	6-0	218	Jr.
QB#14	Jerry Tagge	6-2	215	Sr. Great player, a real winner; a strong runner
RB#35	Jeff Kinney	6-2	210	Sr. Best inside runner we've faced
FB#40	Bill Olds	6-1	215	Jr. Fine quickness, strong blocker
WB #20	Johnny Rodgers	5-10	171	Jr. A real All-American; great athlete

Defense

LE#57	John Adkins	6-3	221	Sr.
LT#75	Larry Jacobson	6-6	250	Sr. Great player, All-American
MG#79	Rich Glover	6-1	234	Jr. Great ability; likes to run around center; All-American.
RT#55	Bill Janssen	6-3	228	Jr.
RE#81	Willie Harper	6-3	207	Jr. Outstanding quickness and size
SLB #45	Bob Terrio	6-2	209	Sr. Fine mobility; real aggressive player
WLB #51	Jim Branch	5-9	203	Jr. Strong and quick; good on pursuit
R#25	Dave Mason	6-0	199	Jr. Real fine secondary; reacts extremely well; aggressive against the run
LC#27	Joe Blalak	5-10	184	Jr. Real fine secondary; reacts extremely well; aggressive against the run
RC#18	Jim Anderson	6-0	180	Sr. Real fine secondary; reacts extremely well; aggressive against the run
S#24	Bill Kosch	6-0	176	Sr. Real fine secondary; reacts extremely well; aggressive against the run [392]

OTHER CRIMSON TIDE NEWS
BEFORE PRACTICE RESUMES

The weekend before practice resumed was filled with Alabama-related news besides that of the current SEC Champions. On Saturday, the first day of signing, the Tide coaching staff signed twenty-seven athletes to scholarships. At least thirteen additional slots would be open for signees before the 1972 fall practice. At the same time as the signing, Livingston University won its first small college national football championship over Arkansas Tech at Legion Field. Mickey Andrews, a former Alabama football star, coached Livingston, which is only 45 miles away from Tuscaloosa. Andrews had been a halfback and linebacker for the Bear during the early sixties. At the Capstone he had lettered in both 1963 and 1964.

Several All-American teams were named during Alabama's mid-December off-week. They included the Associated Press, United Press International, Kodak coaches poll, and Gridiron teams. Johnny Musso, John Hannah, and Robin Parkhouse made at least one of the first two teams published. Musso made the first team in the Kodak, Football Writers, and United Press International polls. Hannah made the first squad in the Kodak and Gridiron as well as the second team in the United Press International. Parkhouse made the first team in the Gridiron and the second team in the United Press International.

BACK TO THE PRACTICE FIELD

Paul Bryant talked to reporters on the weekend before practice resumed. He was still in good spirits, and his coaching staff was getting ready for Nebraska. On Tuesday the squad reported for practice. There was no mention of specifics about the workout except that the players were working hard preparing for Nebraska. Meanwhile B. W. Whittington announced on behalf of the University of Alabama's ticket office that orders for the Nebraska game were the greatest in history for a Crimson Tide bowl game. Twelve thousand five hundred tickets were allotted to each of the teams. Alabama received over 32,000 orders, while Nebraska had over 30,000 requests. The capacity for the Orange Bowl is 75,000. Ernie Seiler, executive director of the Orange Bowl, stated, "We could have easily sold 250,000 seats, if we had the capacity."[393]

Wednesday was a formal "off day" and the players were expected to continue their conditioning on their own. Coach Bryant and Johnny Musso flew to Nashville to receive the awards at the *Nashville Banner* Banquet of Champions. Both were gracious in their remarks to the crowd of over 1,000 assembled for the annual event. Musso spoke first and adopted the fans and players of Tennessee's capital city. "I can assure you that when I take the field from now on I'll not only be representing the University of Alabama, but the coaches who selected me for this honor and the people of Nashville for having me here."[394] Bryant followed his star player and was equally magnanimous in his praise of all who had assisted the Crimson Tide during this wonderful season: "I'm flattered and honored to be here. I've never been around so many champions, and I like it. Johnny and Pat [Sullivan] displayed the qualities off the field that would make those who picked them proud. Of course, I proudly accept for the assistants and players who contributed so much more to this team than I did. As it is with any championship team, many, many people contribute to its success."[395]

The next couple of practices on Thursday and Friday were routine, with almost nothing mentioned about their substance. These workouts were done in sweat clothes and helmets only. Saturday's practice involved some hard hitting and scrimmaging in full pads for the first time since the Auburn victory.

The biggest report coming out of Tuscaloosa over the weekend was the election of the permanent 1971 team captains. It certainly was no surprise to Crimson Tide fans that Robin Parkhouse and Johnny Musso were the recipients of these honors bestowed by their teammates. Coach Bryant gave high praise of the newly elected captains. "They are fine choices to be captains of this team. We've had very good senior leadership all year, and these two were exceptional in a good group of leaders. I think that their election by their teammates is a great tribute to them."[396] Some thirty years later, fellow team member John Croyle would call these two the "Fire and Ice" of the 1971 team. "Parkhouse was definitely the fire with his in-your-face leadership and, Johnny was the ice with his solid contributions you could always depend on. Both of these players were great leaders."[397]

On Monday *Football News* announced its annual superlatives, representing the Crimson Tide well. Bryant won the publication's national Coach of the Year award while Johnny Musso earned the title Player of the Year. The famous pigskin publication named John Hannah to the second team. Like the *Nashville Banner*, this publication did not poll voters until after the end of the regular season.

Bryant consented to an interview with Alf Van Hoose following Monday's practice, the day before the team was to break for the Christmas holidays. He was very upbeat in his comments regarding the Tide's progress: "We have just completed five practices, five good practices. The team worked as if everybody knew what was at stake. I thought we had championship type practice—boom, boom, everybody alert, striking, getting things done. Each player took home sweatshirts and shoes. We asked them to run 15 to 20 minutes a day. If a player loses just a bit off his conditioning edge, we're not going to have time in Miami for him to get it back."[398]

On Tuesday morning the team participated in a light workout before leaving for the holidays. They would return to Tuscaloosa on December

26 and fly to Miami to continue their pre-game preparations. On December 23, as the players returned home to be with their families, the *Birmingham News* announced that Johnny Musso and Pat Sullivan would share the SEC Backs of the Year award presented the following month by the Birmingham Monday Morning Quarterback Club. In addition, the Birmingham Touchdown Club made public that on January 18 vice president Spiro Agnew would attend the annual Governor's Cup Dinner.[399]

ON TO MIAMI

The players came back from the holiday break on Christmas night. They met with the coaches at Coleman Coliseum to discuss the itinerary for their Miami stay. The next morning, the bus carrying the players to the Tuscaloosa airport left Bryant Hall at 10 o'clock for an 11:00 A.M. flight. All the players were present and accounted for except Bill Davis, who had had a kidney stone attack during the Christmas break and spent the next few days in the hospital. He was expected to be in Miami for practice on Tuesday afternoon.

As the players were flying to Florida, the big news in Miami was the arrival of the two teams. A number of stories surrounded the commotion

Lanny Norris and Wilbur Jackson relax at one of the venues before the Orange Bowl game. (Jack White collection)

of the Orange Bowl. This would be the third time that Alabama and Nebraska had played each other. The Crimson Tide had won both of the previous contests in New Year's Day bowl games following the 1965 and 1966 seasons. In the first, the 1966 Orange Bowl, Bama won 39-28 on the way to its second consecutive national title. As it turned out, this game would also determine the national title since the Huskers were ranked third and the Tide fourth going into the game. Arkansas and Ohio State, previously the first- and second-ranked teams, had lost earlier in the day, making this a title game. The next year Alabama again defeated Nebraska 34-7 in the Sugar Bowl en route to a perfect 11-0 season, but the pollsters denied the Tide a third consecutive national title.

This game would mark the first time that two undefeated and untied teams had played each other for the national title since Oklahoma defeated Maryland in 1955. Nebraska had won its first national title during the previous season with a season-ending victory over LSU in the Orange Bowl. It had been four years since the Tide had played in a New Year's Day bowl. Alabama's last four bowl appearances had not been that impressive, as they had gone 0-3-1. Nebraska had won twenty games in a row during the past two seasons and were 6-point favorites to win their second national championship in as many years.

Robin Parkhouse, Jeff Beard, and John Hannah laugh it up in front of the "Sheriff Joe" cutout before practice in Miami for the Orange Bowl. (Jeff Beard collection)

Jimmy Rosser hams it up with Assistant Coach Bob Tyler, as Bill Davis looks on in the lead-up to the Orange Bowl game with Nebraska. (Jeff Beard collection)

ORANGE BOWL WEEK

Historically speaking, bowl game trips are rewards for successful seasons. These forays are usually mixtures of work and play. From the Alabama perspective, this was all about work. Yes, they would do some things for entertainment, but they would be together as a team. This trip was all about taking care of business. Paul Bryant was glad to be back in the national spotlight, hoping to win the Crimson Tide's fourth national championship in eleven years. Given the frustration of the last few seasons, the veteran head coach outlined to the players his idea of what it would take to do just that. The schedule was full for the next seven days. There would be team meetings with position coaches and practices during the daytime. Except on Sunday, every night was taken up with group activities. These scheduled events included outings to movies, concerts, jai-alai games, and dog races. Curfew ranged from 12:00 A.M. to 12:30 A.M. except on Friday night, when players had to be in by 11:30 P.M. The Alabama football team was here to win the Orange Bowl. They could party and celebrate after the game on Saturday night, because everything was secondary to the mission at hand.[400]

The first practice in Miami was held at the nearby Miami Military Academy at 3:00 P.M., just over an hour after the team checked into the Americana Hotel on Sunday afternoon. Four Tide players averted a near disaster when they missed the bus ride over, but they were able to make it to the practice on time thanks to Jack Baldwin. Baldwin was the Orange Bowl team-selection chair and had been in the hotel lobby as the four were rushing to catch the bus. He took the tardy players across the bay to practice, where they arrived right behind the team bus. It would not be an exaggeration to say that Terry Davis, Steve Bisceglia, Morris Hunt, and Billy Sexton were extremely grateful to the Orange Bowl official. The head coach made no comments concerning this incident. The practice was a lively ninety-minute session, conducted in shorts and helmets. The team worked on their quickness. Bryant called the first practice "pretty good."[401]

After dinner, players got together with their position coaches for about an hour to view film. The rest of the evening was the only night off from team events. Many of the players stayed at the hotel and visited with family and friends, but a number of others went out to enjoy the nightlife of Miami. It was here that the Tide's carefully cultivated discipline began to break down. A good many of the players felt that they deserved at least one night out away from the hotel. Starting fullback Ellis Beck, one of several who missed the curfew, explained why this happened:

> A lot of us, thirty-seven if I remember correctly, had missed curfew at the beginning of our time in Miami. The coaches were doing a good job of trying to keep us focused. We kept seeing that Nebraska was being treated like the number-one team, and we were treated second best. We could hardly leave the hotel. Coach Goosetree was in charge of this, and it was a lot of crazy shit that they were doing, and it was driving us nuts. We were down here to win a championship, but the game was six days away. This was supposed to be a reward for winning and now, all of a sudden, we're playing for all the marbles, and everything was so uptight. Everybody just needed to get away from the hotel and blow off some steam.[402]

Jim Goosetree was in charge of enforcing the curfew and had been diligent in his efforts. The following morning Goosetree met with Coach Bryant and told him about the players missing the curfew. Bryant's first response was punitive. He wanted to just send the tardy team members home and let them miss playing for the national championship. It was not that simple, however, given the large number of late players. After meeting with Bryant, Goosetree called together the players who had been late and scolded them. Beck recalled that "Goose" told them he had not told Bryant and was going to let it slide this time but warned the players not to let it happen again. Order and discipline was restored and there were no more curfew violations.

It probably surprised people living in Alabama and Nebraska that the big talk among the Miami natives had little to do with Monday's Orange Bowl. On Sunday the professional Miami Dolphins were playing the Baltimore Colts at the same stadium for the American Football Conference (AFC) championship. The winner of this game would play in the sixth annual Super Bowl. People stood in line for more than ten hours on Monday trying to get tickets for Sunday's game. The game would be blacked out locally. This would be the first time in the team's eleven-year history that the Dolphins would be playing for a championship. The irony of this situation is that two years before, Paul Bryant had turned down the job as head coach of the Dolphins and decided to remain at his alma mater. Both the Dolphins and the Crimson Tide were playing for championships on the same weekend in the same stadium.

There was a lot of hitting during Monday's practice. There were a number of players who felt like baseballs hit by power hitters. This took place in the 80-degree heat and high humidity. Even though it had been several months since the players had experienced high temperatures in Tuscaloosa, they adapted and quickly became used the heat. The squad was in excellent condition.

John David Crow mentioned a small item about Monday's practice in the *Birmingham Post-Herald*. It went unnoticed by the media that covered Alabama football on a daily basis. Crow was quite adamant about the "footing being bad"[403] in the first couple of Miami workouts. Alabama had brought with them turf shoes with rubber soles because they would be playing on turf in the Orange Bowl. Yet they were practicing on a hard-grass field containing many rocks, and the shoes were not suitable for that kind of surface. A number of players were getting blisters on their feet. The University of Alabama had both grass and turf practice fields. In the week leading up to a game, players would practice on the field like the one that would be used in the game. If it did not make any difference where one practiced, then why spend money to have two types of fields? On the other hand, Nebraska was practicing at an area junior college that had a much better practice field. When questioned some thirty years later about the preparations for Nebraska, both Crow and Musso mentioned the sorry practice field and the inappropriate shoes. The workout itself lasted two hours, but the media session that followed lasted another two hours.

On a positive note, some good news emerged from the Tide camp on Monday. Bill Davis arrived a day earlier than expected after a bout with kidney stones. He kicked the ball well and seemed none the worse for missing a few practices.

After the team dinner were the usual team meetings to watch film and discuss questions. These gatherings took about an hour and a half. Next the team assembled in the hotel lobby for a trip to the dog races. A mix-up concerning the times at the track caused the team to go to a movie instead. They saw *Dirty Harry* starring Clint Eastwood. Most of the players thought the police action-drama was a good choice. At the 11:00 evening snack almost all of the players ate sparingly before retiring at the 12:30 curfew.

On Monday another announcement came from the Crimson Tide camp. At a news conference held by both of the head coaches, Paul Bryant disclosed to the press that he had joined with former owner of the New York Jets, Sonny Werblin, to form the Hat Corporation of America. The two planned to manufacture a houndstooth hat known as "The Bear." Bryant even tried one out on Bob Devaney. Devaney laughed at the gesture and put his own hat on the Alabama head coach, which made for a good media photograph. The Nebraska coach told how he was "trapped" into playing the Crimson Tide for the national championship because his previous two contests with Alabama had been losses. He told a funny story about how he had avoided making the mistake of playing the Tide for the third time in five years: "Bryant called me and asked me about playing him in the Liberty Bowl a couple of years ago, and I told him okay, but then I called the Sun Bowl and signed with them just to keep away from them." On hearing this tale the Bear just smiled and laughed.[404]

On Tuesday a luncheon sponsored by the Orange Bowl honored both teams. After the lunch, there was more work for the Alabama players. They went with their position coaches for team meetings before the afternoon workout. Coach Bryant was quite pleased with Tuesday's session in which there was some brief scrimmaging. He hinted to the press that maybe the hard-hitting was over until Saturday night. Bryant said, "We need to get a little quicker before we play Nebraska."[405] That night the squad went to a floor show at the hotel that included a concert by singer Peggy Lee. There were no defections from the 12:30 A.M. curfew.

MID-WEEK BUSINESS AS USUAL

The two mid-week practices were business as usual. Team meetings and general preliminaries continued as they would during a normal game week. These practices involved some hitting but there was less and less of that as the week progressed. The Crimson Tide had no injuries to report and the players were in perhaps their best physical condition since the beginning of the season. Stephen Stills, a big football fan and one of the lead singers of the rock group Crosby, Stills, Nash, and Young (CSNY), attended the mid-week practices. After practice Stills talked with a number of players including Joe Labue and Jim Simmons. The team went to jai-alai games on Wednesday night and attended another movie on Thursday night. After Thursday's practice Paul Bryant announced to the press that his team was "just about ready" as they approached Saturday night's clash. He also stated, "cheek-to-cheek, eyeball-to-eyeball, the players look about even to me. Now, it's about time to crawl in the ring and see who's the best man."[406]

During the middle of the week there were some hints in the press that Alabama might have a surprise up their sleeves for Nebraska on Saturday. That surprise would be an offensive game plan that included much more passing. Bama had thrown only eighty-four times during its eleven victories. Bob Devaney hinted at Bama's throwing by pointing to how successful Oklahoma passing game had been against Nebraska on Thanksgiving. Terry Davis tried to downplay this in his explanation to the media: "I hope I don't have to throw any more against Nebraska than I did during the regular season. We've been running all year and winning that way. I don't know what would happen if we got in a catch-up situation, and I'd have to go out and pass almost every play."[407]

ON THE EVE OF THE NATIONAL
CHAMPIONSHIP SHOWDOWN

On Friday morning, Bryant and Devaney appeared together in an interview by Joe Gargiaola of the *Today Show*. In addition, a segment on *CBS Morning News* featured the coaches' wives and how they were coping with being at the Orange Bowl. The segment showed Mary Harmon Bryant shopping, lying out by the pool, going to the beauty shop, and generally having a good time while her husband toiled, getting his team ready to play for a championship.[408]

On Friday night, the Tide went through their last workout at the Orange Bowl. Paul Bryant thought that his squad was ready to play right then. However, the oddsmakers did not agree, as they increased their point spread to 7 points for Nebraska on Friday. The Bear vehemently disagreed with this assessment. The point-spread was totally meaningless. "Physically, we're in the best position we've been in all season and I think that we'll play the best that we can. I just hope that's enough."[409] He would certainly find out whether his team was ready as the clock ticked closer to the 8:00 P.M. starting kickoff time.

Alf Van Hoose did not agree with those oddsmakers who increased their betting line on the eve of the Orange Bowl and he devoted his New Year's Eve column to just this. Van Hoose predicted that Alabama would win 31-17 over Nebraska and pointed to Alabama's defense, kicking game, and running attitued in tough games.

Van Hoose was one of many who followed the Crimson Tide on a daily basis and did not agree with those in Las Vegas who bet on sporting events. Bob Phillips of the *Birmingham Post-Herald*[410] and Delbert Reed of the *Tuscaloosa News*[411] also picked Alabama to win the Orange Bowl over Nebraska for many of the same reasons Van Hoose cited. It only remained for the game to be played for the truth to be known.

CALM BEFORE THE STORM

The weather forecast in the Miami area predicted highs in the mid-70s with some clouds but only a slight chance of rain. It was overcast and pleasant for most of the day with only a few light showers. However, as most people know, these predictions can often change depending on other weather patterns. People attending the Orange Bowl late Saturday afternoon found this out the hard way, not having access to hourly readings by the National Weather Service. Very few of the 78,000-plus fans brought any rain gear because of the forecasts. Two hours before the game, the slight chance of rain turned into a torrential downpour, very near flash flooding that lasted right until the start of the game. Cheap plastic rain ponchos were selling like hotcakes to the unprepared fans streaming into the stadium. The stadium's Polyturf surface was certainly preferable to the grass field; with all the pre-game festivities the field was still quite slick.

A strange occurrence took place as the Crimson Tide went back into the locker room just before the opening kickoff. While the players changed jerseys, piling up their wet ones, Bryant went to the front of the dressing area to address them one last time before the game. Tom Surlas was on his way to the restroom before they had to return to the field. The Alabama head coach erupted, calling Surlas down for not thinking about the game. The rest of the squad was visibly shaken by the outburst as they returned to the field to compete for the national championship.

The first 11-plus minutes of the 1972 Orange Bowl was relatively even with both sides checking each other out. There was no score in the game until late in the first quarter. Then, just like the heavy rain that preceded the game, bad breaks came for the Alabama footballers.

A bad punt attempt gave Nebraska good field position at the Tide 47. Three plays later, at the Bama 33, Jerry Tagge threw a pass toward the end zone to Woody Cox, who was closely guarded by Steve Williams. Williams was called for a controversial pass interference even though the ball was not catchable by the receiver and was overthrown by at least 7 yards. There was a short discussion among the officials, who were not of the same mind. Williams was seething inside but did not argue with the officials because Coach Bryant had drilled into him that to do so was inappropriate. Finally, the officials called interference and gave the ball to the Cornhuskers on the 2-yard line. Jeff Kinney went over for the first touchdown of the game. After the unsuccessful extra point attempt, Nebraska led 6-0.

Alabama's next offensive possession was fruitless and they had to kick the ball away to Nebraska again. This time, Greg Gantt got a good kickoff that Johnny Rodgers fielded at his own 23-yard line. He proceeded to out-fake and out-run the Tide defenders 77 yards for their second score. This time a Tagge completion in the end zone for the 2 points extended the Cornhusker's advantage to 14-0.

The ensuing kickoff was fielded by Steve Williams at the 2-yard line. He was running as if he had exploded out of a cannon until three Nebraska defenders hit him at his own 30-yard line and fumbled the football. Nebraska recovered it at the Bama 27. Seven plays later, Tagge went over from the 1 for the third score in less than 7 minutes to increase the lead to a disheartening 21-0.

The Crimson Tide got the ball again but was forced to surrender it after only four offensive plays. Nebraska got rolling again, but a fumble recovery by Steve Wade after a Tagge completion to Rodgers gave Bama the ball at its own 1-yard line. Two plays later, Steve Bisceglia fumbled the ball over to Nebraska again after a vicious hit by Rich Glover. This time Rich Dixon ran it over from the 2-yard line to put the Huskers up even further. The extra point was good and the score now read Nebraska 28, Alabama 0.

This all happened in a period of eight minutes and twenty-four seconds—it seemed almost unreal that this had occurred in such a short period. The Tide game seemed to be governed by Murphy's Law. The Alabama offense sputtered for the remainder of the first half and the score stubbornly remained the same. The halftime statistics were also on Nebraska's side, as they had 225 yards of total offense to Alabama's 96. The Cornhuskers had the ball twice as much as the Tide by the count of fifty-three to twenty-six offensive plays. As the proud Crimson Tide limped into their locker rooms at halftime, they felt numb. Rod Steakley, one of the senior players who had not played in the first half, recalled what happened next:

I remember coming in and Coach Bryant kicks over a chair. He said, "I want all the seniors over here. I don't care what you do. You haven't been playing good football anyway. I don't want to even talk to you." He puts us over in this area by ourselves. Guys have tears in their eyes—in shell shock because we've embarrassed ourselves. I know we had made a bunch of mistakes. We had been hard workers and had made almost no mistakes the entire season, until now.... Coach Bryant gets us over in this little corner of the locker room and he says, "Guys, everybody that you know that's important in your life watched the first half of that game. Your mommas, your daddies, and everybody else that is important to you. Most of you guys are going to live and work in Alabama. A lot of the folks that are important to you are not going to watch the second half; they're embarrassed. A lot of people who aren't important to you now but will be important in your lives, they won't watch the second half either. Some of them will because they love you, and they love Alabama. You guys, seniors, you've got 30 minutes to go back out and reclaim your prize because you've won eleven games this year, and they will remember that. They will remember that you had a chance to be a national champion, but you got your butts kicked. You've got 30 minutes left. What are you going to do with them? Not 30 minutes for this football team, but you've 30 minutes for the rest of your life, so you can be able to hold your head up with your friends and your family. You better go out there and reclaim your prize.[412]

Lanny Norris (40), Jeff Rouzie (56) and Chuck Strickland (36) get ready for the Nebraska offense. (Paul W. Bryant Museum)

Johnny Musso catches a pass during his last game of his career for the Crimson Tide. (Paul W. Bryant Museum)

COULD BAMA COME BACK?

Paul Bryant had appealed to his team's sense of pride. He never mentioned anything about winning the game. It was about saving face and trying to make the best of a bad situation. Alabama held the Cornhuskers to three plays and out after the second-half kickoff. Starting on their own 43-yard line, the Tide began to act like an inspired football team. They marched the ball down to the Nebraska 14 before Joe Blahak picked off a Terry Davis pass meant for David Bailey and stopped the best Alabama drive of the night. If the Crimson Tide could have scored on this possession as they did on the next, this might have been a different game.

Again the Tide defense held the Cornhuskers and got the ball right back. The offense was now in harmony for the second series in a row. Davis, Musso, and Biscelgia all had good runs as Alabama scored its first touchdown when Davis went over from the 3-yard line. Bama failed on the 2-point conversion but narrowed the margin to 28-6 with 5:40 left in the third quarter. Maybe they had enough time. The teams on both sides of the football were inspired. Alabama began playing like the team that had made it to this game, not the one who had played the first half.

Nebraska took the wind out of the Tide's sails as they took the kickoff and drove it methodically downfield for the final minutes of the third quarter. Rich Sanger kicked a 21-yard field goal as the whistle blew on the third period. The Huskers now led 31-6 with only 15 minutes left in the game.

The Tide continued to play hard but it would not be enough. They would not win their fourth national championship under Paul Bryant. There were, however, a couple of bright spots in the last half. Robin Parkhouse and Terry Rowell both played tenaciously on the defensive line. Parkhouse would later break his foot. Steve Williams made several strong defensive plays and knocked Johnny Rodgers unconscious with a vicious hit in the middle of the field. Terry Davis played well until his shoulder was broken by Willie Harper at the beginning of the fourth quarter. Davis's replacement, Butch Hobson, played for most of the fourth quarter and did an admirable job. Both sides played many of their reserves in the final quarter. Nebraska intercepted a pass and ran it back to the Alabama 1 before scoring another touchdown. The game clock expired as Alabama was driving for another score, but the effort ended on the 7-yard line as the final horn sounded. The final score was 38-6 in favor of Nebraska.

STATISTICS DO NOT TELL THE STORY

If one did not know the final score of this national-championship battle between the top two teams in the country, when viewing the final statistics it would probably appear that this was a very close game. Alabama had the edge in first downs, sixteen to fifteen, and rushing yardage, 241-133, while the total offense was about the same with Nebraska leading 292-288. Even the return yardage was nearly even at 166-164 in favor of the Cornhuskers. The penalized yards were relatively even, with Bama holding a 58-50 yard advantage. Oh, but those costly turnovers—Alabama had a four-to-two advantage over Nebraska. All four of the turnovers led to scores. The only offensive drive Nebraska sustained was for the field goal at the end of the third quarter. The rest of the scores came from turnovers and a controversial pass interference call.

Beyond mistakes, the single glaring area of concern lay in the lack of an adequate passing game. Alabama had completed only three of thirteen passes for 47 yards and two interceptions. A lot of talk leading up to the game had concerned the Tide opening up the passing game, but this was not to be. In all fairness, this entirely new offense was designed to control the ball and run it downfield. Granted, this was the twelfth game of the year, but the Alabama coaching staff thought they could run the ball on Nebraska. When the team was down 28-0, it was nearly impossible to put in a quick strike offense that could move the ball downfield in just a few passes. The Crimson Tide had only been behind three times all season—a touchdown to Ole Miss, a single point Tennessee, and a field goal to Miami—all in the first quarters of the games. None of the three teams had the kind of defense that Nebraska had, which was very similar to LSU but maybe even quicker.

Rich Glover led a tenacious Nebraska defense that had the Alabama offense off stride, for he seemed to be in the Tide backfield all night long. After the game he received the Most Valuable Lineman award. The key to the wishbone was having a creditable threat at fullback to run the ball up the middle, but Glover was consistently clogging the middle. He was lined up on Jimmy Grammer, who by himself was expected to block a man who was quicker, stronger, and outweighed him by 35 pounds. One of the technical responses to this dilemma came from Jeff Rouzie, who, having spent the bulk of the last thirty years as an assistant coach for the University of Alabama, described what might have been done to alleviate some of Glover's quickness.

Nebraska was a wonderful team, but when you look at the statistics, we probably had as many yards as they did. But when you go back as a coach analyzing it, where Nebraska was at that point in time, you realize some things. For example, we were in the first year in the Wishbone. Well, our blocking schemes weren't up to par with what Nebraska was doing on defense. They were running their linebackers up and playing a nose tackle on our center. We were asking our center to block that nose tackle one-on-one. There was no such thing as zone blocking schemes that were developed just a few years later as a response. Things like that would have helped us a lot. The scheme that Nebraska was playing was a little bit, ahead of what we were doing. So our kids were at a disadvantage there.[413]

The Tide coaching staff did not have an answer in the form of double-teams because of the other problems on the Cornhusker defense, such as Larry Jacobsen, Willie Harper, and Bob Terrio, all of whom had outstanding games. The speed of the defensive ends and linebackers stopped the running game of Alabama. If the Tide had completed some passes down field they might have resolved this somewhat, but unfortunately that was not the case.

COACHES' EXPLANATIONS FOR THE NEBRASKA VICTORY

Bob Devaney was all smiles in the Nebraska locker room. All week he had been very confident that his team would win the game. Devaney knew what it meant to lose a national championship game. Alabama had defeated his team in a championship game six years earlier. As it turned out, this was Devaney's final game as the head coach of the Cornhuskers. What a way to go out—with two national championships in a row. Devaney would remain the athletics director at the university. He described how his Huskers had won the game so handily:

> This is the biggest win of my career. It looked like they had Rodgers cornered for a while and then he broke loose for a touchdown. He's the finest kick return man I have ever seen. Our defense created some breaks with good hard tackling in the first half, which helped us a lot. No, I didn't think it would be this easy. I think we played a real fine first half. The second half we didn't play quite as well—but we did play well enough to stay ahead. I think when you are 28 points ahead at the half, it's kind of hard to keep up your momentum—then I think that Alabama played a lot tougher defense the second half. The president didn't call me at halftime. I hadn't gotten that far yet.[414]

Paul Bryant did not make any excuses for his team's poor performance. He took all the criticism on himself. This loss was the largest margin in his bowl career. One would have to go back to 1954, when he was in his first season at Texas A&M, to find a Bryant-coached team that lost by this many points. Bryant explained his position on why Alabama had lost: "We were beaten soundly by a far superior football team. They were much better prepared than ours. They toyed with us most of the time. They were one of the greatest, if not the greatest team I have ever seen. We came back a little in the second half, but not for long. I must have done a poor job of getting them ready for the game."[415]

OTHER EXPLANATIONS FOR THE LOSS

Alabama players and coaches gave a number of explanations for the big loss to Nebraska. Their assessments were not simply excuses but rather legitimate reasons for the defeat. These elucidations ranged from the obvious (that Nebraska had the better team), overall preparations (certain changes might have produced better results), and a premature peak (if only the game could have been played a day or two earlier). Robin Parkhouse and John Mitchell seemed to buy into the "obvious" argument when talking to reporters after the game. Parkhouse spoke highly of Nebraska when he said, "They were tremendous. They have the best backfield, without a doubt, that we've played. They were very overpowering." Mitchell added, "We knew we would have to stop their inside running—which we didn't do. I guess that hurt us a lot. Actually, they didn't do that much on offense, but what they do, they do with precision."[416]

Many of the Alabama players felt that the loss had much to do with the overall preparations for the game. Terry Davis and Johnny Musso were of this school of thought. Davis put it succinctly when describing what went wrong: "The Nebraska game was one in which the coaches hog-tied us all week. We could not go in the pool, we could not go to the beach, and it was very frustrating. You can't lock sixty or sixty-five guys up in a hotel all week and expect them to stay in their rooms."[417] Recently Musso admitted that he has tried not to think about the Nebraska game for the past thirty years. Nevertheless, when pressed, he added the following:

> The overall preparation was bad. We had a sorry practice field on which we tried to get ready to play. We had the wrong shoes in practice. We had our turf shoes when we practiced on a hard grass and dirt surface. The coaches tried to do some things the last couple of practices that we had done all year, instead of concentrating on what we had done to get here. It just seemed like everything was wrong with the whole preparation. It just carried over to the game.[418]

John Hannah was one of those players who thought Alabama just peaked too soon. He certainly was not alone in that assertion. Hannah agreed with the lack-of-preparation argument but went further in explaining the reasons for the loss: "I think the coaches got scared. They moved me out to tackle and put Bearcat Brown at guard instead of keeping the same alignment we had had all year. They did a lot of different things in practice than we had done all season. I think the coaches panicked."[419] Bubba Sawyer seconded Hannah, adding a number of interesting observations. The senior wide receiver reflected:

> The whole week was so different from the whole season. The coaches were so uptight, and it made us the same way. We had played in a couple of minor bowls the last two seasons that did not mean a whole lot. Now we were playing for the national championship... Coach Bryant had told about the rewards for playing in these types of games. We did not feel that we were being rewarded but were being punished. We could not do anything in Miami. I can remember talking to David Bailey in the pre-game warm-ups about not being fired up. It was a real strange feeling among a lot of us of not being ready to play in the biggest game of our lives. Sure, we wanted to win badly, but something was missing.[420]

For the past three decades Lanny Norris has thought a lot about this game. He has had many bad dreams associated with the loss. Norris agreed with many of the other players as to why Alabama lost so badly, but he went further. His explanation was perhaps the most comprehensive and insightful than any of the others.

> The thing that was so disappointing to all of us is when you look back on it, on how badly we played against Nebraska. The mistakes and the horrendous pass interference call. That call essentially gave them a touchdown, and everything seemed to fall apart after that... While acknowledging that the score was lopsided, in my mind, I was not in awe of them or their talent. Their talent was similar to Southern California. I have wished a million times that I could go back and replay that game. In that era, Coach Bryant had lost several bowl games in a row. In my three years, tying Oklahoma was the best that we could do. The field we practiced on was a sandlot, crappy field. It was a joke. I don't remember any intensity during the practices. Another thing about the films was that Nebraska gave us were in a different speed. They were a lot faster than those films indicated. We thought that they were a big

and slow team and we would beat them to death. The first mistake that we made was agreeing to practice on that field. We went down there too early. There was no focus and intensity. In my mind, it was a collection of screw-ups.[421]

While many of the players had different opinions on why Alabama lost, Norris touched on the most widely reported reasons:

The conventional wisdom of this game was that Nebraska was a much better football team and out-classed Alabama in the Orange Bowl. If one looks at just the score, it would seem to be the case. However… the differences between Alabama and Nebraska were not that great. The score of this game was not indicative of the strength of the two teams. Although, they played no similar opponents in '71, they did the year before. LSU and Oklahoma were like opponents in 1970. Alabama lost to LSU 14-9 and tied Oklahoma 24-24. LSU lost to Nebraska in the 1971 Orange Bowl 17-12. The Oklahoma team that finished second in the nation in '71 and lost 35-31 to Nebraska was essentially the same one that the Crimson Tide had tied the year before in the Astro-Bluebonnet Bowl.[422]

Bryant, Red Blount, Tom York meet with Vice-President Spiro Agnew and his wife in Birmingham after the 1971 season. (Paul W. Bryant Museum)

THE TURNING POINT AND BEYOND

MANY KNOWLEDGEABLE OBSERVERS CONSIDER PAUL "BEAR"
Bryant the greatest college football coach of all time.[423] Some twenty
years after his retirement, his stature and legacy remain unchallenged.

In the long and storied history of the University of Alabama football,
1971 was a turning point. Both the university and Bear Bryant owed a lot
to the 1971 team for their future successes. It is time the team's players
are appropriately acknowledged for their accomplishments.

Alabama finished the decade of the 1970s with 103 wins, more victories than any team in college football history. The Tide won eight
Southeastern Conference championships during the 1970s. They won
national championships in 1973, 1978, and 1979. In 1977 the Crimson
Tide ranked second in the country. They also had several opportunities
to win national championship honors in 1971, 1972, and 1974 but fell
short in these campaigns. Alabama finished in the top five seven times
during the 1970s (See appendix for rankings.). Bryant completed his
coaching career in 1982 with 323 victories, the most in major college
football history. He held the career victories record for twenty years until
coaches Joe Paterno of Pennsylvania State University and Bobby Bowden
of Florida State University passed him in career wins in 2001 and 2002,
respectively.

Bryant, the university, and the football team were all at a crossroads in 1971. Bryant nearly left Alabama to coach in the National Football League. He had two mediocre seasons and was clearly frustrated with the conditions at Alabama. The 1971 team was the Bear's most important team during his twenty-five-year career at the Capstone. This team is noted for changes that laid the foundation for future success during the next twelve seasons. The team's initial break with the past was its first integrated squad. The second notable change was Bryant's attempt to run the wishbone offense. If these changes had not succeeded, he might have gone elsewhere to coach or even retired. When in summer 1971 Bryant traveled to meet with Darrell Royal in Austin, he strongly hinted to the famous Texas head coach his feelings about the Alabama team. Later, in the late 1970s, the Bear essentially told millionaire investor Bunker Hunt that he had thought of giving up on the team. Rod Steakley acknowledges being present for this startling revelation:

> Bunker Hunt asked me if he could visit with Coach Bryant. He asked me if I could call him and see if he could visit with him. So I called Coach Bryant and he said something like, "Yeah, come on up and bring him with you to visit. I've got an hour and a half before the awards banquet. He [Hunt] owns those old Kentucky thoroughbreds, doesn't he? I think I probably won a dollar or two on some of his horses. Bring him on up." We sat down, and I was blown away. I was with two of the most powerful people in just a normal conversation. Bunker Hunt asked him something to the effect of, "You have coached for a long time. Was there a time when thought about giving it up?" He said in return, "There came a point in the late sixties when that young man over there was playing, when I wondered if I could identify with the players, and whether or not I needed to be coaching those kids. I had to prove to myself that winning was winning and the principle still worked." That's what led to 1971.424

Had Bryant not been successful in 1971, the remainder of his career would have been totally uncertain. The changes he made as coach laid the foundation for the greatest decade in college football and propelled Bryant to the status of winningest coach in major collegiate football history. After the 1972 season, at a banquet held in Mobile for John Mitchell and Bobby McKinney, the Bear admitted that he wished he had recruited black athletes earlier in his career.[425] More importantly, even though he was not the first Southern college football coach to integrate his squad, his role in integrating the football team made it easier for other coaches, especially those in the South, to follow his lead. In doing this, the famous coach made an even greater contribution to society by improving race relations.

In 1971 the University of Alabama was also at a crossroads of sorts as they were attempting to make their university more accessible to students of all races. Although they had integrated in 1963, by 1971 the university had only about 400 black students out of a student body of more than 15,000. It is not a stretch to suggest that the greater visibility of black athletes at the University of Alabama would have much more positive connotations for race relations than simply allowing blacks to enroll. This was generally true for all universities but even greater at Alabama, given its role in the struggle for civil rights as well as its strong football tradition. If blacks could be successful in the football program at the University of Alabama, it would be much easier for them to succeed in society as a whole. Wilbur Jackson confirmed this point when he said, "Being a football player at Alabama puts you into a select network that will help you throughout your adult life."[426]

Finally, the Alabama football team had endured the woes of two 6-5 seasons. Yes, they were winning seasons, but this was not the kind of excellence to which the players had grown accustomed in the earlier sixties. The seniors on this 1971 team were determined to make their last season meaningful. Nearly three-fourths of their freshmen class had left the team for a number of different reasons. The remaining group, as seniors, wanted to end on a winning note—one reminiscent of the glory days of just a few years earlier. Although the 1971 team did not win a national championship, they certainly played for one. They won an SEC championship and defeated six top-twenty teams en route to an 11-1 season. Their final rankings in the polls were fourth in the AP and second in the UPI. It would have been virtually impossible for the succeeding teams of the 1970s and beyond to have had the level of prosperity they enjoyed had the 1971 team not laid the groundwork. Paul Bryant has been acknowledged for the credit he so richly deserves in the history of college football. Now is the time for his 1971 squad to receive theirs. The two are inescapably linked.

The author and Coach Clem Gryska at the Paul W. Bryant Museum. Gryska was Bryant's recruiting coordinator from 1960–1982. He is currently a staff member for the Bryant Museum. (Paul W. Bryant Museum)

WHERE ARE THEY NOW?

ON SEPTEMBER 22, 2001, THE 1971 UNIVERSITY OF ALABAMA Crimson Tide football team was honored by the athletics department for the first time. This event marked the 30-year reunion of this squad. This was the first game played 11 days after the events of September 11, which ironically was Coach Bryant's birthday. The spiritied reunion served as a reminder of those players who helped Paul W. Bryant rach a turning point in his career and represented one of the most important teams in Alabama football history. The following list accounts for where the members of that team are today.

Number (Position) Name—Status

01 (kicker) Bill Davis—Dentist in Gadsden, Alabama.

06 (wide receiver) Pete Pappas—Doctor in Birmingham, Alabama

07 (tight end) Glenn Woodruff—In hardware sales in Tuscaloosa, Alabama.

08 (kicker) Greg Gantt—Salesman in Birmingham, Alabama.

10 (quarterback) Terry Davis—Sales manger in Ozark, Alabama.

11 (quarterback) Gary Rutledge—In pharmaceutical sales in Birmingham, Alabama.

14 (quarterback) Billy Sexton—Assistant football coach for Florida State University in Tallahassee, Florida.

15 (quarterback) Benny Rippetoe—In the construction business in Lynchburg, Tennessee.

16 (quarterback) Johnny Sharpless—In the real estate business in Orange Beach, Florida.

17 (quarterback) Butch Hobson—Minor league baseball manager in Nashua, New Hampshire.

18 (defensive back) David McMakin—Computer specialist in Huntsville, Alabama.

19 (defensive back) Slade Rhodes—Unknown.

20 (running back) Phil Murphy—Minister in Anniston, Alabama.

21 (defensive back) Wayne Adkinson—Banker in Birmingham, Alabama.

22 (running back) Johnny Musso—Owner of an investment firm in Chicago, Illinois.

23 (running back) Ron Richardson—Physical therapist in Birmingham, Alabama.

24 (running back) Paul Spivey—Vice president of a cabinets firm in Jasper, Indiana.

25 (defensive back) Jeff Blitz—Attorney in Montgomery, Alabama.

26 (defensive back) Bobby McKinney—In real estate sales in Orange, California.

27 (wide receiver) Bubba Sawyer—Minister in Athens, Georgia.

28 (defensive back) Steve Williams—Middle school teacher and coach in Tuscaloosa, Alabama.

29 (defensive back) Robby Rowan—Insurance agent in Huntsville, Alabama.

30 (running back) Joe Labue—High school teacher and coach in Birmingham, Alabama.

32 (defensive back) Steve Wade—In sporting goods sales in Dothan, Alabama.

34 (running back) Rod Steakley—Attorney and team chaplain for the Huntsville Stars baseball team in Huntsville, Alabama.

35 (running back) Ellis Beck—In office products sales in Mobile, Alabama.

36 (linebacker) Chuck Strickland—Supervisor for Tennessee Valley Authority in Stevenson, Alabama.

39 (running back) David Knapp—In sales in Huntsville, Alabama.

40 (defensive back) Lanny Norris—Insurance agent in Russellville, Alabama.

41 (defensive back) Joe Doughty—Unknown.

42 (linebacker) Tom Surlas—Works for the railroad in Mt. Pleasant, Pennsylvania.

43 (running back) Richard Bryan—Deceased.

44 (running back) Steve Bisceglia—In the wine business in Mission Viego, California.

45 (running back) Joe Cochran—Unknown.

46 (wide receiver) Jerry Cash—High school teacher and coach in Portland, Oregon. He holds the world record for the pole vault in the over-fifty category.

48 (defensive back) Robin Cary—In sales in Greenwood, South Carolina.

49 (defensive back) Steve Higginbotham—Sales manager for sheet metal firm in Birmingham, Alabama.

50 (linebacker) Wayne Hall—In the construction business in Auburn, Alabama.

51 (center) Freddy Marshall—Sportswriter in Montgomery, Alabama.

52 (linebacker) Andy Cross—In the construction business in Birmingham, Alabama.

53 (center) Pat Raines—Dean of the business school at Belmont University in Nashville, Tennessee.

54 (offensive tackle) Jim Krapf—Financial consultant in Newark, Delaware.

55 (center) Jimmy Grammar—Retired middle school principal in Hartselle, Alabama.

56 (linebacker) Jeff Rouzie—In the investments business in Birmingham, Alabama.

57 (defensive tackle) Terry Rowell—In the real estate department for the state of Mississippi.

60 (offensive guard) Morris Hunt—In sales in Orlando, Florida.

61 (offensive guard) John Rogers—In the investments business in Montgomery, Alabama.

63 (offensive guard) Marvin Barron—In heavy equipment sales in Duncanville, Alabama.

65 (offensive tackle) Buddy Brown—Manager for Yelvington Distributors in De Funiak Springs, Florida.

66 (offensive guard) Jack White—Vice president of the Professional Golf Association in Ponte Vedra, Florida.

67 (linebacker) Steve Root—In real estate in Palm Springs, California.

68 (offensive guard) Rick Rogers—In security in Boise, Idaho.

69 (center) Mike Eckenrod—Owner of a Ford dealership in Cullman, Alabama.

70 (offensive tackle) Don Colkley—Lives in Morrisville, North Carolina.

71 (offensive guard) Steve Patterson—Self-employed financial consultant in Westerville, Ohio.

72 (offensive guard) Jimmy Rosser—In security for BellSouth in Atlanta, Georgia.

73 (offensive guard) John Hannah—High school football coach in Chattanooga, Tennessee.

74 (defensive tackle) Mike Raines—In the computer networking in Jacksonville, Florida.

75 (offensive tackle) Allen Cox—Real estate developer in Spanish Fort, Alabama.

76 (offensive tackle) Doug Faust—Owner and operator of a shipping business in Hammond, Louisiana.

77 (defensive tackle) Jeff Beard—Insurance consultant in Birmingham, Alabama.

78 (offensive tackle) Steve Sprayberry—In the insurance business in Sylacauga, Alabama.

79 (offensive tackle) Mike Denson—Financial consultant in Nashville, Tennessee.

80 (running back) Wilbur Jackson—Owner of a landscaping firm in Ozark, Alabama.

81 (defensive end) Tommy Lusk—Pilot in the United States Air Force for twenty-five years. He currently is in office products sales in Clarksville, Tennessee.

82 (wide receiver) Wayne Wheeler—High school teacher and coach in Port Orange, Florida.

83 (defensive end) John Croyle—Founder and president of Big Oak Ranch in Rainbow City, Alabama.

84 (wide receiver) David Bailey—In hardware sales in Meridian, Mississippi.

85 (tight end) Jim Simmons—In the heavy equipment business in Tupelo, Mississippi.

86 (defensive end) Jimmy Horton—In pharmaceutical sales in Atlanta, Georgia.

87 (tight end) Randy Moore—Deceased.

88 (wide receiver) Danny Taylor—Unknown.

89 (defensive end) Ed Hines—Attorney in Brewton, Alabama.

90 (defensive end) Robin Parkhouse—In the construction business in Orlando, Florida.

91* (defensive end) Don Groves—In the insurance business in Mobile, Alabama.

91*(defensive end) Phil Law—In sales in Fairhope, Alabama.

92 (wide receiver) Dexter Wood—High school teacher and football coach in Buford, Georgia.

93 (defensive end) David Watkins—High school teacher and football coach in Buford, Georgia.

94 (linebacker) Noah Miller—Dentist in Gadsden, Alabama.

95 (defensive tackle) Skip Kubelius—Deceased.

96 (defensive tackle) Jim Patterson—Dean in the Escambia County school system in Pensacola, Florida.

97 (defensive end) John Mitchell—Defensive line coach for the Pittsburgh Steelers in Pittsburgh, Pennsylvania.

*Players wore the given numbers at different times during the 1971 season.

The thirty-year reunion of the 1971 Alabama football team at the A-Club before the Arkansas game in 2001. Bottom row (L to R): Jack Rutledge. Ellis Beck. Rod Steakley, Phil Murphy, Joe Labue, Jerry Cash. Terry Rowell. Jack White, Paul Spivey, Bobby McKinney, Bubba Sawyer, and Jimmy Rosser. Middle row: Gary White, Sang Lyda, Dickie Coates, Finus Gaston, Robby Rowan, Gary Rutledge, Jim Simmons, Jeff Rowell, Lanny Norris, Jimmy Horton, Steve Root, Gary Bannister, Jimmy Sharpe, and Mal Moore. Back row: Wayne Adkinson, Phil Law. Noah Miller, Chuck Strickland. Robin Parkhouse, David McMakin. Ed Hines, Benny Rippetoe. Jeff Beard, Steve Sprayberry, and Bill Davis. (Paul W. Bryant Museum, courtesy of Kent Gidley)

APPENDIX

Chronology of the Afro-American Student Association, et al Vs. Paul "Bear" Bryant et al

1969

JUL 02   The suit is filed in the United States District Court for the Northern District of Alabama. (Civil Action 69-422)

JUL 02   Athletics Director Paul W. Bryant issues memorandum for coaches stating no change in recruiting policy.

JUL 07   The student newspaper, the *Crimson-White* endorses the action taken by the Afro-American Student Association against the university.

JUL 15   The article in *Presbyterian Life* written by Wilmina Rowland accuses both the university and athletics department of being racist.

JUL 07–28 Bryant meets with SGA officials on the implications of the lawsuit.

JUL 29   SGA officials send letter to Bryant and Associate Athletic Director Sam Bailey thanking them for the meeting and any support that they could offer.

JUL 31   Bryant sends letter of appreciation back to the SGA.

AUG 28   Bryant sends letter to Warren Herlong, president of SGA, updating him on the progress in recruiting and what black athletes will be offered scholarships the coming year and others that will be evaluated during the coming season.

SEP 28   Judge Frank H. McFadden gives university thirty days to answer the complaint filed by the Afro-American Student Assocation.

OCT 23   Sam Bailey sends list of all black schools visited or contacted in Alabama's recruiting of football players to Dewey E. Dodd of the Department of Health, Education, and Welfare's (HEW) regional office in Atlanta, Georgia.

DEC 02   Andrew Thomas sends letter to Rufus Beale of the motion of the United States attorney Wayman G. Sherrer to dismiss filed on behalf of Robert Finch, secretary of HEW.

DEC 05   Rufus Beale acknowledges the letter from Thomas and agreeing that there should no opposition should be made to the above listed motion to dismiss.

1970

FEB 25   Pretrial hearing in which Judge McFadden called for lists of all persons who have been discriminated against.

MAR 21   Andrew Thomas sends letter to Rufus Beale that lists only three of the original fourteen party plaintiffs being the Afro-American Student Association, Isiah Lockett, and Andrew Pernell.

MAY ??   U. W. Clemon requests interrogatories concerning times, dates, lists, methods, etc. that the athletics department employs in the recruitment of athletes.

MAY ??   The athletics department complies with Clemon's request

JUN 08   Judge McFadden issues an order on the pretrial hearing to furnish a list of all known class members within twenty days of trial. The list will include the following: name of individual; home address; high school attended; name of high school coach; college attended (if any); participation in college athletics (if any). Each list must be received no later than ten days prior to trial, the opposing parties will exchange lists of all witnesses which each side contemplates calling for the purpose of giving testimony at the trial.

JUN 09   Andrew Thomas corresponds with George T. Driver (associate counsel of the University of Alabama), stating that plaintiff's attorney will be furnishing a list of all athletes who accuse the progam of discrimination no later than July 1, 1970.

JUL 08   Deposition of Coach Paul Bryant and Coach Clem Gryska.

JUL 21   Memorandum from Coach Gryska on the recruiting of black athletes making known to the staff that the trial has been postponed until May 10, 1971. As directed by Bryant, he is setting up a complete file on this category. Forms that denote such things as contact, visits, questionnaire, phone calls, transcripts, ball games, evaluation, campus visits, and other correspondence would be filed.

AUG 06   List of expenses incurred by the firm of Thomas, Taliaferro, Forman, Burr, & Murray totaling $8181.53 that was approved and recommended for payment by Rufus Beale.

AUG 19   The athletic department's report to the president of the Afro-American Grievance Committee. The report updated information concerning the recruitment of black athletes since 1968.

NOV 17   Letter from Bryant to firm of Thomas, et al with a check of $8181.53 included for services rendered.

MAY 05   Letter from Andrew Thomas to U. W. Clemon concerning recent information from the University of Alabama on the recruiting of black athletes. It is noted in the letter that Wilbur Jackson and John Mitchell (scholarship black athletes) both played in the May 1 A-Day game. In addition, three other black athletes (Sylvester Croom, George Pugh, Ralph Stokes, and Mike Washington) were signed to play football in fall 1971. Another black athlete, Charles Cleveland was signed to a basketball grant-in-aid.

MAY 10   Letter from Thomas to Beale concerning above information listed on May 5. Thomas also informs Beale of Thomas's discussion with Clemon before Judge McFadden agreeing that the case be dismissed. This was based on an earlier meeting on July 20, 1970, that if, a black football player had been recruited within the next year, the plaintiffs would dismiss the case.

MAY 10   An order signed by Judge McFadden ordering that the case is dismissed and each party will bear its own costs.

MAY 11   Letter from Thomas to Beale acknowledging the dismissal of the lawsuit.

ORIGINAL PLAINTIFFS AND DEFENDANTS*

PLAINTIFFS

PERCY C. JONES, JR. is the duly elected president of the Afro-American Student Association. He is a black graduate of the predominately white Ramsey High School in Birmingham.

EDWARD L. NALL is the outgoing president of the association. He is a graduate of the University of Alabama, and a male Negro citizen of the United States and the State of Alabama.

LINDSEY L. HARRIS is a black student at the University of Alabama. He is a graduate of Druid High School in Tuscaloosa where he played football.

LAWRENCE POELLNITZ was a black athlete at Saint Jude High School in this state and is now a student at the University of Alabama.

ISIAH LOCKETT excelled in football at Ozark High School in Ozark, Alabama, before matriculating at the University of Alabama.

JOHN JORDAN, JR., was a track star at Ullman High School in Birmingham. He is now a student at the University of Alabama.

ANDREW PERNELL played football at Jefferson County's Brighton High School. He now studies at the University of Alabama.

ARTHUR THOMAS, JR., is a senior at Tuscaloosa High School. He is a minor, and a black citizen of the United States and the state of Alabama. He sues through his mother and best friend, Ethel Thomas.

EMMA JEAN HUGHES, a minor, graduated last term from the Druid High School in Tuscaloosa. She sues through her mother and best friend, Mabel Hughes.

TUSCALOOSA CITIZENS ACTION COMMITTEE is an association situated in Tuscaloosa working for better race relations.

DEFENDANTS

PAUL "BEAR" BRYANT is the head football coach and athletics director at the University of Alabama. He makes the final decision regarding recruitment of football players and awarding scholarships and grants-in-aid to football players. He decides which players shall play on the football teams.

JOHN A. CADDELL is the chairman of the executive committee of the board of trustees of the University of Alabama. The business of the University of Alabama is conducted by or under the director of the board. The university is a state institution of higher learning. It is the most prominent institution of higher learning in the state. It is state-supported, and is the recipient of great amounts of federal funds.

DAVID F. MATHEWS is the president of the university. As such he is its chief administrative officer. He is responsible to the board. He administers its policies. Dr. Mathews should have been aware of the desire of black university students to end discrimination against blacks in the university's athletic programs. He has refused to act, or, he has been ineffective, if, indeed, he has attempted to remedy the situation.

ROBERT FINCH is the secretary of health, education, and welfare. His agency is charged with administering federal programs that give financial aid to the University of Alabama. He is charged under Title VI of the Civil Rights Act with the duty of halting the flow of federal aid to institutions of higher learning where and when those funds are used in programs that discriminate on the basis of race or color.

* Descriptions taken from the lawsuit pages 5-7. [DAVID, SEE CHICAGO MOS ON HOW TO CITE LAWSUITS AND GIVE US SOME MORE INFO.]

GENERAL STATISTICS AND INFORMATION

STARTING LINEUPS FOR THE 1971 A-DAY GAME

White Offense
Split End—David Bailey

Weak Guard—John Rogers

Strong Guard—Gary Reynolds

Tight End—Randy Moore

Tailback—Steve Dean

Flanker—Wilbur Jackson

Weak Tackle—Don Cokely

Center—Pat Raines

Strong Tackle—John Hannah

Quarterback—Billy Sexton

Fullback—Joe Labue

Kickers—Randy Moore and Steve Wade

White Defense
Left End—John Croyle

Right End—John Mitchell

Middle Linebacker—Jim Krapf

Strong-side Linebacker—Noah Miller

Right Halfback—Bobby McKinney

Free Safety—Steve Wade

Left Tackle—Jeff Beard

Right Tackle—Jim Patterson

Weak-side Linebacker—Tom Surlas

Left Halfback—Steve Higginbotham

Strong Safety—Jeff Blitz

Red Offense
Split End—Wayne Wheeler

Weak Guard—Marvin Barron

Strong Guard—Morris Hunt

Tight End—Jim Simmons

Tailback—Johnny Musso

Kicker—Greg Gantt

Weak Tackle—Jimmy Rosser

Center—Rand Lambert

Strong Tackle—Jack White

Quarterback—Terry Davis

Fullback—Paul Spivey

Red Defense
Left End—Robin Parkhouse

Right End—Tommy Lusk

Middle Linebacker—Chuck Strickland

Left Halfback—Slade Rhodes

Strong Safety—Lanny Norris

Strong-side Linebacker—Jeff Rouzie

Left Tackle—Mike Raines

Right Tackle—Terry Rowell

Weak-side Linebacker—Andy Cross

Right Halfback—David Knapp

Free Safety—Wayne Adkinson

COMPLETE STATISTICS OF THE 1971 A-DAY GAME

Whites		Reds
19	First Downs	18
182	Yards Rushing	141
108	Yards Passing	179
8-18-1	Passes	19-33-3
5/40.4	Punts/Average	5/41.8
2	Fumbles Lost	2
3/25	Penalties/Yards	2/20

Whites Rushing	Attempts	NetYards	TD
Rutledge	1	7	0
Murphy	8	22	0
Sexton	3	-9	0
Labue	15	49	1
Biscelgia	1	25	0

Reds Rushing			
Davis	10	28	1
Musso	14	70	0
Spivey	14	34	0
Beck	1	15	0

Whites Passing	Att.-Comp.-Int.	Yards	TD
Sexton	6-2-1	22	0
Rutledge	10-5-0	85	0
Hobson	1-0-0	0	0
Wade	1-1-0	1	0

Reds Passing			
Davis	12-6-2	109	1
Rippetoe	20-13-1	70	0
Musso	1-0-0	0	0

Whites Pass Receiving	No.	Yards	TD
Dean	1	13	0
Labue	1	17	0
Jackson	1	1	0
Bailey	5	77	0

Reds Pass Receiving			
Wheeler	7	73	0
Richardson	2	12	0
Spivey	5	-10	1
Musso	2	55	0
Horton	1	20	0
Wood	1	8	0
Beck	1	21	0

Whites Punting	No.	Yards	Average
Wade	5	202	40.4

Reds Punting			
Gantt	5	209	41.8

SEVEN AWARDS INITIATED
AND NAMED AFTER CRIMSON TIDE STANDOUTS

01 The "Lee Roy Jordan Headhunter Award"—Robin Parkhouse

02 The "Jerry Duncan I Like to Practice Award"—David McMakin

03 The "Billy Neighbors Most Improved Defensive Lineman Award"—Jim Patterson

04 The "Paul Crane Most Improved Offensive Lineman Award"—Pat Raines

05 The "Ray Perkins Most Improved Receiver Award"—Wayne Wheeler

06 The "Bobby Johns Most Improved Defensive Back Award"—Steve Wade

07 The "Dixie Howell Memorial Award"—Steve Dean

THE UNIVERSITY OF ALABAMA IN COLLEGE FOOTBALL
RANKINGS IN THE 1970S

Year	Record	Year End Ranking (AP)	Year End Ranking (UPI)
1970	6-5-1	Not Ranked	Not Ranked
1971	11-1	4	2
1972	10-2	7	4
1973	11-1	4	1
1974	11-1	5	2
1975	11-1	3	3
1976	9-3	11	9
1977	11-1	2	2
1978	11-1	1	2
1979	12-0	1	1

Total Record for the 1970s—103-16-1

FIRST BLACK FOOTBALL PLAYERS IN THE SEC

School	Name	Year Signed	First Varsity Year
Alabama	Wilbur Jackson	1970	1971
	John Mitchell	1971	1971
Auburn	James Owens	1969	1970
Florida	Leonard George	1969	1970
	Willie Jackson, Sr.	1969	1970
Georgia	Horace King	1970	1971
	Larry West	1970	1971
	Richard Applebee	1970	1971
	Chuck Kinnebrew	1970	1971
Kentucky	Nat Worthington	1965	1967
LSU	Mike Williams	1971	1972
Ole Miss	Ben Williams	1971	1972
Mississippi State	Robert Bell	1970	1971
	Frank Dowsing	1970	1971
Tennessee	Lester McClain	1967	1968
Vanderbilt	Taylor Stokes	1970	1971

Source: SEC Office: Birmingham, Alabama

SELECTIVE BIBLIOGRAPHY

Banks, Jimmy. *The Darrell Royal Story*. Austin: Eakin Press, 1994.

Brooker, Tommy. *Coach Bryant's Football Family*. Tuscaloosa: Taylor Press, 1987.

Browning, Al. *Bowl, Bama, Bowl*. Nashville: Rutledge Hill Press, 1987.

———. *Third Saturday in October*. Nashville: Cumberland House, 2001.

Bryant, Paul W. *Building a Championship Team*. Englewood Cliffs: Prentice-Hall, 1960.

———, and John Underwood. *Bear: The Hard Life and Good Times of Alabama's Coach*. New York: Bantam Books, 1974.

Clark, E. Culpepper. *The Schoolhouse Door: Segregation's Last Stand at the University of Alabama*. New York/Oxford: Oxford University Press, 1995.

Dent, Jim. *The Junction Boys: How Ten Days in Hell with Bear Forged a Championship Team*. New York: St. Martin's Press, 1999.

Dunnavant, Keith. *Coach: The Life of Paul "Bear" Bryant*. New York: Simon & Schuster, 1996.

Dye, Pat. *Inside the Arena*. Montgomery: Black Belt Press, 1992.

Ford, Thomas C. *Alabama Family Tides*. Birmingham: The Alabama Sports Network, 1992.

Forney, John. *Above the Noise of the Crowd: Thirty Years Behind the Alabama Microphone*. Huntsville: Albright and Company, 1986.

Bama and the Bear. Salt Lake City: Great American Sports; Orem UT: Randall Books, 1983.

Groom, Winston. *The Crimson Tide: An Illustrated History of Football at the University of Alabama*. Tuscaloosa: University of Alabama Press, 2000.

Hayman, John. *Richmond Flowers and the Civil Rights Revolution*. Montgomery: Black Belt Press, 1996.

Herskowitz, Mickey. *The Legend of Bear Bryant*. Austin: Eakin Press, 1987.

Lesher, Stephen. *George Wallace: American Populist*. Reading MA: Addison-Wesley, 1994.

Permaloff, Anne, and Carl Crafton. *Political Power in Alabama: The More Things Change...* Athens: University of Georgia Press, 1995.

Reed, Delbert. *Paul 'Bear' Bryant: What Made Him a Winner*. Tuscaloosa: Vision Press, 1995.

Rogers, William Warren, Robert David Ward, Leah Rawls Atkins, and Wayne Flynt. *Alabama: The History of a Deep South State*. Tuscaloosa: University of Alabama Press, 1994.

Stoddard, Tom. *Turnaround: The Untold Story of Bear Bryant's First Year as Head Coach at Alabama*. Montgomery: Black Belt Press, 1994.

Townsend, Steve. *Tales from 1978–79 Alabama Football: A Time of Champions*. Chicago: Sports Publishing, LLC, 2003.

CAREER IN CRISIS

NOTES

[1] Paul W. Bryant and John Underwood, *Bear: The Hard Life and Good Times of Alabama's Coach* (New York: Bantam Books, 1974) 17.

[2] Mickey Herskowitz, *The Legend of Bear Bryant* (Austin TX: Eakin Press, 1987) 115.

[3] Tom Stoddard, *Turnaround: The Untold Story of Bear Bryant's First Year at Alabama*, 2nd ed. (Montgomery AL: Balck Belt Press, 2000) 38–39.

[4] Jack Rutledge, interview with the author, Tuscaloosa AL, May 17, 2000, audiocassette, in author's possession, Morristown TN.

[5] William F. Reed, "Football's Week," *Sports Illustrated*, October 27, 1969, 51.

[6] Tom Siler, "Rockne Crowned King of Coaches," *Sporting News*, September 13, 1969, 51–52. Tom Siler Collection, 1931–1986, Special Collections Library, Hoskins Library, the University of Tennessee, box 4, folder 34. This poll was conducted by Tom Siler, who served as the national college football correspondent for *Sporting News*. In the poll Paul Bryant was the only active coach listed in the top ten of the "greatest college coaches since 1869"; the only other active coach listed in the top-twenty poll was Woody Hayes of Ohio State. Knute Rockne, Robert Neyland, Amos Alonzo Stagg, Pop Warner, and Bud Wilkinson were the top five coaches listed in this poll. The special collections folder includes the original ballots, many of which bear the voter's name. Paul Bryant's ballot did not include himself and listed Frank Thomas, Robert Neyland, and Bud Wilkinson as his first three choices for the honor. A number of notable participants (Bobby Dodd, Bud Wilkinson, and Tonto Coleman) did not list Bryant in the top ten of all time. However, there were many who also had Bryant listed in their top ten, including Vince Lombardi (second), Johnny Vaught (first), and Red Grange (third).

[7] 1969 University of Alabama football press guide, Paul W. Bryant Museum (PWB), Tuscaloosa, Alabama, 3.

[8] Pat Dye, interview by author, Auburn AL, March 13, 2001, audiocassette, in author's possession, Morristown TN.

[9] Clem Gryska, interview by author, Tuscaloosa AL, March 16, 2000, audiocassette, in author's possession, Morristown TN.

[10] John David Crow, telephone interview witht he author, Tuscaloosa AL, April 13, 2002, audiocassette, in author's possession, Morristown TN.

11 Jack Rutledge, interview by author Tuscaloosa AL, May 17, 2000, audiocassette, in author's possession, Morristown TN.

12 Bryant and Underwood, *Bear*, 297.

13 Keith Dunnavant, *Coach: The Life of Paul "Bear" Bryant* (New York: Simon and Schuster, 1996) 270.

14 Gryska, interview by author, Tuscaloosa AL, March 16, 2000, audiocassette, in author's possession, Morristown TN.

15 Larry "Dude" Hennessey, interview by author, Tuscaloosa AL, March 16, 2000, audiocassette, in author's possession, Morristown TN.

16 Jimmy Rosser, interview by author, Atlanta GA, December 2, 2000, audiocassette, in author's possession, Morristown TN.

17 Jack Doane, "Bryant Rebuilds at Bama," *Montgomery Advertiser*, September 2, 1970, 15.

18 Jim Murray, "End of a Charade," *Los Angeles Times*, September 13, 1970, C1.

19 *Bear: The Legend of Paul W. Bryant*, Prod. and Dir. Bob Bodzinger and Erik Kesten, 90 min., Black Canyon Productions, CBS Sports, December 26, 2001, videocassette. In this video, the writers claim that Paul Bryant convinced Sam Cunningham to come to the Alabama locker room after the 1970 contest to show his players what a real player looked like. None of the Alabama players or coaches interviewed for this book remembered this occurrence. Although thirty years has passed since the game, if something like this had happened someone would have remembered it. Such an incident would have been completely out of character for Bryant and would have humiliating to the Alabama players. CBS made matters worse when they interviewed Sam Cunningham on the sideline of the Southern California-Auburn game in 2003 and got him to talk about the supposed incident. It seemed clear to me that the network had put Cunningham up to it as he did not look comfortable discussing it. He acted as if something happened but not exactly the way that the CBS interviewer put it. I guess not considering that it did not happen was not an alternative to the network.

20 Jeff Prugh, "Trojans Fall on Alabama," *Los Angeles Times*, September 13, 1970, C1.

21 David Bailey, interview by author, Orange Beah, AL, June 8, 2001, audiocassette, in author's possession, Morristown TN.

22 Johnny Musso, interview by author, Tuscaloosa AL, April 14, 2000, audiocassette, in author's possession, Morristown TN.

23 Hennessey interview.

24 Doug Layton, interview by author, Tuscaloosa AL July 14, 2000, audiocassette, in author's possession, Morristown TN.

25 Mal Moore, interview by author, Tuscaloosa AL May 18, 2000, audiocassette, in author's possession, Morristown TN.

26 Pat Dye and John Logue, *In the Arena* (Montgomery: Black Belt Press, 1992) 96–97.

27 Jimmy Sharpe, interview by author, Destin FL, December 29, 2000, audiocassette, in author's possession, Morristown TN.

28 Kirk McNair, interview by author, Tuscaloosa AL March 16, 2000, audiocassette, in author's possession, Morristown TN.

29 Jack Rutledge, interview by author, Tuscaloosa AL, May 17, 2000, audiocassette, in author's possession, Morristown TN.

30 Hennessey interview.

31 Paul W. Bryant, and John Underwood, *Bear: The Hard Life and Good Times of Alabama's Coach* (New York: Bantam Books, 1974) 316–24.

32 *Brown v. Board of Education of Topeka, II*, 339 US 294, 75 S.Ct. 753, 99 L. Edition, 1083, 757 (US Supreme Court).

33 Stephen Lesher, *George Wallace: American Populist* (Reading MA: Addison-Wesley Publishing Company, 1994) 128–29, 174.

300

CAREER IN CRISIS

[34] Andrew Doyle, "An Atheist in Alabama Is Someone Who Doesn't Believe in Bear Bryant: A Symbol for an Embattled South." In Miller, Patrick B., *The Sporting World of the Modern South* (Urbana IL: University of Illinois Press, 2002) 265.

[35] Clark, E. Culpepper, *The Schoolhouse Door: Segregation's Last Stand at the University of Alabama* (New York/Oxford: Oxford University Press, 1995) xi.

[36] Paul W. Bryant deposition, in *Afro-American Association of the University of Alabama, et al., vs. Paul "Bear" Bryant, Athletic Director and Head Football Coach of the University of Alabama, et al.*, US District Court for the Northern District of Alabama, Western Division. 404 Federal Building, Birmingham, AL. (July 8, 1970) 48–54.

[37] Dunnavant, *Coach*, 254.

[38] Gerald Astor, "Southern Football: Bear of Alabama," *Look*, November 16, 1965, 101–109.

[39] Frank Rose presidential papers, university archives, W. S. Hoole Special Collections, university libraries, the University of Alabama.,Box 002, Location 084-078.

[40] Donna Bible, "Judge Gives UA 30 Days to Answer Afro Complaint," *Crimson-White*, September 29, 1969, 1.

[41] David S. Mathews presidential papers, university archives, W. S. Hoole Special Collections, university libraries, the University of Alabama, box 005, location 085-046.

[42] U. W. Clemon, interview by author, Birmingham AL, June 23, 2000, audiocassette, in author's possession, Morristown TN.

[43] "Support for Afros," *Crimson-White*, July 7, 1969, 2.

[44] Wilmina Rowland, "Gifts Sought for Scholarship Program," *Presbyterian Life*, July 15, 1969, 25.

[45] Mathews papers, n.p.

[46] Ibid., n.p.

[47] J. Rufus Beale, interview by author, Tuscaloosa AL, June 1, 2000, audiocassette, in author's possession, Morristown TN.

[48] Bryant deposition, 13–15.

[49] Ibid., 65–66.

[50] Bryant deposition, 79–80.

[51] Mathews papers, n.p.

[52] Ibid., n.p.

[53] Bryant and Underwood, *Bear*, 322.

[54] David S. Mathews, interview by author, Tuscaloosa AL, June 19, 2004, audiocassette, in author's possession, Morristown TN.

[55] Clemon interview.

[56] Bobby Stanford, interview by author, Tuscaloosa AL, March 28, 2003, audiocassette, in author's possession, Morristown TN.

[57] Rod Steakley, interview by author, Huntsville AL, August 22, 2001, audiocassette, in author's possession, Morristown TN.

[58] Roy Riley, "Tide Defense Shafted Tough Tenn.," *Birmingham News*, October 18, 1971, 10.

[59] Clemon interview.

[60] Clem Gryska, interview by author, Tuscaloosa AL, March 16, 2000, audiocassette, in author's possession, Morristown TN.

[61] Bryant and Underwood, *Bear*, 299–300.

[62] Clemon interview.

[63] Beale interview.

[64] Theodore Roosevelt, *Theodore Roosevelt: An Autobiography* (New York: Charles Scribner's Sons, 1943) 50–53.

[65] Paul W.Bryant and John Underwood, *Bear: The Hard Life and Good Times of Alabama's Coach* (New York: Bantam Books, 1974) 193.

[66] Jim Dent, *The Junction Boys: How Ten Days in Hell with Bear Bryant forged a Championship Season* (New York: St. Martin's Press, 1999).

[67] I met Graning in the early 1980s in Knoxville, Tennessee. I discussed the incident with him and he never blamed Paul Bryant for what happened. However, he did not let Holt off the hook completely.

[68] Furman Bisher, "College Football Going Berserk," *Saturday Evening Post,* October 20, 1962, 10-11

[69] Frank Graham, Jr., "The Story of a College Football Fix," *Saturday Evening Post,* March 22, 1963, 80–87.

[70] Mickey Herskowitz,, *The Legend of Bear Bryant* (Austin: Eakin Press, 1987) 129–42.

[71] ABC Sports, *Alabama's Bear: Coach Bryant,* New York, October 1967, produced by R.F. Siemanowski.

[72] Chapter 6 of Tom Stoddard's *Turnaround: The Untold Story of Bear Bryant's First Year at Alabama* (Montgomery AL: Black Belt Press, 2000) gives much greater detail. Although this season is thirteen years later, the same basic program was still in place.

[73] Jimmy Rosser, interview by author, Atlanta GA, December 2, 2000, audiocassette, in author's possession, Morristown TN.

[74] Ibid.

[75] Terry Davis, interview by author, Atlanta GA, January 25, 2001, audiocassette, in author's possession, Morristown TN.

[76] Dexter Wood, interview by author, Atlanta GA, January 20, 2002, audiocassette, in author's possession, Morristown TN.

[77] John Mitchell, interview by author, Pittsburgh PA, February 1, 2001, audiocassette, in author's possession, Morristown TN.

[78] Bubba Sawyer, interview by author, Athens GA, January 2, 2003, audiocassette, in author's possession, Morristown TN.

[79] John Croyle, interview by author, Springville AL, November 17, 2000, audiocassette, in author's possession, Morristown TN.

[80] Jimmy Grammer, interview by author, Huntsville AL, November 25, 2000, audiocassette, in author's possession, Morristown TN.

[81] Terry Rowell, interview by author, Tuscaloosa AL, October 28, 2000, audiocassette, in author's possession, Morristown TN.

[82] Jeff Rouzie, interview by author, Tuscaloosa AL, March 16, 2000, audiocassette, in author's possession, Morristown TN.

[83] Gary White, interview by author, Tuscaloosa AL, October 20, 2001, audiocassette, in author's possession, Morristown TN.

[84] Delbert Reed, interview by author, Tuscaloosa AL, October 27, 2000, audiocassette, in author's possession, Morristown TN.

[85] Paul W. Bryant, audio interview with Bill Clark, March 1971, Tuscaloosa AL.

[86] Ed Darling, "We've Got to Get Off the Bottom—Bryant," *Tuscaloosa News,* March 28, 1971, 1B.

[87] Ed Darling, "Carnival Atmosphere Takes Over at Alabama Practice," *Tuscaloosa News,* April 15, 1971, 9.

[88] Ibid.

[89] 1971 University of Alabama: football press guide, PWB, Tuscaloosa AL, 9.

[90] Johnny Musso, interview by author, Tuscaloosa AL, April 14, 2000, audiocassette, in author's possession, Morristown TN.

[91] Paul Spivey, interview by author, Tuscaloosa AL, April 13, 2001, audiocassette, in author's possession, Morristown TN.

[92] Joe Labue, interview by author, Tuscaloosa AL, November 16, 2000, audiocassette, in author's possession, Morristown TN.

[93] Ellis Beck, interview by author, Orange Beach AL, June 8, 2001, audiocassette, in author's possession, Morristown TN.

[94] Steve Bisceglia, interview by author, Orange Beach AL, June 9, 2001, audiocassette, in author's possession, Morristown TN.

[95] David Bailey, interview by author, Orange Beach AL, June 8, 2001, audiocassette, in author's possession, Morristown TN.

[96] Clark interview with Bryant.

[97] Jim Simmons, interview by author, Tuscaloosa AL, September 21, 2001, audiocassette, in author's possession, Morristown TN.

[98] Terry Davis, interview by author, Atlanta GA, January 25, 2001, audiocassette, in author's possession, Morristown TN.

[99] Benny Rippetoe, interview by author, Tuscaloosa AL, September 22, 2001, audiocassette, in author's possession, Morristown TN.

[100] Paul W. Bryant, audio interview with Bill Clark, March 1971, Tuscaloosa AL.

[101] Jimmy Rosser, interview by author, Atlanta GA, December 2, 2000, audiocassette, in author's possession, Morristown TN.

[102] Jimmy Grammer, interview by author, Huntsville AL, November 25, 2000, audiocassette, in author's possession, Morristown TN.

[103] Jack White, interview by author, Ponte Vedra FL, December 28, 2000, audiocassette, in author's possession, Morristown TN.

[104] Mike Eckenrod, interview by author, Orange Beach AL, June 8, 2001, audiocassette, in author's possession, Morristown TN.

[105] Marvin Barron, interview by author, Tuscaloosa AL, June 20, 2000, audiocassette, in author's possession, Morristown TN.

[106] Paul W. Bryant, *Building A Championship Football Team* (Englewood Cliffs: Prentice-Hall, 1960) 24.

[107] Paul W. Bryant, audio interview with Bill Clark, March 1971, Tuscaloosa AL.

[108] 1971 University of Alabama football press guide, PWB, Tuscaloosa AL, 2.

[109] Jeff Rouzie, interview by author, Tuscaloosa AL, March 16, 2000, audiocassette, in author's possession, Morristown TN.

[110] Chuck Strickland, interview by author, Tuscaloosa AL, September 30, 2000, audiocassette, in author's possession, Morristown TN.

[111] Wayne Hall, interview by author, Auburn AL, March 14, 2001, audiocassette, in author's possession, Morristown TN.

[112] Steve Root, interview by author, Tuscaloosa AL, September 22, 2001, audiocassette, in author's possession, Morristown TN.

[113] Robin Parkhouse, interview by author, Orlando FL, December 27, 2000, audiocassette, in author's possession, Morristown TN.

[114] Ibid.

[115] David Watkins, interview by author, Buford GA, October 19, 2001, audiocassette, in author's possession, Morristown TN.

[116] Jeff Beard, interview by author, Birmingham AL, May 25, 2001, audiocassette, in author's possession, Morristown TN.

[117] Jim Patterson, telephone interview by author, Kingsport TN, September 28, 2005.

[118] Steve Higginbotham, interview by author, Birmingham AL, August 15, 2001, audiocassette, in author's possession, Morristown TN.

[119] Steve Williams, interview by author, Tuscaloosa AL, September 30, 2000, audiocassette, in author's possession, Morristown TN.

[120] Ed Darling, "Routine Opener for Bryant, Tide Gridders," *Tuscaloosa News*, April 1, 1971, 7.

[121] Ed Darling, "Quarterback Solution Easy One," *Tuscaloosa News*, April 4, 1971, 1B.

[122] Ed Darling, "Weeb Ewbank in Town: The Subject? Football," *Tuscaloosa News*, April 15, 1971, 9.

[123] John Pruett, "Joe's Back in Tide Camp," *Huntsville Times*, April 15, 1971, 30.

[124] Steve Sprayberry, interview by author, Tuscaloosa AL, September 22, 2001, audiocassette, in author's possession, Morristown TN.

[125] Ed Darling, "Tiders Make Bryant Happy Again," *Tuscaloosa News*, April 18, 1971, 1B.

[126] Ibid.

[127] Ed Darling, "Tiders Make Bryant Happy Again," 1B.

[128] Ed Darling, "Schnellenberger Latest Visitor to Tide Camp," *Tuscaloosa News*, April 20, 1971, 6.

[129] Ibid.

[130] Mike McKenzie, "Jeff Blitz(es) Show," *Huntsville News*, April 20, 1971, 14.

[131] Ed Darling, "Both Offense and Defense Draw Praise from Bryant," *Tuscaloosa News*, April 22, 1971, 17.

[132] "Injuries Worry Bryant," *Tuscaloosa News*, April 24, 1971, 5.

[133] Ed Darling, "Bryant Happy with Defense," *Tuscaloosa News*, April 25, 1971, 1B, 4B.

[134] John Pruett, "A-Day Named, Seem Even on Paper," *Huntsville News*, April 29, 1971, 36.

[135] Ed Darling, "Reds Get Davis, Sexton on Whites," *Tuscaloosa News*, April 29, 1971, 13, 14.

[136] Charles Land, "Opposing Coaches Impressed by Tide," *Tuscaloosa News*, May 2, 1971,1B.

[137] Ed Darling, "Tide Resumes Practice, Bryant Reviews Game," *Tuscaloosa News*, May 4, 1971, 6.

[138] Bill Easterling, "Whites Outscore the Reds; Rutledge Bids for QB Job," *Huntsville News*, May 2, 1971.

[139] Ed Darling, "Tide Resumes Practice, Bryant Reviews Game," *Tuscaloosa News*, May 4, 1971, 6.

[140] Ibid.

[141] Ed Darling, "Tide Resumes Practice, Bryant Reviews Game," *Tuscaloosa News*, May 4, 1971, 6.

[142] Ed Darling, "Routine Tide Session: Final Scrimmage Slated," *Tuscaloosa News*, May 7, 1971, 9.

[143] Ed Darling, "Big Plays Mark Final Scrimmage," *Tuscaloosa News*, May 8, 1971, 5.

[144] Gary White, interview by author, Tuscaloosa AL, October 20, 2001, audiocassette, in author's possession, Morristown TN.

[145] Ibid.

[146] Gary White interview.

[147] Bob Tyler, interview by author in Jackson MS, June 25, 2002, audiocassette, in author's possession, Morristown TN..

[148] Ibid.

[149] Clem Gryska, interview by author, Tuscaloosa AL, March 16, 2000, audiocassette, in author's possession, Morristown TN.

[150] Kirk McNair, interview by author, Tuscaloosa AL, March 16, 2000, audiocassette, in author's possession, Morristown TN.

[151] Darrell Royal, telephone interview by author, April 1, 2002, audiocassette in author's possession, Morristown TN.

[152] Ibid.

[153] Ibid.

[154] Royal interview.

[155] John David Crow, telephone interview by author, Tuscaloosa AL, April 13, 2002.

[156] Jimmy Sharpe, interview by author, Destin FL, December 29, 2000, audiocassette, in author's possession, Morristown TN.

[157] Paul W. Bryant and John Underwood, *Bear: The Hard Life and Good Times of Alabama's Coach* (New York: Bantam Books, 1974) 330

[158] Mal Moore, interview by author, Tuscaloosa AL, May 18, 2000, audiocassette, in author's possession, Morristown TN.

[159] Royal interview.

[160] Clyde Bolton, "Supermen Not Needed to Pull Big Half of Wishbone," *Birmingham News*, August 5, 1971, 34.

[161] Jimmy Bryan, "Return to Greatness: Bama Theme This Fall," *Birmingham News*, August 15, 1971, 1C.

[162] John Clark, "Johnny Vaught Day—Mississippi Pays to a Winner," *Birmingham News*, August 15, 1971.

[163] Ray Maxwell, interview by author, Tuscaloosa AL, September 19, 2003, audiocassette, in author's possession, Morristown TN.

[164] Rod Steakley, interview by author, Huntsville AL, August 22, 2001, audiocassette, in author's possession, Morristown TN.

[165] Bill Oliver interview by author, Tuscaloosa AL, April 13, 2003, audiocassette, in author's possession, Morristown TN.

[166] Bill Lumpkin, "Alabama's Red Tide Rides Again," *Birmingham Post-Herald*, August 16, 1971, 9.

[167] Delbert Reed, "Musso Hopes for Better Tide, Better Musso," *Tuscaloosa News*, July 28, 1971, 1B.

[168] Jimmy Bryan, "Tide's Musso, Ready for Football," *Birmingham News*, July 11, 1971, 1C, 5C.

[169] Wilbur Jackson, interview by author, Ozark AL, March 14, 2001, audiocassette, in author's possession, Morristown TN.

[170] "It's Quitting Time for Alabama Boys," *Birmingham News*, August 18, 1971, 33.

[171] Alf Van Hoose, "Terry Davis Looking Sharp at Tide QB," *Birmingham News*, August 20, 1971, 9.

[172] Alf Van Hoose, "Tide Coach Admits to Fun in '71," *Birmingham News*, August 22, 1971, 1C.

[173] Steve Dean, interview by author, Birmingham AL, January 5, 2002, audiocassette, in author's possession, Morristown TN.

[174] Steve Williams, interview by author, Tuscaloosa AL, September 30, 2000, audiocassette, in author's possession, Morristown TN.

[175] Tom Couchman, "Thus Far, No Growling from Crimson Tide's Bear," *Tuscaloosa News*, August 21, 1971.

[176] Alf Van Hoose, "Bryant First Week Label: Impressive," *Birmingham News*, August 22, 1971, 1C.

[177] Allen Cox, interview by author, Orange Beach AL, June 10, 2001, audiocassette, in author's possession, Morristown TN. | Tom Couchman, "What Can Happen in a Weekend?" *Tuscaloosa News*, August 24, 1971, 6.

[178] Chuck Strickland, interview by author, Tuscaloosa AL, September 30, 2000, audiocassette, in author's possession, Morristown TN.

[179] Paul W. Bryant, audio interview with Bill Clark, March 1971, Tuscaloosa AL.

[180] "Tidesmen Finish Two-a-Day Work," *Birmingham News*, August 25, 1971, 36.

[181] "Davis Throws Three TD's," *Birmingham News*, August 27, 1971, 10.

[182] Tom Couchman, "Wayne Hall: A Beginning," *Tuscaloosa News*, August 28, 1971, 5.

[183] Tom Couchman, "Defense Better, Attack Sputters," *Tuscaloosa News*, August 29, 1971, 1B.

[184] Robin Parkhouse, interview by author, Orlando FL, December 27, 2000, audiocassette, in author's possession, Morristown TN.

[185] Delbert Reed, "Bryant Says Time Running Out of Time," *Tuscaloosa News*, August 31, 1971, 6.

[186] Delbert Reed, "Alabama Defense Still Out Front," *Tuscaloosa News*, September 3, 1971, 7.

[187] Wilbur Jackson, interview by author, Ozark AL, March 14, 2001, audiocassette, in author's possession, Morristown TN.

[188] Pat Dye and John Logue, *In the Arena* (Montgomery: Black Belt Press, 1992) 96–97.

[189] Jackson interview.

[190] John Mitchell, interview by author, Pittsburgh PA, February 1, 2001, audiocassette, in author's possession, Morristown TN.

[191] Paul W. Bryant and John Underwood, *Bear: The Hard Life and Good Times of Alabama's Coach* (New York: Bantam Books, 1974) 303.

[192] Mitchell interview.

[193] Glenn Woodruff, interview by author, Tuscaloosa AL, July 14, 2000, audiocassette, in author's possession, Morristown TN.

[194] Rod Steakley, interview by author, Huntsville AL, August 22, 2001, audiocassette, in author's possession, Morristown TN.

[195] Woodruff interview.

[196] Jerry Cash, interview by author, Tuscaloosa AL, September 22, 2001, audiocassette, in author's possession, Morristown TN.

[197] Jack White, interview by author, Ponte Vedra FL, December 28, 2000, audiocassette, in author's possession, Morristown TN.

[198] Delbert Reed, interview by author, Tuscaloosa AL, October 27, 2000, audiocassette, in author's possession, Morristown TN.

[199] Kirk McNair, interview by author, Tuscaloosa AL, March 16, 2000, audiocassette, in author's possession, Morristown TN.

[200] John Clark, "LSU Gets Solid Vote Over Vols and Auburn," *Birmingham News*, September 7, 1971, 13.

[201] McNair interview.

[202] Morris Hunt, interview by author, Orange Beach AL, June 9, 2001, audiocassette, in author's possession, Morristown TN.

[203] Tom Couchman, "Bama Captains Remember 1970 Plan: Different Game This Time," *Tuscaloosa News*, September 8, 1971, 15.

[204] Jimmy Horton, interview by author, Atlanta GA, July 21, 200, audiocassette, in author's possession, Morristown TN.

[205] Jimmy Sharpe, interview by author, Destin FL, December 29, 2000, audiocassette, in author's possession, Morristown TN.

[206] "4000 Students Cheer Crimsons," *Birmingham Post-Herald*," September 9, 1971, 10.

[207] John David Crow, "Southern Cal Bigger, Better, Tide Aide Says," *Tuscaloosa News*, September 5, 1971, 2B.

[208] Fred Girard, "Tide...To Ride with Wishbone," *St. Petersburg Times*, September 8, 1971, 3C.

[209] Dwight Chapin, "Bama May Spring Wishbone T Attack Against Wary Trojans," *Los Angeles Times*, September 9, 1971, Section III, G1.

[210] Alf Van Hoose, "Tide to Have Spivey-Musso Available for USC," *Birmingham News*, September 9, 1971, 36.

[211] Tom Siler, "First of 12 for Tide?" *Knoxville News Sentinel*, September 10, 1971, 15.

[212] Larry Norris, interview with the author, Tuscaloosa, AL, October 28, 2000, in author's possession, Morristown TN.

[213] John Croyle, interview by author, Springville AL, November 17, 2000, audiocassette, in author's possession, Morristown TN.

[214] Joe Labue, interview, audiocassette, in author's possession, Morristown TN.

[215] Jim Murray, "Custer Comes Back for More with Replacements," *Los Angeles Times*, September 9, 1971, sec. 3, 1. 9C.

[216] Rosser interview.

[217] John Hannah, telephone interview by author, Kingsport TN, June 13, 2002, audiocassette, in author's possession, Morristown TN.

[218] Jeff Beard, interview by author, Birmingham AL, May 25, 2001, audiocassette, in author's possession, Morristown TN.

[219] Jimmy Grammer, interview by author, Huntsville AL, November 25, 2000, audiocassette, in author's possession, Morristown TN.

[220] "Guessperts Go with Trojans," *Birmingham News*, September 10, 1971, 9.

[221] Delbert Reed, "Guessing Game," *Tuscaloosa News*, September 10, 1971, 11.

[222] Wayne Adkinson, interview by author, Birmingham AL, November 16, 2000, audiocassette, in author's possession, Morristown TN.

[223] John Mitchell, interview by author, Pittsburgh PA, February 1, 2001, audiocassette, in author's possession, Morristown TN.

[224] Rod Steakley, interview by author, Huntsville AL, August 22, 2001, audiocassette, in author's possession, Morristown TN.

[225] Chuck Strickland, interview by author, Tuscaloosa AL, September 30, 2000, audiocassette, in author's possession, Morristown TN.

[226] Joe Labue, interview by author, Tuscaloosa AL, November 16, 2000, audiocassette, in author's possession, Morristown TN.

[227] Ellis Beck, interview by author, Orange Beach AL, June 8, 2001, audiocassette, in author's possession, Morristown TN.

[228] Steve Wade, interview by author, Tuscaloosa AL, April 13, 2001, audiocassette, in author's possession, Morristown TN.

[229] Jimmy Rosser, interview by author, Atlanta GA, December 2, 2000, audiocassette, in author's possession, Morristown TN.

[230] Doug Layton, interview by author, Tuscaloosa AL, June 27, 2000, audiocassette, in author's possession, Morristown TN.

[231] Robin Parkhouse, interview by author, Orlando FL, December 27, 2000, audiocassette, in author's possession, Morristown TN.

[232] Ibid.

[233] Alf Van Hoose, "Bryant Beams Over Tide in Trenches," *Birmingham News*, September 11, 1971, 1.

[234] Delbert Reed, "Tide Players Now Believers," *Tuscaloosa News*, September 12, 1971, 1B.

[235] John David Crow, telephone interview by author, Tuscaloosa AL, April 13, 2002, audiocassette, in author's possession, Morristown TN.

[236] Terry Davis, interview by author, Atlanta GA, January 25, 2001, audiocassette, in author's possession, Morristown TN.

[237] Bryant and Underwood, 332.

[238] Steve Bisceglia, interview by author, Orange Beach AL, June 9, 2001, audiocassette, in author's possession, Morristown TN.

[239] Al Thomy, "With USC Upset, Tide Back," *Atlanta Journal-Constitution*, September 12, 1971, 11D.

[240] Bud Furillo, "Bear Is Walking on Water Again," *Los Angeles Herald-Examiner*, September 11, 1971, 1 (Sports).

[241] Jim Murray, "Bear's No Legend," *Los Angeles Times*, September 13, 1971, sec. 3, 1, 8.

[242] Kirk McNair, interview by author, Tuscaloosa AL, March 16, 2000, audiocassette, in author's possession, Morristown TN.

[243] Delbert Reed, "Little Breathing Room," *Tuscaloosa News*, September 13, 1971, 6.

[244] Wilbur Jackson, interview by author, Ozark AL, March 14, 2001, audiocassette, in author's possession, Morristown TN.

[245] Paul W. Bryant's football practice schedules 1971 ("Red Book"), Southern Mississippi Week, Paul W. Bryant Museum, Tuscaloosa AL.

[246] Delbert Reed, "Parkhouse Says Tide Has It Going," *Tuscaloosa News*, September 14, 1971, 6.

[247] Ibid.

[248] Harriet Swift, "Bryant Gets Bob Hope; UA Center Takes Blame," *Crimson-White*, September 13, 1971, 1.

[249] Ibid. | Delbert Reed, interview by author, Tuscaloosa AL, October 27, 2000, audiocassette, in author's possession, Morristown TN.

[250] Bill Oliver, "Southern Miss Has Most Returning," *Crimson Tide Illustrated*, September 18, 1971, 4.

[251] Delbert Reed, "Stage Set Here for Tide Upset?" *Tuscaloosa News*, September 16, 1971, 9.

[252] "Bryant Announces at Rally," *Tuscaloosa News*, September 17, 1971, 11.

[253] Jimmy Rosser, interview by author, Atlanta GA, December 2, 2000, audiocassette, in author's possession, Morristown TN.

[254] Jackson interview.

[255] "Hope Entertains After Southern Mississippi Victory," *Crimson-White*, September 20, 1971, 3.

[256] Delbert Reed, "Coach Bryant Says Tide Getting to Meat of Schedule," *Tuscaloosa News*, September 20, 1971, 6.

[257] Tom Siler, "UT Seeks Coach as Dickey Heads Home," *Knoxville News-Sentinel*, December 30, 1969, 11.

[258] "WHA-A-A-T-T," *Knoxville News-Sentinel*, January 1, 1970.

[259] Mal Moore, "Tide Aide Sees Gators as Ready," *Tuscaloosa News*, September 22, 1971, 13.

[260] Ibid.

[261] Labue, interview.

[262] Roy Riley, "Benched Reaves Still Says He Can Compete with the Best," *Birmingham Post-Herald*, September 27, 1971, 8.

[263] Terry Davis, interview by author, Atlanta GA, January 25, 2001, audiocassette, in author's possession, Morristown TN.

[264] "Familiar Setting for Soph.," *Tuscaloosa News*, September 26, 1971, 6B.

[265] Jeff Rouzie, interview by author, Tuscaloosa AL, March 16, 2000, audiocassette, in author's possession, Morristown TN.

[266] Jack White, interview by author, Ponte Vedra FL, December 28, 2000, audiocassette, in author's possession, Morristown TN.

[267] Andy Cross, interview by author, Birmingham AL, August 14, 2001, audiocassette, in author's possession, Morristown TN.

[268] Bob Tyler, "Rebs Impressive, Tide Aide Says," *Tuscaloosa News*, September 29, 1971, 13.

[269] Ed Shearer, "Bama's Hannah Gets Honor," *Tuscaloosa News*, September 28, 1971, 6.

[270] John Vaught, "Vaught See His Former Rebels Taking the Tide," *Tuscaloosa News*, September 29, 1971, 15.

[271] Sang Lyda, interview by author, Tuscaloosa AL, April 13, 2002, audiocassette, in author's possession, Morristown TN.

272 Davis interview.

273 David Bailey, interview by author, Orange Beach AL, June 8, 2001, audiocassette, in author's possession, Morristown TN.

274 Clem Gryska, interview by author, Tuscaloosa AL, March 16, 2000, audiocassette, in author's possession, Morristown TN.

275 Jim Simmons, interview by author, Tuscaloosa AL, September 21, 2001, audiocassette, in author's possession, Morristown TN.

276 Ellis Beck, interview by author, Orange Beach AL, June 8, 2001, audiocassette, in author's possession, Morristown TN.

277 Tom Couchman, "Bryant Says Crimson Tide Not Great Football Team," *Tuscaloosa News*, October 5, 1971, 7.

278 Tom Couchman, "Tide's Rosser Turns Out to Be a Hero," *Tuscaloosa News*, October 7, 1971, 9.

279 Paul Bryant's 1971 football practice schedules ("Red Book"), Vanderbilt Week, Paul W. Bryant Museum, Tuscaloosa AL.

280 Ibid.

281 Mike Denson, interview by author, Nashville TN, August 18, 2001, audiocassette, in author's possession, Morristown TN.

282 John Vaught, "Vaught Believes in Alabama Now," *Tuscaloosa News*, October 6, 1971, 13.

283 Al Browning, *Third Saturday in October* (Nashville: Cumberland House, 2001) 217.

284 Bert Bank, interview by author, Tuscaloosa AL, October 20, 2001, audiocassette, in author's possession, Morristown TN.

285 Delbert Reed, "Bryant Says Nothing Counts but the Vols," *Tuscaloosa News*, October 11, 1971, 8.

286 Richard Williamson, interview by author, Spartanburg SC, July 31, 2002, audiocassette, in author's possession, Morristown TN.

287 Richard Williamson, "Vols Have Ingredients of Great Ball Club," *Crimson Tide Illustrated*, October 16, 1971, 4.

288 Marvin West, "Tide's Strickland Is Primed for Vols," *Knoxville News-Sentinel*, October 14, 1971, 29.

289 Chuck Strickland, interview by author, Tuscaloosa AL, September 30, 2000, audiocassette, in author's possession, Morristown TN.

290 Ken Donahue, interview by author, Knoxville TN, September 29, 2000, audiocassette, in author's possession, Morristown TN.

291 Rick Young, "Bama-Vol Series Tied at 23-23-7," *Crimson-White*, October 14, 1971, 7.

292 Terry Davis, interview by author, Atlanta GA, January 25, 2001, audiocassette, in author's possession, Morristown TN.

293 David Bailey, interview by author, Orange Beach AL, June 8, 2001, audiocassette, in author's possession, Morristown TN.

294 Jimmy Grammer, interview by author, Huntsville AL, November 25, 2000, audiocassette, in author's possession, Morristown TN.

295 Jimmy Rosser, interview by author, Atlanta GA, December 2, 2000, audiocassette, in author's possession, Morristown TN.

296 John Hannah, telephone interview by author, Kingsport TN, June 13, 2002.

297 Sang Lyda, interview by author, Tuscaloosa AL, April 13, 2002, audiocassette, in author's possession, Morristown TN.

298 Jeff Beard, interview by author, Birmingham AL, May 25, 2001, audiocassette, in author's possession, Morristown TN.

299 Roy Riley, "Tide Defense Shafted Tough Tenn..," *Birmingham Post-Herald*, October 18, 1971, 10.

300 Wayne Martin, "It Was Just One of Musso's Days," *Birmingham News*, October 17, 1971, 6C.

301 Tom Couchman, "Happiness Is Big Win," *Tuscaloosa News*, October 17, 1971, 3B.

302 Tom Siler, "Tide Could've Been Had," Knoxville *News Sentinel*, October 17, 1971, D1.

303 Tom Couchman, "Happiness Is Big Win," *Tuscaloosa News*, October 17, 1971, 3B.

304 Jerry Wizig, *Eat 'Em Up, Cougars* (Huntsville: The Strode Publishers, 1977).

305 Paul Bryant's 1971 football practice schedules ("Red Book"), Houston Week, Paul W. Bryant Museum, Tuscaloosa AL.

306 Pat Dye, "Houston's Offense Explosive," *Tuscaloosa News*, October 20, 1971, 15.

307 Delbert Reed, "Bryant: Tide Not Ready to Play," *Tuscaloosa News*, October 21, 1971, 11.

308 Ibid.

309 Reed, "Bryant," 11.

310 Ibid.

311 Reed, "Bryant," 11.

312 "No Bear Facts," *Knoxville News-Sentinel*, October 20, 1971, 40.

313 Larry Norris, interview by author, Tuscaloosa AL, October 30, 2000, in author's possession, Morristown TN.

314 Jeff Beard, interview by author, Birmingham AL, May 25, 2001, audiocassette, in author's possession, Morristown TN.

315 Tom Couchman, "Bear Unhappy with Defense," *Tuscaloosa News*, October 24, 1971, 2B.

316 Wayne Martin, "Defeated Cougars Think This Year's Tide Is Better," *Birmingham News*, October 24, 1971, 6C.

317 Delbert Reed, "Tiders Begin to Feel Pressure," *Tuscaloosa News*, October 28, 1971, 11.

318 Jimmy Bryan, "Defense Won It for Us, Says Bear After Bruising Game," *Birmingham News*, October 31, 1971, 8C.

319 Ibid.

320 Bryan, "Defense Won It for Us," 8C.

321 Delbert Reed, "Bryant: Tide Has Shot at Something Big," *Tuscaloosa News*, November 1, 1971, 6.

322 Ibid.

323 Bubba Sawyer, interview by author, Athens GA, January 2, 2003, audiocassette, in author's possession, Morristown TN.

324 Mal Moore, "Typical LSU Team—A Good One," *Tuscaloosa News*, November 3, 1971, 17.

325 Tom Couchman, "All Terry Davis Needed Was a Chance," *Tuscaloosa News*, November 5, 1971, 13.

326 Townsend, Steve, *Tales from 1978–79 Alabama Football: A Time of Champions* (Chicago: Sports Publishing LLC, 2003) 3.

327 Jimmy Grammer, interview by author, Huntsville AL, November 25, 2000, audiocassette, in author's possession, Morristown TN.

328 John Hannah, telephone interview by author, Kingsport TN, June 13, 2002, audiocassette, in author's possession, Morristown TN. | Wayne Adkinson, interview by author, Birmingham AL, November 16, 2000, audiocassette, in author's possession, Morristown TN.

329 John Hannah, telephone interview.

330 Jim Simmons, interview by author, Tuscaloosa AL, September 21, 2001, audiocassette, in author's possession, Morristown TN.

331 Paul Spivey, interview by author, Tuscaloosa AL, April 13, 2001, audiocassette, in author's possession, Morristown TN.

332 Jimmy Rosser, interview by author, Atlanta GA, December 2, 2000, audiocassette, in author's possession, Morristown TN.

333 Glenn Woodruff, interview by author, Tuscaloosa AL, July 14, 2000, audiocassette, in author's possession, Morristown TN.

[334] Joe Labue, interview by author, Tuscaloosa AL, November 16, 2000, audiocassette, in author's possession, Morristown TN.

[335] Greg Gantt, interview by author, April 12, 2002, audiocassette, in author's possession, Morristown TN.

[336] Fred Marshall, interview by author, March 14, 2002, audiocassette, in author's possession, Morristown TN.

[337] Paul Davis, "Patching-Up Time, Happy Bear Says," *Tuscaloosa News*, November 7, 1971, 4B.

[338] Ibid.

[339] Delbert Reed, "Bryant Says Miami in Fine Position for Upset," *Tuscaloosa News*, November 8, 1971, 8.

[340] Tom Couchman, "Musso to Miss Miami," *Tuscaloosa News*, November 9, 1971, 8.

[341] Reed, "Bryant Says Miami," 8.

[342] John David Crow, "Miami Features Reckless Backs," *Tuscaloosa News*, November 10, 1971, 17.

[343] Delbert Reed, "Tide Games Just Keep Getting Bigger and Better," *Tuscaloosa News*, November 17, 1971, 11.

[344] Ibid.

[345] Reed, "Tide Games," 11.

[346] Ibid.

[347] "Defense Leaves Musso Smiling," *Tuscaloosa News*, November 14, 1971, 1B.

[348] Alf Van Hoose, "Miami Coach Says Tide Much Better than Notre Dame," *Birmingham News*, November 14, 1971, 8C.

[349] "Not One of Better Games, but Bear Happy to Win It," *Tuscaloosa News*, November 14, 1971, 2B.

[350] Delbert Reed, "Auburn Great Team, Tide's Bryant Says," *Tuscaloosa News*, November 15, 1971, 11.

[351] Terry Smith, "Bama Must on Preparation," *Tuscaloosa News*, November 17, 1971, 16.

[352] Ibid.

[353] Delbert Reed, "Alabama Gridders Back at Work," *Tuscaloosa News*, November 18, 1971, 17.

[354] Paul Spivey, interview by author, Tuscaloosa AL, April 13, 2001, audiocassette, in author's possession, Morristown TN.

[355] Tom Couchman, "Uncomfortable Feeling Helps Make This Game," *Tuscaloosa News*, November 23, 1971, 8.

[356] Ibid.

[357] Ibid.

[358] Steve Wade, interview by author, Tuscaloosa AL, April 13, 2001, audiocassette, in author's possession, Morristown TN.

[359] Bill Oliver, "Oliver: Sullivan Still Improving," *Tuscaloosa News*, November 21, 1971, 1B.

[360] Kirk McNair, "Bama Made a Wish(bone) and Everything Came True," *Huntsville Times*, November 21, 1971, 52.

[361] Paul Wappler, "No Wishbone, No Terry Davis," *Alabama Journal*, November 23, 1971, 15.

[362] Roy Riley, "Musso Has Special Fan in AU's No. 7," *Birmingham Post-Herald*, November 23, 1971, 11.

[363] Sang Lyda, interview by author, Tuscaloosa AL, April 13, 2002, audiocassette, in author's possession, Morristown TN.

[364] Hoyt Harwell, "State Sports Editors Lean Toward Auburn, 9-7," *Tuscaloosa News*, November 26, 1971, 12.

[365] "How Post-Herald Writers See It," *Birmingham Post-Herald*, November 27, 1971, 10.

[366] "Tigers, Huskers Given 8-3 Nods," *Birmingham News*, November 24, 1971, 18.

[367] John Vaught, "Vaught Predicts Victory for Tide," *Tuscaloosa News*, November 25, 1971, 7B.

368 Jack White, interview by author, Ponte Vedra FL, December 28, 2000, audiocassette, in author's possession, Morristown TN.

369 Terry Davis, interview by author, Atlanta GA, January 25, 2001, audiocassette, in author's possession, Morristown TN.

370 Jimmy Rosser, interview by author, Atlanta GA, December 2, 2000, audiocassette, in author's possession, Morristown TN.

371 John Hannah, telephone interview by author, Kingsport TN, June 13, 2002.

372 Paul W. Bryant's 1971 football practice schedules ("Red Book"), Auburn Week, Paul W. Bryant Museum, Tuscaloosa AL.

373 Bill Oliver, interview by author, Tuscaloosa AL, April 13, 2003, audiocassette, in author's possession, Morristown TN.

374 Steve Williams, interview by author, Tuscaloosa AL, September 30, 2000, audiocassette, in author's possession, Morristown TN.

375 Steve Higginbotham, interview by author, Birmingham AL, August 15, 2001, audiocassette, in author's possession, Morristown TN.

376 Wade interview.

377 Larry Norris, interview by author, Tuscaloosa AL, October 30, 2000, audiocassette, in author's possession, Morristown TN.

378 Robin Parkhouse, interview by author, Orlando FL, December 27, 2000, audiocassette, in author's possession, Morristown TN.

379 Jimmy Bryan, "It Was Worth Everything for This, Exults Tide's Jeff Beard," *Birmingham News*, November 28, 1971, 1C, 4C.

380 Oliver interview.

381 Ibid. | Jeff Rouzie, interview by author, Tuscaloosa AL, March 16, 2000, audiocassette, in author's possession, Morristown TN.

382 Jimmy Bryan, "Proud Bear Showers Praise on Everybody," *Birmingham News*, November 28, 1971, 4C.

383 "Shug Says Tide Worthy Champ," *Tuscaloosa News*, November 28, 1971, 6B.

384 Alf Van Hoose, "Think We Can Entertain Anybody," *Birmingham News*, November 29, 1971, 30, 31.

385 Ibid.

386 "Awards Piling for Bama Stars," *Birmingham News*, November 30, 1971, 14.

387 Ibid.

388 Jack White private collection, Ponte Vedra FL

389 Alf Van Hoose, "McKay Talks of Alabama, Auburn, Foes," *Birmingham News*, December 12, 1971, 1C.

390 Ibid.

391 Mal Moore, "Huskers Toughest Foe Yet," *Tuscaloosa News*, December 19, 1971, 1B.

392 Paul W. Bryant 1971 football practice schedule ("Red Book"), Nebraska Week, Paul W. Bryant Museum, Tuscaloosa AL.

393 "Tigers, Tide Take It Easy in Workouts," *Birmingham News*, December 15, 1971, 38.

394 Delbert Reed, "Musso Adds New Fans in Addition to New Trophy," *Tuscaloosa News*, December 16, 1971, 9.

395 Ibid.

396 Clyde Bolton, "Parkhouse, Musso Lead the Tide," *Birmingham News*, December 19, 1971, 1F.

397 John Croyle, interview by author, Springville AL, November 17, 2000, audiocassette, in author's possession, Morristown TN.

398 Alf Van Hoose, "Busy Bryant Likes the Looks of Tide's Work," *Birmingham News*, December 21, 1971, 18.

399 Jimmy Bryan, "Musso, Sullivan to Share Award," *Birmingham News*, December 23, 1971, 22.

400 "Orange Bowl itinerary," Jimmy Rosser private collection, Atlanta GA.

401 Alf Van Hoose, "Tiders Hold First Miami Workout," *Birmingham News*, December 28, 1971, 18.

402 Ellis Beck, interview by author, Orange Beach AL, June 8, 2001, audiocassette, in author's possession, Morristown TN.

403 Bill Lumpkin, "Beat Busy Running Errands for Namath," *Birmingham Post-Herald*, December 26, 1971, 13, 15.

404 Delbert Reed, "Bear Hats Cause Orange Stir," *Tuscaloosa News*, December 28, 1971, 6.

405 Ibid.

406 Alf Van Hoose, "Tide Labels, 'Just About,'" *Birmingham News*, December 31, 1971, 25.

407 Ibid.

408 Alf Van Hoose, "Tide's Oliver a Winner on His Press Day," *Birmingham News*, December 30, 1971, 11.

409 Delbert Reed, "Dream-Like Finish Appproaches," *Tuscaloosa News*, January 1, 1972, 1.

410 Alf Van Hoose, "A Guess Is Made, It's Alabama 31, Nebraska 17," *Birmingham News*, December 31, 1971, 25. | Bob Phillips, "On the Roof," *Birmingham Post-Herald*, December 30, 1971, 11.

411 Delbert Reed, "A Vote for Tide," *Tuscaloosa News*, December 31, 1971, 13.

412 Rod Steakley, interview by author, Huntsville AL, August 22, 2001, audiocassette, in author's possession, Morristown TN.

413 Jeff Rouzie, interview by author, Tuscaloosa AL, March 16, 2000, audiocassette, in author's possession, Morristown TN.

414 Paul Davis, "Bryant: Nebraska a Great Team," *Tuscaloosa News*, January 2, 1972, 1B.

415 Ronald Weathers, "Defeated Bamas Agreed: Nebraska 'Does It All Well,'" *Birmingham News*, January 2, 1971, 3C.

416 Ibid.

417 Terry Davis, interview by author, Atlanta GA, January 25, 2001, audiocassette, in author's possession, Morristown TN.

418 Johnny Musso, interview by author, Tuscaloosa AL, April 14, 2000, audiocassette, in author's possession, Morristown TN.

419 John Hannah, telephone interview by author, Kingsport TN, June 13, 2002, audiocassette, in author's possession, Morristown TN.

420 Bubba Sawyer, interview by author, Athens GA, January 2, 2003, audiocassette, in author's possession, Morristown TN.

421 Larry Norris, interview by author, Tuscaloosa AL, October 30, 2000, audiocassette, in author's possession, Morristown TN.

422 Weathers, "Defeated Bamas Agreed," 3C.

423 A number of reputable sports organizations in the last few years have named Bryant the greatest coach in college football history. These include ABC Sports (1999), *Sports Illustrated* (2000), and Pigskin.com (2001).

424 Rod Steakley, interview by author, Huntsville AL, August 22, 2001, audiocassette, in author's possession, Morristown TN.

425 Ben Nolan, "Glimpses from the Scorebook," *Mobile* (AL) *Register*, February 20, 1973, 1C.

426 Wilbur Jackson, interview by author, Ozark AL, March 14, 2001, audiocassette, in author's possession, Morristown TN.

INDEX

319

321

INDEX